OTHER BOOKS IN THE CREATIVE MACHINE ARTS SERIES, AVAILABLE FROM CHILTON:

OTHER BOOKS IN JAN SAUNDERS' TEACH YOURSELF TO SEW BETTER SERIES, AVAILABLE FROM CHILTON:

CONTENTS

by Robbie Fanning

Have you wanted to know how your Viking works without having to go to school to become a mechanic? What about those gadgets that came with your machine? This is a crash course to clear up misunderstandings you may have about threading, tension adjustments, and needle and thread selection. You will also find simple care and maintenance information and learn how to use the basic presser feet and stitches. Also see how various tools can make sewing easier and a lot more fun.

Learn the proper stitches and presser feet to sew woven and knit fabrics by making a pair of woven pull-on shorts and a knit top with ribbing. Once you complete this project, you'll have the basic skills to tackle more challenging ones.

Practice the basics of machine appliqué and embroidery by making a tote bag with a compass design. Embellish a pocket for your shorts and knit top made in Chapter 2 with Pictograms™ and other machine-stitched embroideries.

Make Envelope Placemats and matching "Lapkins" to master buttonholes, mitered corners, and professional edge finishes.

Stitch a small quilt to perfect free-machine quilting, piecing, borders, straight-stitch quilting, and tying a quilt.

Create stuffed fabric blocks and a hobbyhorse while mastering thread fringe, yarn fringe, gusset insertion, gathering over a cord, and more.

Surprise your family and friends with quick-to-stitch key rings and a fabric game board and pouch. At the same time you'll learn zipper insertion, edgestitching, and topstitching techniques, along with new ways to use your decorative stitches.

Part Three:

See utility and decorative stitch applications for common stitches available on most Vikings made within the last 15 years. Also includes the 197 stitches available on the Viking 1100. The stitches introduced here are cross-referenced throughout the projects in Part II and in the Encyclopedia of Presser Feet.

Learn how to use presser feet for utility and decorative applications. Presser feet available for current Viking models as well as those made in the last 15 years are covered. The presser feet applications are cross-referenced throughout the projects in Part II and in the Encyclopedia of Stitches.

PREFACE

In most sewing books the word "sewing" means making garments. Such books spend pages showing you how to measure yourself, choose patterns, lay out fabric, cut, and mark.

This book is different. I approach a project by considering the fabric and how to use the stitches, presser feet, and techniques I've learned on my Viking to create something unique—unlike most sewing books that approach sewing with the emphasis on everything but the sewing machine.

To me, the word "sewing" implies using your sewing machine to its fullest potential. You may want to use your Viking to make garments, but that's only part of The World of Sewing. In this book you'll learn to use your Viking wisely not only for making clothing, but also for appliqué and embroidery, home decoration, quilt making, toys and games, and gifts.

1.
Sew Fashion

2.
Sew Embellishments— Machine Appliqué and Embroider

3.
Sew for Your Home

4.
Sew a Quilt

5.
Sew Toys

6.
Sew Gifts

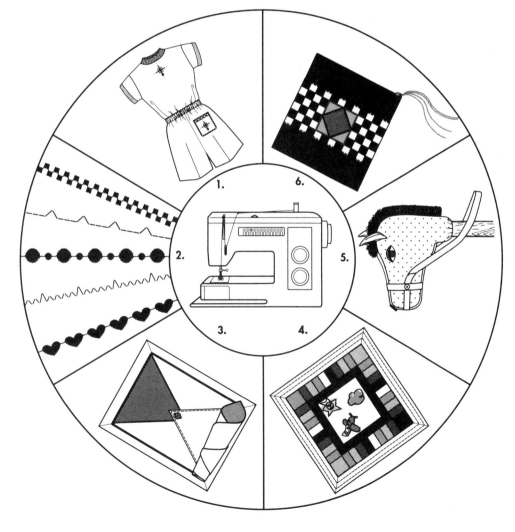

A *Step-by-Step Guide to Your Viking* takes a broad look at sewing and is written so you can complete each project successfully, regardless of which Viking model you own. In Part I, Meet Your Viking, you will take a look at the parts of your Viking, at tools necessary for respectable results, and at basic stitches. You will also preview the way the projects in Part II are constructed by completing three simple exercises.

Part II, The World of Sewing, is divided into six chapters—like spokes in a wheel, with the sewing machine at the hub.

You may wonder how The World of Sewing can be covered in one book. I don't pretend to cover each area in infinite detail. But just as you don't need to know every landmark to follow directions to a place you've never been before, you don't need to know everything about one area of sewing to complete the project. Each chapter covers how to use some part of your Viking and guides you step-by-step through a project. The projects were selected and designed to appeal to almost anyone, regardless of age or gender. Instructions for many projects are written as a "master recipe." The variations for each project should enable you to tailor it for your needs.

Even if you don't plan to make a project, read through the directions and make the project in your mind. You will learn many valuable techniques that can be transferred to other projects in this book and others. Look for **Transferable Learnings** as a checklist of what you have learned by making the project, and a chapter review.

Also look for the **Sew-How** tips sprinkled throughout the book. Think of them as a sewing smorgasbord: keep what you like and discard the rest. **Sew-How** tips are designed to give you insight into a particular technique—a kind of "did you know?" or "don't forget" department. Other **Sew-How** information should enhance your knowledge and understanding of sewing.

 Don't think I've ignored the benefits of using the serger for fast professional results. However, I couldn't cover everything about sewing in this book. If there is a particular technique or step that could be completed as well on the serger as on your Viking, you will see a serger symbol in the margin.

Part III is an encyclopedia of the undiscovered treasures available for your Viking—stitches and presser feet. Each major stitch and foot is illustrated. The text explains settings and uses, and the projects in Part II are cross-referenced to both stitch and presser feet encyclopedias in Part III.

This book is for anyone who wants to sew . . . better. Whether you're a beginner or have been sewing for years, whether you need a refresher course or an advanced look at your Viking, this book shows you how to sew more efficiently by learning to use your machine better. Some of the information you may know already; some may be enlightening. My hope is that you'll sew more (and encourage others to do the same) by enjoying your Viking, stitches, and feet as much as I do.

Jan Saunders
Columbus, Ohio

ACKNOWLEDGMENTS

When you read a book, you remember the subject matter, maybe the author, you may recognize the name of those quoted on the back cover and the editor, but there are many other people who selflessly lend their knowledge and expertise so a book . . this book. . . can be the best it can be.

I wish to acknowledge and thank the following people who are very much a part of this book: Audrey Griese, Marsha Fredrickson, Ron and Barbara Goldkorn, Janet Penwell, Kathy Thompson, and Ann Williams for their candid comments on their businesses and their retail customers; Carol Ahles, Sue Bagley, Sandra Betzina, Gail Brown, Clotilde, David Coffin, Louise Garigk, Lois Gotwals, Sue Hausmann, Carl Jorden, Kathy Embry, Nancy Rice, Cheryl Robinson, Ann Wallace, and Nancy Zieman for their insightful comments on our industry at large, and their interest and love for sewing in their own lives.

Also a big thanks to McCall Pattern Company for use of their patterns and pattern graphics, and VWS, Inc. for use of their sewing machines.

A special thanks goes to Pam Poole for her willingness to make each drawing as clear and understandable as possible, even at the expense of many corrections. Also to Carl Moffet and Timm Flagg of Carl's Sewing Center, who answered Pam's questions and made the equipment available so her drawings could be as technically correct as they are beautiful.

As always, thanks to Robbie Fanning for crafting this book, polishing my writing style, and helping me when I really needed it.

FOREWORD

It had been a long, hard, hot day at work—interruptions, backtracking, emergencies, deadlines. I came home at 6 pm, pooped. But within an hour, I was rejuvenated, relaxed, peaceful. Why? Because I was machine-piecing a quilt for my daughter. You see, I truly love to sew. Like a kid's blankie, sewing is my Best Thing. (And best of all is to listen to recorded books as I sew.)

But I was lucky. My mother sewed as we grew up and we learned by osmosis. Later came seventh grade home ec and some sewing classes at the local fabric store.

Today, people are not as lucky as me. Sewing is rarely taught in home ec and many stores do not have classes. (Thank heavens for 4-H, where teaching sewing is still strong.) At the same time that fabrics have improved, machines have become easier to use, and speedy techniques have revolutionized sewing, fewer people know how.

Jan's book should help. For each of the six main sewing areas, it contains simple projects for any age. She then explains how the skills learned in each chapter can be transferred to more ambitious projects. The more experienced sewer will appreciate Jan's "Encyclopedia of Stitches and Presser Feet" in Part III.

Still, I propose you take one further step: share your love of sewing with someone else. You don't need teaching credentials to do this. Simply challenge yourself to help someone else learn to sew. It may be as simple as inviting a neighborhood child in to help you thread your machine. If he or she wants to run the machine, use the warm-up exercises in Chapter 1.

There are many other imaginative ways to share our mutual love of sewing. Set up a machine at work and let interested people use it on lunch breaks. Join 4-H and learn to teach sewing. Take your machine to a local school and show the students what you have made. Volunteer to teach sewing costumes to community theater. Demonstrate sewing at the church bazaar or county fair. Spend a day in the children's ward of a hospital, machine-embroidering patients' initials on bean bags.

As Diana Davies, a member of the Minneapolis chapter of the American Sewing Guild, suggested, "Each one teach one."

Jan and I would like to hear about your experiences. Please write us at the address below.

Robbie Fanning
Series Editor, Creative Machine Arts

Are you interested in a quarterly newsletter about creative uses of the sewing machine, serger, and knitting machine? Write to The Creative Machine, PO Box 2634, Menlo Park, CA 94026.

MEET YOUR VIKING

Part I

MEET YOUR VIKING

MEET YOUR VIKING

- *Step One: Identify the Parts of Your Viking*

- *Step Two: Assemble Your Tools*

- *Step Three: Learn the Basic Stitches*

- *Transferable Learnings*

EVERY TIME I SIT DOWN TO SEW, I want my Viking to perform perfectly. But it can't take care of itself. This section will acquaint you with the common parts of your Viking and briefly explain their function. You will also brush up on how to take care of your machine, so it takes care of you. Note that the Viking Education Department has a comprehensive collection of educational materials for specific models. The purpose of this book is to acquaint you with the many feet, accessories, and stitches you may have available for your Viking. See the bibliography for a complete listing of educational materials for your model.

Although the Viking Operating Manuals are generally well written and illustrated, to help you understand the basics of your machine, I've designed this section as a workbook to accompany your Operating Manual. If your manual has disappeared, call your local dealer to get another one (or see the Sources of Supply). You will also make stitch samples, so have a variety of fabrics such as cotton kettle cloth, T-shirt knit, and light- and medium-weight wovens, cut into 7" (18 cm) squares. To keep your samples straight, buy a large three-ring binder and clear pocket-type pages to document your successes and failures. Why keep your failures? So you don't make the same mistake twice.

Step One:

IDENTIFY THE PARTS OF YOUR VIKING

Regardless of the model or sophistication, Viking machines have many parts in common. Review Figs. 1.1 (computerized Viking 1100) and 1.2 (mechanical Viking 150E) and compare them with your Viking.

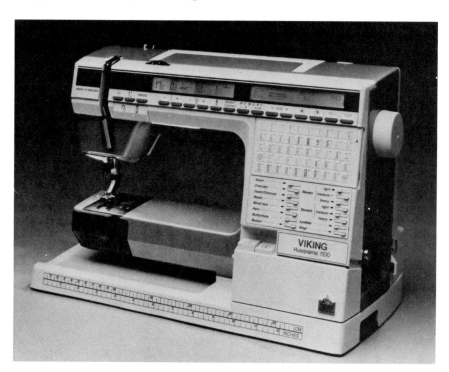

Fig. 1.1.
Viking 1100
computerized sewing
machine.

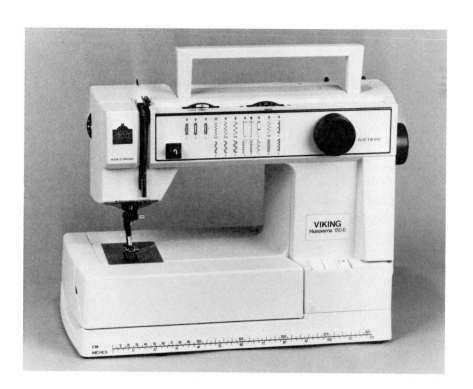

Fig. 1.2.
Viking 150E
mechanical sewing
machine.

Table 1.1. Viking Needle, Fabric, Stitch, and Presser Foot Sewing Advisor. If you don't have a Viking 1100, this guide helps you select the appropriate stitch, stitch setting, and presser foot for your fabric.

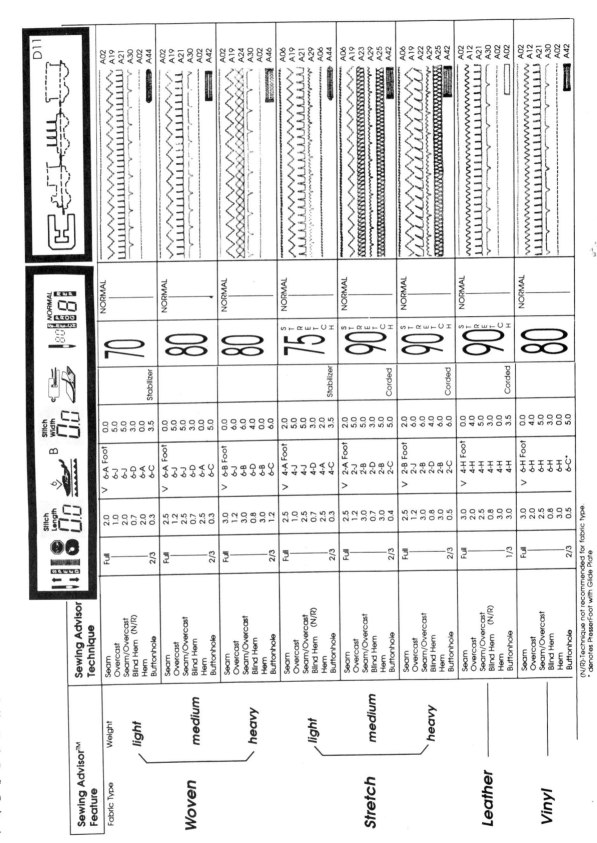

Fabric Type	Weight	Sewing Advisor Technique		Stitch Length	B Foot	Stitch Width	Feature	Needle	NORMAL	Stitch Code
Woven	light	Seam	Full	2.0	> 6-A Foot	0.0		70	NORMAL	A02
		Overcast		1.0	6-J	5.0				A19
		Seam/Overcast		2.0	6-J	5.0				A21
		Blind Hem (N/R)		0.7	6-D	3.0				A30
		Hem	2/3	2.0	6-A	0.0				A02
		Buttonhole		0.3	6-C	3.5	Stabilizer			A44
	medium	Seam	Full	2.5	> 6-A Foot	0.0		80	NORMAL	A02
		Overcast		1.2	6-J	5.0				A19
		Seam/Overcast		2.5	6-J	5.0				A21
		Blind Hem		0.7	6-D	3.0				A30
		Hem	2/3	2.5	6-A	0.0				A02
		Buttonhole		0.3	6-C	5.0				A42
	heavy	Seam	Full	3.0	> 6-B Foot	0.0		80	NORMAL	A02
		Overcast		1.2	6-J	6.0				A19
		Seam/Overcast		3.0	6-B	5.0				A24
		Blind Hem		0.8	6-D	4.0				A30
		Hem	2/3	3.0	6-B	0.0				A02
		Buttonhole		1.2	6-C	6.0				A46
Stretch	light	Seam	Full	2.5	> 4-A Foot	2.0		75 STRETCH	NORMAL	A06
		Overcast		1.0	4-J	5.0				A19
		Seam/Overcast		2.5	4-J	5.0				A21
		Blind Hem (N/R)		0.7	4-D	3.0				A29
		Hem	2/3	2.5	4-A	2.0				A06
		Buttonhole		0.3	4-C	3.5	Stabilizer			A44
	medium	Seam	Full	2.5	> 2-A Foot	2.0		90 STRETCH	NORMAL	A06
		Overcast		1.2	2-J	5.0				A19
		Seam/Overcast		3.0	2-B	5.0				A29
		Blind Hem		0.7	2-D	3.0				A25
		Hem	2/3	3.0	2-B	5.0				A42
		Buttonhole		0.4	2-C	5.0	Corded			
	heavy	Seam	Full	2.5	> 2-B Foot	2.0		90 STRETCH	NORMAL	A06
		Overcast		1.2	2-J	6.0				A19
		Seam/Overcast		3.0	2-B	5.0				A22
		Blind Hem		0.8	2-D	4.0				A29
		Hem	2/3	3.0	2-B	6.0				A25
		Buttonhole		0.5	2-C	6.0	Corded			A42
Leather		Seam	Full	3.0	> 4-H Foot	0.0		90	NORMAL	A06
		Overcast		2.0	4-H	4.0				A12
		Seam/Overcast		2.5	4-H	5.0				A21
		Blind Hem (N/R)		0.8	4-H	3.0				A30
		Hem	1/3	3.0	4-H	0.0				A02
		Buttonhole		3.0	4-H	3.5	Corded			A02
Vinyl		Seam	Full	3.0	> 6-H Foot	0.0		80	NORMAL	A02
		Overcast		2.0	6-H	4.0				A12
		Seam/Overcast		2.5	6-H	5.0				A21
		Blind Hem		0.8	6-H	3.0				A30
		Hem	2/3	3.0	6-H	0.0				A02
		Buttonhole		0.5	6-C*	5.0				A42

(N/R)-Technique not recommended for fabric type.
* denotes PresserFoot with Glide Plate

A. The **needle** is the most important part of the machine.

Sew-How: *To prevent skipped stitches and snagging, use a new needle for each garment or project. Use a fine needle for fine fabric, heavier needles for heavier fabric (see Table 1.1).*

B. The **needle plate**, sometimes referred to as a throat plate, rests on the bed of the machine over the feed dogs and has a round or oblong hole for the needle to pass through.

Sew-How: *Use the needle plate with the oblong hole for most of your sewing. If the fabric puckers and you are using the appropriate needle and stitch length for the fabric, decenter the needle to the far left or right. This offers support around three sides of the needle and often solves a puckering problem. If the puckering continues, use the needle plate with the round hole (but only for straight stitching).*

C. The **bobbin** and **bobbin case** are necessary to make a stitch. The bobbin holds thread necessary for sewing; the bobbin case holds the bobbin and is positioned in the front or side of the machine in the race area (see Fig. 1.9). When top and bobbin threads lock, a stitch is formed.

D. **Feed dogs,** often referred to as feed teeth, are the teeth under the presser foot that move the fabric through the machine.

Sew-How: *Keep the lint cleaned out from under the feed dogs to prevent skipped stitches (see Care and Maintenance later in this chapter).*

E. The **presser foot**, sometimes incorrectly referred to as the pressure foot, holds the fabric firmly against the feed dogs for proper stitch formation. There are many types of presser feet each designed for specific purposes (see Chapter 9, Encyclopedia of Presser Feet).

Sew-How: *To determine the use of a presser foot, examine its underside. Even if you have lost your Operating Manual, you may understand its intended use just by looking.*

F. The **free-arm**, often called an open arm, enables you to stitch tubular areas, such as cuffs, armholes, or pant legs, without ripping out a seam.

G. **Stitch length** used to be calibrated in stitches per inch (spi); Viking sewing machines are calibrated in millimeters (mm). In the Machine Readiness Checklists throughout this book, stitch length is described in millimeters (mm). The following chart shows you what stitch length really means:

setting in mm	stitches per inch (spi)
0.5	60
1	24
2	13
3	9
4	6
5	5
6	4

Sew-How: *Instead of adjusting thread tensions, remember this rule for selecting the proper stitch length:*

*If the fabric **puckers** when you sew, **shorten** the stitch length. Shortening the length adds thread to the stitch, allowing the fabric to relax and eliminating puckers.*

*If the fabric **waves out of shape** as you sew, **lengthen** the stitch. Lengthening the stitch eliminates thread from the stitch, preventing the thread from pushing the fabric out of shape.*

H. **Stitch width** is what gives the sewing machine its creative possibilities. Add width to a straight stitch to get a zigzag stitch.

I. The **flywheel**, also called a hand wheel, is found on the right end of the machine and turns as you are sewing. The flywheel either helps drive the machine or coordinates needle swing with the action of the feed dogs to create a stitch. Move the flywheel by hand to place the needle exactly where you want it for stitch-by-stitch control.

J. The **stitch selector** indicates stitches available on your machine. Rather than creating a variety of stitches manually, most machines have a way of selecting built-in stitches with a dial, lever, push button, or touch pad.

K. **Top thread tension** is one of the most misunderstood parts of your machine. I prefer the term "thread control." Thread control is necessary on both top and bobbin for proper stitch formation. On most machines, both can be changed without damaging your machine to create many interesting effects (see Part II, The World of Sewing). The Viking 900 and 1100 series machines automatically adjust top tension for each stitch.

L. The **take-up lever** is what pulls the thread through the upper tension as the stitch is being formed.

Sew-How: *Prevent your machine from unthreading the needle by stopping with the take-up lever at the highest position.*

M. The **presser foot pressure dial** regulates the amount of pressure the presser foot exerts on the fabric. The normal setting is usually well marked on each model. Pressure is released when darning freehand, or for free-machine stitchery.

Sew-How: *The Viking 1100 has a unique pressure system. The pressure adjustment is recommended for each function on the Infodisplay above the recommended presser foot.*

FEATURES AND COMPUTER TERMINOLOGY

If you have a computerized Viking 1100, or a model in the 900 series, you have computerized features and function buttons on your machine. The following explanations should help you identify the functions, and the symbols used in the Machine Readiness Checklists found throughout this book.

The **Infodisplay™ Window** (Fig. 1.3) is found on the Viking 1100. The panel, which looks like a mini-computer screen, tells you the preferred stitch length and width, recommended pressure, the best presser foot and needle size to use for a particular stitch and fabric, and whether you need a fabric stabilizer or interfacing under your work. Pretty amazing, isn't it? The Infodisplay also calls out the other functions for programming decorative stitches and Pictograms (see your Operating Manual).

Fig. 1.3.
Viking 1100
Infodisplay.

Next to the Infodisplay Window, is the **Programdisplay™ Window.** The Programdisplay shows you what a Pictogram (see below) or combination of decorative stitches and/or letters and numbers look like before you stitch.

Needle stop enables you to keep your hands on your work rather than turning the flywheel by hand to stop the needle where you want it. With this function, you can select whether the needle will stop in the "up" position for easy removal of the fabric or in the "down" position for pivoting.

The **instant reverse button** is touched to backstitch at the beginning and end of a seam. It is also used to program stitch combinations (see **Automatic one-step buttonhole** below).

With the **Automatic one-step buttonhole,** once the buttonhole type and length is put in the memory on the 990 or 1100, the Viking makes the same buttonhole in one step, time after time; additional steps such as pivoting the fabric or readjusting the stitch width are eliminated. The buttonhole function is controlled by the **instant reverse button.**

Sewing speed or "cruise control" means the sewing speed can be preset, so when sewing accuracy is crucial, acceleration surges are eliminated. On the 900 series, use the right, center, and left ends of the foot control for slow, medium, and fast speeds. On the 1100, set the speed control by pushing the appropriate function button. Note the computer selects speed automatically for a number of the stitches and stitch programs on the 1100.

Pushing the **STOP display** or **finishing** button automatically ties off a stitch and stops the needle at the end of the pattern. Find this feature on the 990 and 1100 Vikings.

The utility, stretch, and decorative stitches and the alphabet and numerals have a **preprogrammed width and length.** However, if you want to fine-tune the width and length for specific uses, you can override the programming.

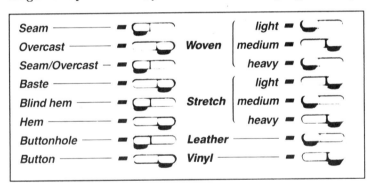

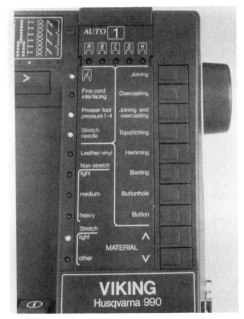

Fig. 1.4.
Viking 1100 and
Viking 990 Sewing
Advisors.

The **Sewing Advisor**™ is available on a cassette on the the 990, and is built in on the Viking 1100 (Fig. 1.4). It's designed to take the guesswork out of selecting a stitch appropriate for the fabric. When you tell the Sewing Advisor what types of fabric you are sewing on and what you want to do, it automatically selects the best stitch, sets the length and width, and suggests a presser foot. If necessary, it adjusts the upper thread tension. The Sewing Advisor on the 1100 also tells you if you need a stabilizer under the fabric and suggests the best needle on the Infodisplay.

The **double-needle width indicator** automatically narrows the stitch width so you don't break a double needle when using a utility or decorative stitch.

The **select function button** is used to program stitch combinations and Pictograms (see below) on the 1100. The **P** or **PM** program button has a similar function on the 900 series machines. See your Operating Manual for your model for specific information.

A machine with **memory** remembers stitches when they have been combined. The 990 series machines all have memory.

The 1100 has a **retained stitch memory bank.** This means you can program up to 63 stitch combinations into one of the nine memories. When the machine is turned off, the memory is retained.

Push the **stitch elongation** button and a stitch pattern can be lengthened while maintaining the stitch density on the Pictograms.

Program cassettes are available for the 990 and 1100 (see your Operating Manual). Each program cassette has a variety of stitches, Satin Elements™, letters, and numerals to choose from.

Pictograms (original decorative stitch combinations) are created by combining **Satin Elements** (stitches 31 – 49 on the D cassette) available on program cassettes for the 1100 and 990 Vikings. This enables the user to create an almost endless variety of decorative stitch combinations.

Single pattern selection means that a single stitch pattern can be isolated. For instance, if you want to stitch a daisy on the top of a stem, you can program the machine to make one complete daisy, then stop and tie off at the end of the pattern.

If your Viking has **mirror imaging** you can create a mirror image of a stitch, important when designing Pictograms, or for centering designs. On the 990, the mirror image is done horizontally. On the 1100, mirror imaging is done both horizontally and end-to-end, increasing decorative possibilities. This way you can create a stitch combination that is symmetrical.

Cursor buttons, found on the 1100 Viking, are used for programming stitches. After you select a stitch, you enter it in the program by pressing the cursor and reverse arrow button.

With **audio feedback,** found on the 1100, a beep lets you know when the machine is on, when the bobbin is low, or when you have done something incorrectly.

THREADING

Upper Threading

Although every machine threads a little differently, each follows a similar threading procedure. From the spool, threading usually follows this order (Fig. 1.5). Note there may be a thread guide or two between one or more of the following:

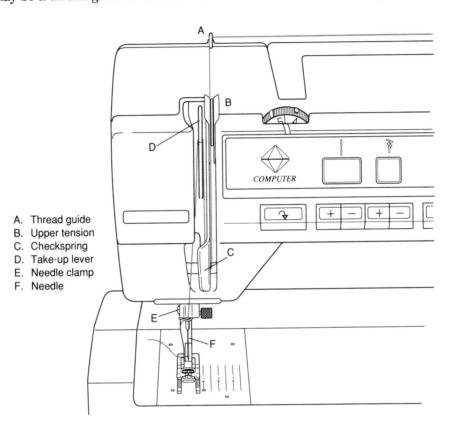

A. Thread guide
B. Upper tension
C. Checkspring
D. Take-up lever
E. Needle clamp
F. Needle

Fig. 1.5.
Upper threading.

Bobbin Winding and Threading

Bobbin winding varies from model to model, so check your Operating Manual.

Sew-How: *Bobbin cases should be threaded so that when the thread is pulled, the bobbin turns clockwise. This prevents the bobbin thread from backlashing, which can cause uneven tension and thread breakage.*

Sew-How: *With older model Vikings, you need to bring the bobbin thread up by hand. Place top thread under the presser foot and hold it against the bed of the machine with the index finger of your left hand. Starting with the take-up lever at the highest position, turn the flywheel one complete turn so the top thread pulls up the bobbin thread loop. Rather than scraping over the feed dogs with a pair of scissors to free the bobbin thread, pull out a longer length of top thread, grasp in both hands a length about 5" (1.3cm) long, then pass it under the foot to free the bobbin thread.*

THREAD CONTROL (TENSION)

What do you think when you hear the word "tension"? A tension headache? I remember a sign in the home ec. lab that read "Don't Touch the Tension!" and my shoulders automatically tightened up. That's why I prefer to call thread tension "thread control."

If you have a removable bobbin case, set your bobbin tension first, then adjust the upper tension to it.

1. Place bobbin in bobbin case. When you pull the thread, the bobbin should turn clockwise.

2. Some bobbin cases have one scew on the side of the bobbin case to adjust tension. Others have two screws on the side of the bobbin case. If yours has two screws, locate the one closest to the thread. This screw is used to adjust bobbin tension. With the tiny screwdriver that came with your machine, carefully loosen this screw on the side of the case, without removing it, so there is no drag on the thread. When you pull the thread, it should slide out easily.

3. By quarter turns, tighten the screw until the thread supports the weight of the bobbin and bobbin case, but there is still a little bit of slipping when you jerk on the thread (Fig. 1.6).

4. Tighten screw *another* quarter to half a turn.

For balanced thread control, top and bobbin thread should lock in the middle of the fabric. It's easier to check if you use one color thread in the top and a different color in the bobbin. (Make sure they are the same weight and brand.) To test this, set your straight stitch on a 2.5 – 3 length and sew on the bias, using a double thickness of medium-weight fabric. Pull stitch on the bias. Thread should break on both top and bobbin side of the stitch.

If only the top thread breaks, loosen the upper tension. If only the bobbin thread breaks, tighten the upper tension. Now stitch a 3 length, 3 width zigzag stitch. Turn the fabric over. Stitches should lock perfectly on one side of the stitch. A slight loop on the other side of the stitch is permissible (Fig. 1.7).

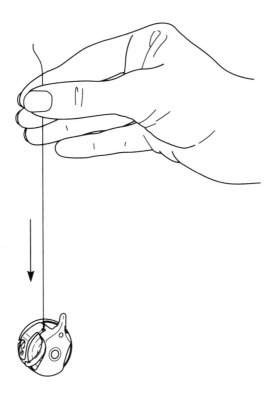

Fig. 1.6.
For proper bobbin
tension, tighten screw
until thread supports
the weight of the
bobbin and bobbin
case, then tighten
screw another quarter
to half turn.

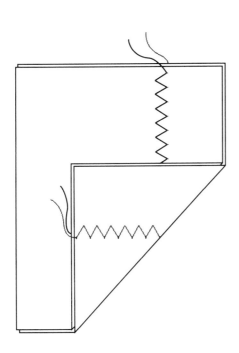

Fig. 1.7.
Zigzag stitch should
lock between the two
layers of fabric on
one side.

PRESSURE

Pressure is the amount of force the presser foot exerts against the fabric and feed dogs.
Most sewing is done with full pressure. However, lighter pressure is advisable when
sewing certain delicate fabrics and for decorative treatments. The pressure is released
completely for freehand darning and free-machine embroidery.

NEEDLE SELECTION

The purpose of the needle is to poke a hole in the fabric big enough for the thread to pass through without fraying. Choose your thread to match the weight of fabric; the needle to match the size of the thread; and the point of the needle to match the type of fabric (review Table 1.1).

The best needle to use for any project is a new one. For the sewer, a new needle for every project is like a clean, sharp scalpel for each operation for the surgeon. New needles prevent skipped stitches, snags, puckering, and unnecessary holes in your fabric.

Needles are sized by the European or American systems and are identified by numbers and letters. The number identifies the size; the letters, the type of point. Tables 1.2 and 1.3 will help you in selecting your needles.

Sew-How: *The Machine Readiness Checklist for each technique and project in the book lists the correct needle for the job. The Viking 1100 also recommends a needle on the Infodisplay when you select a stitch or use the Sewing Advisor.*

Table 1.2
European and American Needle Sizes

European	American	Suggested Fabrics
60	8	silk organza, chiffon, georgette, sheers
70	10	blouse and lightweight dress fabrics
75	11	available in "stretch" needle type only—knit interlock, Lycra, swim wear, knit sheers, Ultrasuede™, and other synthetic leathers and suedes
80	12	suit-weight silks, linens, and wool
90	14	denim, topstitching with topstitching thread, heavy duck cloth, real leather
100	16	use only if the size 90/14 breaks
120	18	hemstitching

Table 1.3.
Needle Point Types.

Table 1.3
Needle Point Types

H	**Universal:** cross between a sharp and ballpoint tip; use on most knits and wovens.
H-S	**Stretch:** sharper point than a universal needle with a deeper scarf, which aids in stitch formation to prevent skipped stitches. Recommended for swim wear knits and synthetic suedes.
H-J	**Jeans:** sharp point to penetrate closely woven fabrics easily without breaking the needle. Recommended on denim, corduroy, and upholstery fabric. Sometimes colored blue to avoid confusion with the other size 14/90 needles.
N	**Topstitching:** eye is twice the size of a normal 90/14 needle to accommodate heavy topstitching thread.
NTW	**Wedge:** large-eyed needle with a wedge point to penetrate genuine leather. The point slices into leather rather than perforating it.

TWIN NEEDLES

Twin needles, also called double needles, have one shank and two needles fixed to a crossbar. They are sized by two numbers and a letter. For example, a 2.0/80(12)H means the needles are 2mm (1/16") apart, are size 80/12, and have a universal point; a 4.0/90(14)H means the needles are 4mm (1/4") apart, are size 90/14, and have a universal point.

RULES FOR THREAD SELECTION

When selecting thread, read the label and unwrap a little, then take a close look at it. It should have a smooth, even appearance.

Throughout this book, you will see a *Machine Readiness Checklist* for each technique. One of the following thread types is recommended:

- 100% cotton sewing
- all-purpose sewing
- cotton embroidery
- rayon embroidery
- nylon monofilament

One hundred percent cotton sewing thread works well for most garment construction provided it is colorfast and mercerized against shrinkage. It has a lot of sheen, so it can also be used for embroidery, topstitching, and buttonholes. Cotton fibers are long and smooth, so you shouldn't experience tension problems. Cotton thread is not as strong as cotton-wrapped polyester or 100% polyester; however, if used with the correct stitch for the fabric, cotton thread is strong enough for most projects. The only other disadvantage with cotton thread is that it is not as readily available as the others. Look for these brand names: D.M.C., Mettler Metrosene, Zwicky.

All-purpose cotton-wrapped polyester thread, referred to in the Machine Readiness Checklist as "all-purpose" thread, is also colorfast and mercerized and is recommended for garment construction. All-purpose thread has slightly less sheen than the 100% cotton thread. It is also stronger and stretches more than the all-cotton thread because of its polyester core, and so it requires some tension adjustments. All-purpose thread is widely available. Look for these brand names: J. & P. Coats (Dual Duty), Mettler Metrosene, Zwicky.

Cotton embroidery thread is finer than the cotton sewing thread, so it is not recommended for construction of seams. However, it is great for machine blind hemming and for machine embroidery. It is recommended for blind hemming because, when used with a fine needle and a loosened top tension, the stitches become almost invisible. Cotton embroidery thread is also colorfast, mercerized, and fills in a design smoothly and with less bulk than the all cotton sewing thread. Look for these brand names: D.M.C., Mettler Metrosene, Zwicky.

Rayon is not as strong a fiber as cotton or polyester, but it has a lot of shine. Therefore, **rayon embroidery thread** is not recommended for construction, but is beautiful for machine embroidery. To prevent the thread from shredding and breaking, use a size 90/14 stretch needle and a loosened top tension. Look for these brand names: Madeira, Natesh, Paradise, Sulky.

Nylon monofilament thread looks like very fine fish line, and blends with any color—helpful because you don't have to rethread your machine when using different color fabrics in the same project. It can also be used on the bobbin so that to change thread color you need only rethread the top. However, some kinds of nylon monofilament thread are wiry, won't hold a knot, and may irritate sensitive skin. Therefore, look for "Invisible Wonder Nylon Thread" available through mail order sources.

Buy your thread at the fabric store or your sewing machine dealer, and stick with the major brands (see Sources of Supply). Buying five spools for a dollar is not a bargain when the thread breaks, fuzzes, and causes the fabric to pucker. Remember, match your thread to the weight of your fabric. If you're sewing on lightweight woven fabric, for example, you want the thinnest thread possible—machine embroidery thread.

STANDARD PRESSER FEET AND ACCESSORIES

Do you know where the accessories are that came with your machine? Do you know what each item is for? The following information may refresh your memory. Specific techniques and usage for these and extra accessories are covered thoroughly in Chapter 9, Encyclopedia of Presser Feet.

Today's Vikings come with the feet and accessories listed in Table 1.4 and shown in Fig. 1.8. Those in Table 1.5 are available as a separate purchase.

Fig. 1.8. Standard Viking accessories—1, standard A metal zigzag foot; 2, utility B foot; 3, buttonhole C foot; 4, blind hem D foot; 5, zipper E foot; 6, raised seam F foot; 7, transparent B (appliqué) foot; 8, Teflon H foot; 9, overcast J foot; 10, raised seam guide; 11, edge (quilting) guide; 12, button reed.

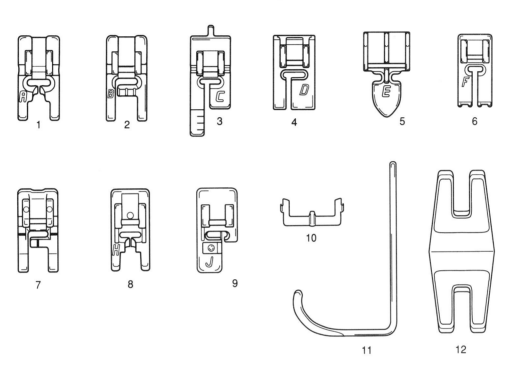

- The **standard A metal zigzag foot** is used for general straight seams and topstitching of lightweight and heavy fabrics. The needle hole is oblong, and the underside is smooth and flat to keep the needle from pulling the fabric up and down with each stitch. The front is also notched to give more places on the foot to guide your fabric for precise topstitching.

- The **utility B foot** has a wide channel behind the needle so it rides smoothly over decorative stitching. It offers more support on the fabric than the transparent B appliqué foot and can also be used for seaming light- to medium-weight fabrics such as T-shirt knits, wool jersey, and interlock knits.

- The **buttonhole C foot** has two narrow channels on the underside behind the needle. This way, the foot rides over the first row of stitching, so the two sides of the buttonhole are parallel. The long toe is marked for easy reference and the prong on the back makes cording a buttonhole easy.

Table 1.4					
Presser Feet and Accessories Included with Viking Machines					
Lettered Feet	Manufacturer's Number	100/600 Series	900 Series	6000 Series	1100 Series
"A" Standard	411 73 86 45	●	●	●	●
"B" Utility	411 73 88 45	●	●	●	●
Transparent "B" Appliqué Foot	412 00 16 45	●	●	●	●
"C" Buttonhole	411 73 89 45	●	●	●	●
Buttonhole Sensor	412 17 84 01				●
"D" Blind Hem	411 73 91 45		●		●
"D" Blind Hem	411 53 31 45	●			
"E" Zipper	411 73 93 45	●	●	●	●
"E" Zipper	411 29 89 01			●	
"F" Raised Seam	411 73 99 01	●	●	●	●
"H" Teflon	411 85 30 45	●	●	●	●
"J" Overcast	411 85 27 45	●	●	●	●
"J" Overcast	411 42 47 01			●	
Standard Machine Accessories					
Edge Guide	401 54 20 01			●	
Edge Guide	411 73 95 01	●	●		●
Attachment Screw	411 13 99 01			●	
Glide Plate	411 77 93 01		●	●	●
Glide Plate	411 77 91 01	●	●	●	●
Glide Plate	411 42 43 01			●	
Button Reed	411 17 32 01	●	●	●	●
Bobbins, Transparent	411 44 01 01	●	●	●	
Bobbins, Transparent	412 09 75 45				●
Raised Seam Guide	411 39 25 01	●	●	●	●

Table 1.4.
Presser Feet and
Accessories
Included with
Viking Machines.

Sew-How: *Sue Hausmann, Chicago, Illinois, uses the long toe of her buttonhole foot to tighten the needle clamp screw instead of hunting for the screwdriver. "I always know where my buttonhole foot is, and it is a lot stronger to use than the screwdriver."*

• The **blind hem D foot** has a wide toe on the right and the underside is higher on the left side for easier guiding and more precise blind hemming.

• The **zipper E foot** snaps off and can be moved to sew either side of the zipper. The deep grooves on the underside ride smoothly over the coil so stitching is straight.

• The **raised seam F foot and guide** is designed for pintucking with twin needles. The foot and guide can also be used to lay down and couch over cord.

• The **transparent B (appliqué) foot** has a similar function to the utility B foot, but is made of a transparent material so it is easy to see what is going on under it. The wide

Table 1.5 — Presser Feet and Accessories Available for Viking Models as Separate Purchase					
	Manufacturer's Number	100/600 Series	900 Series	6000 Series	1100 Series
Bias Binder	411 85 04 45	●	●	●	●
Braiding Foot	411 85 00 45	●	●	●	●
Braiding Foot	409 30 05 01			●	
Braiding Foot, Narrow	411 85 09 45	●	●	●	●
Braiding Guide	411 85 01 45	●	●		●
Buttonholer	2021			●	
Circular Sewing Attachment	411 85 26 45		●		●
Circular Sewing Attachment	411 58 13 01			●	
Cording Foot — 5 Hole	411 45 38 01			●	
Cording Foot — 7 Hole	411 85 11 01	●	●		●
Darning Foot	411 28 98 61			●	
Darning Foot	411 73 90 45	●	●		●
Darning Plate	411 85 14 45	●	●		●
Darning Plate	411 85 14 02	●			
Dual Feeder	411 85 84 45		●		●
Dual Feeder	411 42 94 01			●	
Edgestitching/Lace Joining Foot	412 28 02 01		●		●
Eyelets Plates — 4mm	412 00 69 01		●		●
Eyelets Plates — 6mm	412 00 69 02		●		●
Eyelets Plates — 4mm	411 58 55 01			●	
Eyelets Plates — 6mm	411 58 55 02			●	
Eyelets Plates — 4mm	412 00 71 01	●			
Eyelets Plates — 6mm	412 00 71 02	●			
Gathering Foot	411 85 02 45	●	●		●
Gathering Foot	411 43 81 01			●	
Glide Plate Zipper and Buttonhole	412 01 41 45	●	●	●	●
Hemmers — 2mm	411 85 22 45	●	●	●	●
Hemmers — 5mm	411 85 17 45	●	●	●	●
Hemmers — 3mm	411 85 20 45	●	●	●	●
Hemmers — 2mm	411 85 24 45	●	●	●	●
Hemstitcher	401 53 67 45	●	●	●	●
Open Toe Appliqué Foot	412 27 70 01		●		●
Piping	411 85 10 45	●	●	●	●
Raised Seam Foot and Guide	412 01 42 45	●	●	●	●
Roller Presser Foot	411 85 29 45	●	●	●	●
Roller Presser Foot	411 39 01 01			●	
Ruffler	409 30 20 01			●	
Ruffler	411 85 88 45		●		●
Rug Foot	411 29 64 01	●	●	●	●
Seven Hole Foot and Threader	412 01 43 45	●	●		●
Special Marking Foot	411 85 03 45	●	●	●	●
Special Marking Foot	411 39 31 01			●	
Straight Stitch Foot	411 85 35 45	●	●	●	●
Weavers Reed — 30mm	411 34 58 01	●	●	●	●
Weavers Reed — 45mm	411 34 58 02	●	●	●	●

Table 1.5.
Presser Feet and
Accessories Available
for Viking
Models as Separate
Purchase.

channel behind the needle allows the foot to ride smoothly over decorative stitches without pushing them into the fabric. Also use the appliqué foot for seaming medium to heavyweight fabrics such as sweater knits, velour, and stretch terry cloth.

• The **Teflon H foot** is white in color and has a flat underside which offers a lot of support around the needle. The Teflon surface slides smoothly over sticky fabrics such as leather, vinyl, Ultrasuede™ and Ultraleather™. This foot is also helpful when sewing very fine, slippery fabrics such as nylon tricot or acetate linings because it helps both layers of fabric to feed evenly.

• **Glide plates** are Teflon strips with an adhesive backing, and shaped to stick on the bottom of presser feet so they ride smoothly over sticky fabrics (see Teflon H foot explanation, above).

• The **overcast J foot** is generally used for overcasting a raw edge on a single layer of fabric. The stitch forms over the bar on the right to prevent the fabric from tunneling under the stitch.

• The **quilting** or **edge guide** slides behind the foot shank and rides over a row of stitching, or next to an edge, so successive rows of stitching are evenly spaced.

• The **button reed** is used to create space between the button and fabric when sewing buttons on by machine. It can also be used as a wedge when sewing up and over uneven thicknesses.

• The **buttonhole sensor** comes standard with the Viking 1100 and is designed to measure one-step buttonholes precisely when stitching on uneven fabric thicknesses like those on a front tab, cuff, or collar stand (see Fig. 9.9).

CARE AND MAINTENANCE

Cleaning

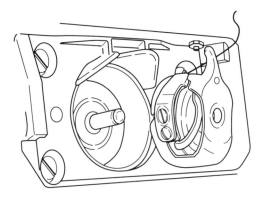

Fig. 1.9.
Viking race.

Next to changing the needle with each project, cleaning the lint from the area under the feed dogs and the race area is most important (Fig.1.9). (Remember, the race is the area that houses the bobbin and bobbin case.)

1. Remove your bobbin, bobbin case, presser foot, needle, and needle plate (see your Operating Manual).

2. Fluff out your lint brush so that each bristle can reach into a lint-infested area to pull the lint out. Dust the big chunks out of the race with the brush. Finish the job by blowing out the finer particles with canned air rather than using your breath. The moisture from your breath may cause parts to rust.

DID YOU KNOW? There has been some controversy about the use of canned air. An ozone safe brand called TAC Air Blast is available through mail-order sources (see Sources of Supply).

Oiling

In 1972, Viking was the first company to make a sewing machine that did not require oiling. If your Viking is newer than that, disregard the information in this section. Older Vikings should be oiled between every eight and twelve hours of sewing time or once a month to keep your machine running smooth and quiet. To find out if your machine needs oiling, rub you finger on the needle bar—you should get a little oil on your finger. If it's dry, oil it with sewing machine oil. This oil is fine, pure, and won't "gum up" the parts. To oil:

1. Unplug machine. Remove the bobbin, bobbin case, presser foot, needle, and needle plate. Remove the top cover and race.

2. Dust out the lint from race.

3. Turn the flywheel by hand, and put a drop of oil on every metal part that moves against another metal part. Repeat for the race area.

Note: If your machine is a flatbed model, tip it back in the cabinet or carrying case. Turn the flywheel and oil every metal part that moves against another metal part.

Don't oil the nylon gears or the belt on the flywheel.

4. Put race back together. Plug machine in and run it without the needle for a couple of minutes until the oil has a chance to work. Wipe off excess oil from bed of machine.

5. Put in new needle and stitch on a scrap to check if oil comes off on the fabric. If it does, stitch on a piece of fabric until stitches are dry; then don't use as much oil the next time.

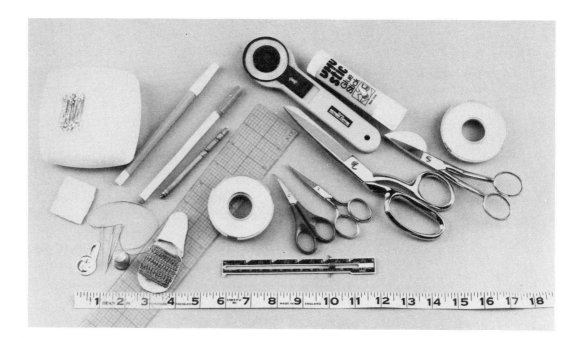

Fig. 1.10.
Measuring, cutting,
marking, and
sewing tools.

Step Two:

ASSEMBLE YOUR TOOLS

Besides your sewing machine, you will need a few tools and notions to measure, cut, mark, sew, and press your completed projects (Fig. 1.10). I refer to many of these throughout the book, so refresh your memory and check your sewing inventory. Besides the items below, there are hundreds of other notions to make sewing easier. See the Sources of Supply for mail-order companies.

MEASURING TOOLS

• Use a **tape measure** so pattern pieces are cut on-grain and for other quick measurements as you lay out a pattern. Choose one that is made of paper or plastic-coated fabric, so it won't stretch with continued use. Most tapes are 5/8" (1.5mm) wide—the width of a standard seam allowance.

Sew-How: *Wear your tape measure around your neck while sewing, for ready reference.*

• A **sewing gauge** has a sliding guide for measuring hem depth, button and buttonhole spacing, trim placement, and pleat width; ear length and eye spacing for toys and appliqués; and more. A must for anyone who mends or sews.

• A **see-through cutting ruler** is thick enough to cut against using the rotary cutter. The O'Lipfa™ ruler is 24" (61cm) long and 1/8" (3mm) thick and has a lip edge. This lip hangs off the edge of the cutting mat and is used like a T-square. It is 5" (12.5cm) wide and is marked every 1/2" (1.3cm) the length of the rule.

Sew-How: *For accuracy, use the same rule to measure and cut all quilting strips and borders.*

CUTTING TOOLS

• **Shears** have a thumb hole and an oblong hole for two or more fingers. They are designed for the best grip and extended usage, so you can cut for long periods of time without straining your hand. The bend provides a place to rest your index finger and allows you to cut without raising the fabric off the table.

Shear blades are made of hot-forged steel, stainless steel, or aluminum. Steel blades can be resharpened more often than their aluminum counterparts, but are heavier to use.

Some shears are joined by a rivet; others by a screw and nut. Generally, riveted shears cannot cut as heavy a fabric as those joined by a screw and nut. When purchasing a pair of shears, test them by cutting through at least two thicknesses of medium-weight fabric. They should cut to the tip.

• **Scissors** have a thumb and finger hole and are used for smaller jobs such as trimming and clipping. There are specific scissors for specific jobs. For general-purpose sewing, use 5" (12.5cm) scissors with one pointed and one round-tipped blade. This way you are less likely to snip a hole where it isn't wanted, or to push scissors through the fabric while pushing out a collar or pocket point.

• A **rotary cutter** and **mat** are for the more serious home sewer. They are more expensive than shears, and you still need shears for cutting intricate designs and pattern pieces. However, the cutter cuts through multiple layers of fabric at one time—great for cutting quilt blocks, strips, and long, straight pattern pieces—but it must be used with a special mat to protect the layout surface.

Rather than sharpening the cutter, you change the blade. If you're looking for a faster way of cutting, this is it.

HOLDING TOOLS

• **Pattern weights** speed up the layout and cutting process. Rather than pinning the pattern pieces to the fabric, weights have pin-like tacks on the underside to hold the pattern tissue and fabric while cutting. If you are using a fabric that snags easily, use the weights with the smooth side down.

• **Pins** are necessary for sewing. If your pins are a collection scavenged from men's dress shirts or the floor of the home ec room at school, buy some new ones. My favorites are fine, glass-headed quilting pins. They are extra long, and the glass heads won't melt if pressed over. They are also easy to find when accidentally dropped on the floor or carpet.

• A **pin cushion,** or magnetic Grab-It™ is an ideal home for your pins. I use a wrist pin cushion while sewing. A Grab-It sits on the table and on the ironing board during layout, cutting, and pressing. This way, I have a place for my pins, no matter where I am in the construction process.

• **Tweezers** are handy for grabbing too-short threads when you have to rip something out, removing tear-away stabilizer, or retrieving a needle or pin that accidentally fell into the workings of your machine. They also help you hold threads, appliqué edges, and tricky seam allowances and can be used to remove lint and broken threads from the race and bobbin area. My favorite tweezers are those that came with my serger. They have a sharp nose which is bent at a slight angle for easy use and visibility. If you don't have a serger, purchase a pair of tweezers through your local serger dealer.

MARKING TOOLS

• **Dressmaker's chalk** or a sliver of soap marks well on dark fabrics, but is sometimes difficult to remove. I like Clo-Chalk (see Sources of Supply) because it marks well, comes with its own sharpener, and disappears in five days on its own or immediately when washed or ironed. Use chalk to transfer pattern markings.

• A **water-erasable marker** is like a felt-tipped marker for fabric and marks well on light-colored fabrics. Marks erase with clear water.

Sew-How: *Use a water-erasable marker to transfer pattern markings by resting the tip on the pattern tissue. The ink bleeds through the tissue, first layer of fabric, then second layer of fabric for an accurate mark.*

• A **vanishing marker** is similar to the water-erasable marker, except the mark disappears within 24 to 48 hours, depending on the humidity. Mark darts and dots, transfer an appliqué pattern, or copy a monogram on the right side of the fabric. If you make a mistake, the ink disappears, and no one is the wiser.

• **Transparent tape** is another handy marking and basting tool. Stitch next to it for straight topstitching, to sew a straight dart, or to stitch in a zipper. Stick a button or appliqué in place before stitching. Just remember to hide your supply from your family, or it may disappear like the vanishing marker.

Sew-How: *I like the type that has a cloudy appearance because it is less sticky and easier to see on dark fabrics than the shiny type.*

SEWING TOOLS

• As ye sew, so must ye rip." A **seam ripper** is essential for fixing mistakes or "unsewing." The point picks the stitch out of the seam, while the blade cuts the thread. Like pins and needles, a ripper wears out occasionally, so replace it when it dulls. The best quality I've found is available through your local sewing machine dealer. Look for the little arrow etched on the blade.

• Rather than tying off threads or backstitching, use a **liquid seam sealant** called Fray Check™ to prevent threads from fraying and coming unstitched.

Sew-How: *Use sealant on the edge of ribbons, trims, and lace to prevent raveling.*

• A **glue stick** is a basting aid. Use it to stick a button, appliqué, lace, or trim in place before sewing.

• As much as I like to stitch everything by machine, **a hand needle and thimble** are necessary in your sewing stash. Use a needle for pulling threads through to the wrong side of the fabric before tying them off, to sew on hooks, eyes, snaps, and other odds and ends. Use a thimble on the middle finger of your right or left hand, to push the needle comfortably through the fabric.

Sew-How: *There is nothing more annoying than hunting for a hand needle when you need one, so store your needle on one end of your wrist pin cushion away from the pins or make yourself a needle case.*

• A **large-eye tapestry needle** is used to pull heavier threads and cord to the wrong side of the fabric before tying it off. Thread cord ends from a corded buttonhole through the large eye of the needle, then pull cords between the facing and garment front to tie them off. Also tape a button to the fabric with a tapestry needle between the holes to create a shank when the button is stitched on by machine (see Fig. 8.17, 8.55).

• A **needle threader** is helpful not only for threading hand and machine needles, but for pulling threads, embroidery floss, and pearl cotton cord to the wrong side of the fabric so it can be tied off.

• A **spring hoop** holds the fabric taut to minimize puckering for free-machine embroidery, free-machine quilting, and appliqué. It is also narrow enough to fit under the foot without removing the needle.

• **Waxed paper** is used to make alterations, redraw a pattern, and to trace off patterns. Use an old, dry ballpoint pen or tracing wheel to transfer the marks onto the waxed paper. Make a roll of waxed paper part of your sewing supplies.

PRESSING TOOLS

The art of pressing is essential to the art of sewing, so you need a few pressing tools (Fig. 1.11).

Fig. 1.11.
Pressing tools.

• A **hand iron** is used to smooth yardage that has been preshrunk before cutting, to press seams and darts, and for countless other uses in the world of sewing.

Sew-How: *If your iron has a rough, uneven surface, clean it with hot iron cleaner, available through your local fabric store. After cleaning, put a piece of brown paper on your ironing board, then a piece of waxed paper over it. Run the warm iron over the waxed paper to restore the shine and smoothness to the soleplate.*

• An **ironing board** is essential for pressing. A muslin cover works better for shaping and pressing a project than the heat-reflective type.

Sew-How: *If the pad under your ironing board cover is flattened, make another one, as Sara Bunje of San Mateo, California, did. She used the old pad as a pattern and cut a new pad from an army blanket.*

• A **Husky Press** is a small, commercial-type press, great for sewing as well as for pressing the rest of the laundry. For more information on the Husky Press and its uses, see *Sew, Serge, Press—Speed Tailoring in the Ultimate Sewing Center* by Jan Saunders, Chilton, 1989.

• To prevent shine and overpressing, place a **press cloth** over the fabric before pressing or ironing on the right side of the fabric. Use a piece of 100% cotton unbleached muslin or a press cloth, available through your fabric store or mail-order source (see Sources of Supply).

Table 1.6   Interfacing Selection Chart

Fabric Type	Interfacing "Hand"	Recommended Interfacing	Fusible or Sew-In	Other Information	Colors
Sheer to light-weight fabrics, such as chiffon, georgette, crepe de chine, charmeuse, voile, batiste, gauze, lace, silk broadcloth	Sheer	Self-fabric Organza Pellon #906F Bridal illusion, netting, or veiling Pellon sheer weight #905 HTC Sheer D'Light™ Featherweight Armo® Sheer-Shape™ Pellon #905	S S F S S F S S	Matches color and hand Available in many colors Light, crisp hand, nonwoven, Adds crispness, won't show through Nonwoven, softer than 906F Crosswise give; soft and drapable Soft and drapable Soft and drapable	— — Wht, bge, chrcl — Wht, bge Wht, chrcl Wht Wht, bge
Featherweight to midweight wovens, such as gingham, challis, tissue faille, jersey, polyester, silk crepe Knits: cotton and cotton blend interlocks, jersey, lightweight sweater knits	Soft	Pellon Sof-Shape® Armo® So-Sheer™ Stacy Easy-Knit® Dritz Knit Fuze™ HTC Fusi-Knit™ J & R Quick Knit™ Armo® Intra-Face™ Bias Featherweight Pellon #910 Featherweight HTC Sew Shape™ Featherweight Armo® Press Soft Pellon #910 Featherweight	F F F F F F S S S S S	Nonwoven, all-bias Nonwoven Nylon tricot knits with crosswise stretch and lengthwise stability. Use on knits and wovens. All-bias for knits and wovens Crosswise stretch, lengthwise stability Gentle control on lightweight knits and wovens Soft shaping for lightweight wovens All-bias gentle support	Wht, chrcl Wht, bge, chrcl Wht, bge, blk Wht, bge, blk Wht, ivy, blk, gry Wht, bge, blk, gry Wht Wht Wht Wht Wht
Other featherweight to midweight wovens: shirtings, broadcloth, oxford, muslin, seersucker, chambray, poplin, pincord, madras, lightweight linen (Heavier) knits: double knits, stretch terry, velour, regular weight and heavy sweatshirt fleece	Firm	Armo® PressSoft Pellon #911FF Stacy Shape-Flex® Armo® Uni-Stretch® Lightweight HTC Sheer D-Light™ Lightweight	S F F F F	Woven, permanent press All bias; soft supple shaping for midweight knits and wovens. Woven Crosswise give, stretch & recovery for knits and stretch-wovens.	Wht Wht, gry Wht Wht Wht, chrcl
	Crisp	Pellon Shapewell® (#70) Dritz Shape Maker™ Pellon ShirTailor® (#905F) Armo®Shirt-Shaper™ Dritz Shirt Maker™ J & R Shirt Bond™	S S F F F F	100% cotton; crisp shaping for oxford cloth, poplin, calico and other light to medium weight dress & blouse fabrics. For shirt collars, cuffs and other details where firmness is desirable for a crisp tailored look.	Wht Wht, blk Wht Wht Wht Wht
Skirt, pants, or suiting fabrics, such as gabardine, chino, linen, linen blends, wool and wool-like crepe, duck, cotton and cotton blends, faille, velvet, velveteen	Soft	Armo® PressSoft Pellon Sof-Shape® Stacy Easy-Knit® Armo® Whisper Weft™ Pellon Shapewell® (#70F) Pellon Easy-Shaper® Dritz Shape-Up Lightweight™ HTC Sheer D'Light™ Medium Weight J & R Stretch 'N Shape™	S F F F F F F F F	Woven, permanent press For tailoring loosely woven light- to midweight fabrics Knit Weft insertion 100% cotton; use in lightweight wovens for soft shaping Soft supple controlled shaping for light and midweight knits and wovens	Wht Wht, chrcl Wht, bge, blk Wht, bge, gry Wht Wht, chrcl Wht, chrcl Wht, chrcl Wht, blk

Table 1.6. Interfacing Selection Chart.

• A **tailor's ham** is a curved, stuffed cushion used to press curved areas. A good ham has cotton drill cloth on one side and wool on the other. The cotton side is used to press cotton, cotton blends, and linens that require higher temperatures. The wool side is for wool, silk, and wool blends and, if used properly, will minimize shine.

FABRIC STABILIZERS

• **Interfacing** is used to stabilize areas in a garment that are likely to stretch out and wear—armholes, necklines, front tabs, plackets, cuffs, collars, and waistbands, to name a few. Fusible interfacing is applied to the fabric with heat, moisture, and pressure. Sew-in interfacing is usually hand- or machine-basted into place. To select the appropriate interfacing, refer to the Interfacing Selection Chart (Table 1.6).

Interfacing Selection Chart (cont.)

Fabric Type	Interfacing "Hand"	Recommended Interfacing	Fusible or Sew-In	Other Information	Colors
Other skirt, pants, or suiting fabrics: denim, poplin, flannel, wool, mohair, coating, corduroy	Crisp	Stacy Shape-Flex® Universal HTC Form-Flex™ Universal J & R Classic Woven	F F F	100% cotton, use in light- to midweight wovens for crisp support	Wht, blk Wht, blk Wht
		Dritz Suitmaker ™ J & R Tailor Fuse™	F F	Lengthwise and crosswise stability and bias give like a woven. Use in mid- to heavyweight tailoring projects.	Natural Wht, blk
		HTC® SRF™ Pellon Stretch-Ease (#921F)	F F	Stretch and recovery for midweight knits, wovens, and stretch wovens	Wht, chrcl Wht, chrcl
		Armo® Uni-Stretch® Suitweight	F	Use for collars, lapels and cuffs	Wht
		Pellon #930 Armo® Press Firm	S S	Firm to very firm shaping of medium- to heavyweight knits and wovens.	Wht Wht
		HTC Sta-Form™ Durable Press HTC Veri-Shape™ Durable Press Dritz Sew-In DuraPress™ J & R Woven Form™	S S S S	Crisp shaping in midweight wovens, stable knits.	Wht, blk Wht Wht Wht
Heavy, tailoring-weight wools and wool coating.	Tailored	HTC Fusible Acro Armo® Weft Pellon #931 TD Midweight (MVF)	F F F	Washable hair canvas Weft insertion For firm support in midweight kntis	Natural Wht, bge, blk, gry Wht
		Pellon Pel-Aire® (#881F) Dritz Shape-Up Suitweight™	F F	Textured surfaces and heavier adhesive coating provides better adhesion to suit and coat-weight fabrics for tailoring.	Natural, gry Wht, chrcl
		HTC (Armo) Acro	S	Washable hair canvas for medium to heavy tailoring: 52% rayon/ 43% polyester/ 5% goathair	Natural
		HTC (Armo) Fino II	S	Hair canvas for fine couture tailoring: 35% wool/35% rayon/ 15% polyester/ 15% goathair	Natural
		HTC P-26 Red Edge	S	Economy hair canvas: 57% cotton/ 32% rayon/ 11% goat hair	Natural
		Pellon Sewer's Choice™ (#90H)	S	Traditional hair canvas: 43% cotton/ 36% rayon/ 21% goat hair	Natural
Fur, fake fur, fleece	Stabilizing	Armo® Press Firm HTC (Armo) Acro Pellon Sewer's Choice™	S S S	Woven, permanent press Washable hair canvas Traditional hair canvas	Wht Natural Natural

Pellon® and Stacy® are registered trademarks of The Pellon Company, a division of Freudenberg Nonwovens Limited Partnership. The Stacy® products listed were purchased by Pellon when Stacy Industries went out of business. Armo® is a registered trademark of Crown Textile Company; Handler Textile Corporation (HTC) sells Armo products to the home sewing market.

Colors	White = Wht	Ivory	= Ivy
Legend:	Black = Blk	Beige	= Bge
	Grey = Gry	Charcoal = Chrcl

• **Paper-backed fusible web** is a stabilizer and adhesive used in appliquéing. With adhesive side against the wrong side of fashion fabric, iron with a dry iron. Draw the appliqué shape on the paper backing, cut out shape, remove paper, and the shape is ready to fuse to the base fabric. See Chapter 3 for specific application and use. There are many brands, but Wonder-Under™ is most widely available.

• **Plastic-coated freezer wrap**, available through your local grocery store, is generally used to rewrap food for storage in the freezer. It's also ironed to the wrong side and used to stabilize fabric for embroidery, appliqué, or quilting, so you rarely need a hoop. Remove wrap after stitching by peeling it off the back of the fabric.

• **Tear-away stabilizer** is used to stabilize fabric and to minimize puckering in machine embroidery and monogramming. Use it on top of or under the work and tear it away after stitching.

• **Water-soluble stabilizer** is a plastic film which is clamped in the hoop and placed on top of the fabric. It can be drawn upon and is removed by rinsing with warm water.

Step Three:

LEARN THE BASIC STITCHES

By now you have cleaned your Viking. You have changed the needle. You have wound a bobbin, threaded it in the bobbin case, completed the upper threading, and balanced top and bobbin tensions. You have also assembled your tools, important notions, and supplies, so let's look at some basic stitches, and sew something.

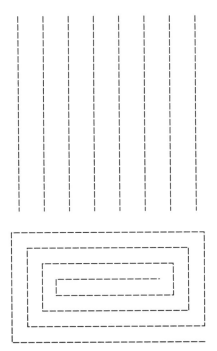
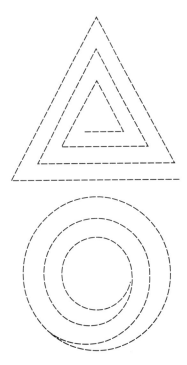

Fig. 1.12.
On a piece of paper, stitch lines, rectangle, circles, and triangle to practice sewing straight, pivoting, and sewing curves. Pattern is 1/2 size.

STRAIGHT STITCH

New Sewer's Note: *If you have never operated a sewing machine before, you may want to practice sewing straight lines, pivoting corners, and sewing curves with an unthreaded machine, stitching on paper. Paper will dull the needle, so be sure to put in a new one when you switch to fabric. (If you have done a similar exercise in the past, or simply need to brush up on your skills, advance to the next exercise.) If you use waxed paper, you can hang it up in a window, for pretty patterns of light. To practice, enlarge the designs in Fig. 1.12 to twice the original size at your local copy center. Trace the lines, rectangle, circles, and triangle on a piece of tracing paper. Press two sheets of waxed paper together with a moderately hot iron. This way the paper is stiff and easier to maneuver. Place waxed paper over tracing paper so you see the stitching lines. Tape corners together with transparent tape.*

WARM-UP EXERCISE

Supplies

- waxed paper (optional)
- tracing paper
- water-erasable marker

1. Set the stitch length to 2.5, the most common stitch length used in sewing. Put the standard A metal foot on your machine. Place edge of paper under the foot and put the needle into the work. The needle is unthreaded.

2. Lower the presser foot and start sewing.

3. To pivot a corner, turn the flywheel by hand so needle is in the waxed paper. Lift the presser foot, pivot, then lower presser foot to continue.

4. To sew inside and outside curves, slow down and guide the fabric by using your fingers like the center point in a compass.

5. Press over waxed paper again to flatten and set the holes. Put this sampler in your notebook, or hang it in a window. Now you're ready for the first exercise.

EXERCISE 1: PRESSED FABRIC LEAVES

The best part of fall is its color. Whether or not it's fall in your neck of the woods, create colorful leaves any time of year while perfecting straight stitching, sewing inside and outside curves, and pivoting. This time, use thread and fabric.

Sew-How: *Throughout this book you will see Machine Readiness Checklists. As you can see, each list contains information to ensure that each technique is successful. After the stitch name, you will see a letter and number. This corresponds to the cassette and stitch number as it is shown on the Viking 1100 cassettes (see Fig. 8.1). If you don't own an 1100, your stitches are not identified this way. Therefore, photocopy Fig. 8.1 and post it so you can identify each stitch by what it looks like and compare it to what you have available for your Viking.*

Machine Readiness Checklist	
Stitch:	straight (A2)
Length:	2 – 4
Width:	0
Foot:	standard A metal zigzag
Needle:	80/12 universal
Thread:	100% cotton or all-purpose one shade darker than fabrics
Fabric:	sheers (e.g., organdy, organza, batiste) in colors you like (I used light pink, blue, lavender, and peach.)
Accessories:	tear-away stabilizer or tracing paper, water-erasable marker, waxed paper, iron

1. Enlarge leaf patterns in Fig. 1.13 two hundred percent at your local copy center. Trace leaf patterns on tracing paper or tear-away stabilizer. Cut two small leaves and one oak leaf.

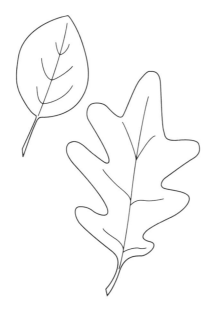

Fig. 1.13.
Leaf pattern for
Pressed Fabric Leaves
exercise. Pattern is
1/2 size.

2. Layer two or three colors of sheer fabric, and pin them together so stabilizer with leaf pattern is on top.

3. Stitch around the leaf, including the veins, one complete time. Practice using a 2 stitch length on the curves and stitch length 3 or 4 on the veins.

4. Repeat sewing around the leaf three or more times, practicing curves and pivots and changing the stitch length.

5. Remove the stabilizer. Cut out leaf and clip threads close to the fabric.

6. Repeat for other small leaf and oak leaf.

Sew-How: *For variation in color, trim away one or more underlayers from various sections of each leaf.*

---

7. Arrange and sandwich leaves between two pieces of waxed paper.

8. Press over leaves and waxed paper with a moderately hot iron. **Pressing** means moving the iron in an up-and-down motion, lifting the iron off the paper, then putting it down next to where you just pressed. After pressing, iron over the piece to eliminate wrinkles and creases. **Ironing** means sliding the iron back and forth with a long, smooth motion.

Hang your creation in a window to see the colors made by layering sheer fabrics.

Variations on Exercise

Layer two or three sheer fabrics and stitch geometric shapes, your initials, flower petals, or any other shape. Arrange shapes, add glitter, crayon shavings, and/or dried flowers, then press between waxed paper.

AUTOMATIC STITCHES

Adding width to the straight stitch creates the zigzag stitch. To achieve this with your machine, you may have to select the zigzag stitch by moving a dial or lever, or by touching a button or pad.

On a double layer of medium-weight fabric, stitch a sample for your notebook using the transparent B (appliqué) foot and zigzag stitch on a 1 length and 1 width. Stitch another row on a 2 length and a 2 width, the next row on a 3 length and 3 width, and so on.

Next stitch rows of zigzag stitches, keeping the stitch length on 0.5 and changing only the width. Start on a 1 width, then sew rows using a 2, 3, 4, and 5 width zigzag. This is called a satin stitch. It is used around appliqués, on napkin edges, in cut work, and in many other decorative ways (Fig. 1.14).

Fig. 1.14.
Satin stitch sampler
showing various stitch
widths.

Sew-How: *If your fabric tunnels under the satin stitch, loosen the upper tension slightly. If tunneling continues, iron plastic-coated freezer paper to the wrong side of the fabric.*

Finally, set the width on 4 and change only the stitch length. Start on a 1 length and work your way through a 2 to 6 stitch length.

This exercise demonstrates the difference between width and length as it affects the zigzag stitch. You can also create designs by moving the width as you sew. However, it's almost impossible to stitch an even pattern with the unpracticed hand.

Automatic stitches are variations on the zigzag and are controlled by your Viking. Examples are the woven blind hem, knit blind hem, three-step zigzag, ball, diamond, and scallop (Fig. 1.15). Once the automatic stitch is selected, with the proper stitch width and length set, the machine stitches them *automatically.*

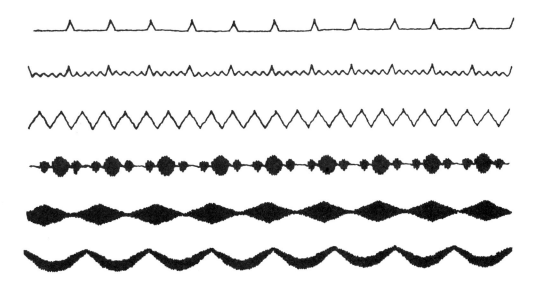

Fig. 1.15.
Automatic
stitches—woven blind
hem, knit blind hem,
three-step zigzag, ball,
diamond, and scallop.

TRIMOTION™ STITCHES

Other types of stitches available on Viking sewing machines since 1960 are called Trimotion™ stitches. While the needle zigzags from side to side, the feed dogs move the fabric forward and back, creating tracery patterns such as the double overlock, flatlock, overedge, stitch-and-overcast, smocking, and clover (Fig. 1.16).

Exercise 2 will familiarize you with what is available on your model Viking, as well as help you practice upper threading and winding and threading a bobbin.

EXERCISE 2: STITCH SAMPLER

A good way to become familiar with the stitches on your machine is to make a sampler. In this exercise, your sampler will feature automatic and Trimotion stitches. Then you'll turn it into a pin cushion.

Machine Readiness Checklist

Stitch:	automatic; Trimotion stitches
Length:	automatic stitches—0.5 – 2; Trimotion stitches—varies
Width:	3 – widest
Foot:	transparent B (appliqué)
Needle:	80/12 universal
Thread:	100% cotton or all-purpose sewing in color that matches fabric
Fabric:	striped cotton or cotton/poly blend with a white stripe (pillow ticking works well)
Accessories:	lightweight fusible interfacing, straight edge, vanishing marker, hand needle, polyester fiberfill (used to stuff toys), coffee mug, and rubber band

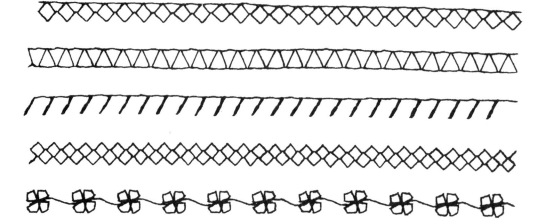

Fig. 1.16. Trimotion stitches—double overlock, flatlock, overedge, smocking, and clover.

1. Cut striped fabric 10 X 5" (25.5 X 12.5cm), so the stripes are going the short way. Fuse lightweight interfacing to wrong side of fabric.

Sew-How: *For the interfacing to bond permanently, use heat, moisture, and pressure. Place fabric on ironing board, wrong side up. Cut interfacing a little smaller than fabric so it will not stick to the ironing board. Place interfacing, fusible (rough) side down. Use the cotton setting on your iron.*

With a very damp press cloth over the work, firmly press 10 to 20 seconds in one spot. Let the steam escape, then press again for a few seconds. Lift up the iron and press again, overlapping iron on previously fused section. Repeat this bonding technique the length of your fabric until the interfacing has been applied (Fig. 1.17).

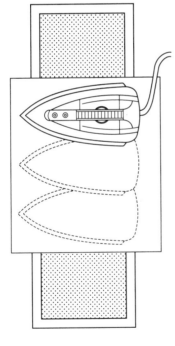

Fig. 1.17.
To fuse interfacing, use a damp press cloth, set iron on cotton setting, then press for 10 to 20 seconds in one spot. Lift iron then press, overlapping iron on previously fused section.

Sew-How: *If you have a Husky Press, use it to fuse interfacing on the wrong side of your fabric as described above. The press exerts 100 pounds (45kg) of pressure and fuses interfacing on a larger surface, faster and more permanently, than a hand iron and press cloth.*

---

2. Decide which stitches you want on your sampler. The Viking 1100 has an almost unlimited number to select from, so find your favorites.

3. Stitch a different automatic stitch on every other light stripe. Remember, for automatic stitches, the fabric feeds through the machine in one direction.

4. On the remaining light stripes, stitch a different Trimotion stitch. For extra color, change the top thread and slightly loosen top tension. (The bobbin thread shouldn't show.)

5. Place the sampler in your notebook or finish it as explained below.

FINISHING

Easiest Pin Cushion

1. Cut your sampler in half to make two 5" (12.5cm) squares. Overcast the four edges of each piece with the three-step zigzag (A19) stitch on a 1 – 1.2 length and the widest stitch width. Guide the raw edge so the needle stitches just off the edge at the right. Put one sampler piece in your notebook.

2. Wrap a small handful of fiberfill with the second half of your sampler and put a rubber band around the bottom to keep stuffing in place.

Fig. 1.18. Wrap fiberfill with stitch sampler and put rubber band around the bottom. Set stuffed sampler in a coffee mug and use as a pin cushion.

3. Stick the fabric-covered stuffing in a coffee mug, rubber band side down (Fig. 1.18).

Note: If the stuffed sampler gets pushed down too far in the mug, stuff with more fiberfill. Set your pin cushion next to your machine, on the cutting table, or on the ironing board.

BUTTONHOLES

Contrary to popular opinion, buttonholes are not difficult and you don't have to avoid a pattern because it calls for them.

Each machine company keeps improving the method by which its machine makes buttonholes. If you are sewing on a new machine, or the machine is new to you, take a few minutes to read your Operating Manual and see how truly easy it is. The next project is designed to help you practice.

EXERCISE 3: BUTTONHOLE SAMPLER

Stitch your buttonhole sampler and put it in your notebook, or finish it by making a pattern weight or paperweight.

Sew-How: *The Viking 990 makes six buttonhole styles. The 1100 makes ten. Use this exercise to practice the different styles, programming the length so they are made the same length.*

Machine Readiness Checklist

Stitch:	zigzag or buttonhole
Length:	0.4 – 0.8
Width:	3.5 – widest
Foot:	buttonhole C or buttonhole sensor (1100)
Needle:	80/12 universal
Thread:	all-purpose in four or five primary and secondary colors
Fabric:	white medium-weight cotton or cotton/poly blend, cut 6" (15cm) square
Accessories:	Wonder-Under cut 6" (15 cm) square, cardboard, small glass ashtray or paperweight globe available at cross-stitch shops, craft glue, colorful buttons (optional), vanishing marker

1. Wind bobbins for each thread color.

2. Fuse Wonder-Under on wrong side of fabric square.

Sew-How: *Place fabric wrong side up on the ironing board. Place Wonder-Under with rough side down, paper side up. Set dry iron on cotton and press for three seconds.*

3. On the right side of the fabric, stitch four or five different sized buttonholes in each color all over your fabric square. (The Wonder-Under paper acts as a stabilizer on the underside of the sampler.) Space buttonholes far enough apart so that your foot will not ride on another buttonhole. Place sampler in your notebook or finish it as explained below.

FINISHING

1. Place the ashtray upside down on the right side of sampler, and trace its outline with the vanishing marker.

2. Cut out ashtray shape from sampler.

3. Remove the Wonder-Under paper from the wrong side of sampler. Now it's ready to fuse to the cardboard.

4. Fuse the cut sampler to the cardboard using a dry iron on wool setting. After the cardboard cools, cut out the cardboard in the shape of the ashtray.

Fig. 1.19.
Buttonhole sampler
pattern weight or
paperweight.

5. Place a few colorful buttons of varying sizes over the sampler (optional). They are loose, not sewn. Drop a few beads of craft glue on the rim of the ashtray and smooth it around. Lay ashtray, upside down, over sampler so buttonholes are seen through the glass (Fig. 1.19). Place a heavy book over paperweight and let the glue dry for 24 hours.

If you don't want to make a pattern weight or paperweight, use this patch as a pocket and stitch it to a T-shirt or sweatshirt.

TRANSFERABLE LEARNINGS

The information and techniques you have learned and practiced in this chapter have given you the skills necessary to sew many other projects. You have learned:

• **Pressing vs. ironing**—when you pressed your leaves between the waxed paper, you used both an up-and-down pressing motion and a side-to-side ironing motion. Pressing helps give a project a finished, professional look during construction. Ironing is done to smooth out wrinkles after the project is complete.

• **Straight stitching**—necessary for sewing seams and topstitching. Standard stitch length is 2.5mm.

• **Inside and outside curves**—necessary for sewing any curve at a neckline, armhole, collar, pocket, or seam.

• **Pivoting**—necessary for turning any corner at a pocket, collar, seam, or for topstitching.

• The **satin stitch**, is used to appliqué, finish napkin edges and cutwork, and for other decorative techniques.

• **Stitch length and stitch width** must be adjusted for both utility and decorative stitches if you have an older Viking model. Many of the new Vikings have a preset width and length that can be fine-tuned for specific needs.

• **Fusible interfacing** is used in many areas to add stability and increase wear. Proper bonding and application is important so interfacing stays put once a project is washed or cleaned.

• **Sewing in a straight line is important.** If you can sew a straight line by stitching accurately between stripes, you can seam or topstitch almost anything.

• **Buttonholes** are seen everywhere on clothing, crafts, and gifts. After practicing, you are ready to make buttonholes whenever the pattern calls for it.

• **Wonder-Under** is a paper-backed fusible web used to bond appliqués so they don't shift when stitched. You will use this product and technique again for machine appliqué and for many other projects in this book.

Now that you have gotten to know your Viking a little better, understand what many sewing notions and tools are for, and have practiced some basic stitches, let's see how this applies to the World of Sewing.

Part II walks you chapter by chapter through six World of Sewing categories—you will "Sew Fashion," "Sew Embellishments—Machine Appliqué and Embroider," "Sew for Your Home," "Sew a Quilt," "Sew Toys," and "Sew Gifts." Stitch through each in order, or skip to the one of most interest. Happy sewing!

THE WORLD OF SEWING

Part II

THE WORLD OF SEWING

THE WORLD OF SEWING

This part of the book explores six areas of sewing. Although you may know something about each area, you may not know the best way to complete a project utilizing the stitches, presser feet, and features of your Viking. Rather than making stitch samples, the objective here is to complete a project using all the tools available, so you can apply the techniques and shortcuts to any other project you attempt in The World of Sewing.

Each chapter in this part has a series of steps. Step One: Planning Your Project helps you with fabric selection, layout, cutting, marking—the all-important preliminaries.

The next steps take you through the project and show you the shortcuts and professional finishing techniques not usually covered in the pattern instructions.

Each technique has a *Machine Readiness Checklist* that lists the stitch, length and width settings, recommended presser foot, and other information to insure your success. The stitch is identified by name and by the stitch number as it is described in Fig. 3.1 for the Viking 1100 and Viking 990 models. Sometimes I couldn't describe a stitch on the 990 by number because it is built in. Therefore, you might want to photocopy Fig. 3.1 and post it in front of you so you can easily identify each stitch by the picture of it.

At the end of each chapter you'll find **Transferable Learnings,** a review of what you've learned and a guide to how you can use the techniques in other areas of sewing.

If you have never sewn before, pay attention to **New Sewer's Notes.** This should help you avoid common pitfalls so your experience is fun, and the projects successful.

Before starting, however, let's organize some efficient work space for the three functions in sewing—cutting, sewing, and pressing.

CUTTING AREA

The cutting area can be as simple as a cardboard cutting board on a bed or dining room table, or as fancy as a cutting table designed specially for the area or room you sew in. Some people like to cut on the floor. To save the carpet and your back, cutting is a lot easier if the table is at least 30" (76cm) high, and if you can get around all four sides of it.

On or near the cutting area, have a yardstick or straight edge of some kind and a tape measure. This enables you to check grain lines, measure and mark strips and quilt blocks, check fabric width and length, plan your pattern layout—the list goes on—without hunting for measuring tools.

An extra station for pins is also helpful. I load my Grab-It with pins so the supply in my wrist pin cushion isn't totally depleted after pinning a pattern to the fabric.

One of my best investments was a tall wastebasket. It's large enough to hold a lot of pattern and fabric scraps, I empty it less, and it's close enough to the height of the table so I can brush scraps into it without dropping them all over the floor. My family also understands it's not for the disposal of food or unfinished drinks. (I never know when I'll have to dig through it for a scrap or something that fell into it by mistake.)

SEWING AREA

Set your machine accessory box to the right of your machine so you don't have to hunt for a foot when you need it. A sewing caddy with marking tools, threads, extra scissors, and accessories is also helpful. If you don't have a caddy, empty checkbook boxes are a good substitute.

To me, a pattern is like toothpaste—once it's out of the envelope, it's almost impossible to put back. Tape a gallon-size resealable plastic bag on the table, and to the right of your machine, for pattern storage. Keep the envelope, extra pattern pieces, and the pattern pieces that come off your fabric in this bag. Everything fits, and you can find your pattern pieces easily. If you teach, have students put their names on all pattern pieces before cutting them apart. This way one student won't end up with another student's pattern piece.

Sew-How: *Fold tissue pattern pieces so the name and number of each is on top. This way if you need to find it again, you don't have to fish around and unfold every one. It's also easier to get pattern pieces back in the envelope when they are folded this way.*

You'll need a place for pattern instructions. If your sewing machine faces a wall, you can tape pattern instructions to the wall, or tack them to a bulletin board in front of you. Nancy Zieman, president of Nancy's Notions Ltd., recommends taping an acetate sheet to the table and slipping the pattern instructions underneath. If you don't have an acetate sheet, try a dry cleaner bag instead.

Finally, have another wastebasket near your sewing machine for threads and fabric clippings.

PRESSING AREA

Here you'll need an ironing board, iron, tailor's ham, and press cloth. Position your ironing board to one side of your machine and lower it so you can press while seated. This way you don't have to get up and down from your machine each time you press. Store the ham, iron, and press cloth at the wide end of the board.

Are you ready to make something? The first project is an outfit—a pair of elastic-waist, woven shorts and a knit top. After completing them, you'll have the skills to make a pair of pants, culottes, skirt, or sweatshirt. Let's get started.

SEW FASHION

- *Step One: Plan Your Projects*

- *Step Two: Sew Woven Pull-on Shorts*

- *Step Three: Sew a Knit Top with Ribbing*

- *Step Four: Project Variations—Instant T-Shirts*

- *Transferable Learnings*

Step One:

PLAN YOUR PROJECTS

A TRIP TO THE FABRIC STORE

Once you have mastered the skills to make a pair of woven shorts and a knit top, you can use those skills to make a pair of woven pants, culottes, or elastic waist skirt as well as a knit shirt, sweatshirt, or knit dress. The style and fabric will be up to you. Before shopping for your fabric and pattern, however, take some measurements to determine your pattern size.

Dress in your underwear or a leotard. Tie a piece of elastic around your waist to find your natural waistline, and ask a friend or spouse to take your measurements, filling in the chart below (Table 2.1). When taking circumference measurements, the measuring tape should be loose enough to get a finger between the tape and your body. Once you have taken measurements, determine your pattern category.

Table 2.1	Measurement and Ease Chart			
WOMEN		Your Measurement	Ease to be Added	Tissue Paper Measurement to Seam Line
Bodice	High bust		3-5"	
	Bust		3-5"	
	Center front bodice length		1/2"	
	Length center back, neck to waist		3/4"	
	Back shoulder width		1/2"	
Sleeves	Upper arm circumference		2-3"	
	Arm length, shoulder to elbow		—	
	Arm length, shoulder to wrist		—	
	Wrist circumference		3/4"	
Skirt	Waistline		3/4"	
	High hip, 3" below waist		3/4"	
	Hips at fullest part, parallel to floor		2-3"	
	Waist to fullest part of hips		—	
	Thighs, parallel to floor		2-3"	
	Shirt length, waist to desired length		—	
Pants	Waistline		3/4"	
	Thigh circumference		2"+	
	Calf circumference		2"+	
	Inseam		—	
	Crotch depth (sitting)		1"	
	Crotch depth (standing)		1"	
MEN				
Upper body	Neck		1/2"	
	Chest		3-5"	
	Center front waist length		1/2"	
	Center back waist length		1/2"	
	Back width		1"	
	Shoulder width		—	
Sleeves	Shirt sleeve length		—	
	Upper arm circumference		2-3"	
	Arm length		—	
	Wrist circumference		3/4"	
Lower body	Waist		3/4"	
	Waist to fullest part of hips		—	
	Hips (seat)		1-2"	
	Thigh		1-2"	
	Trouser outseam (side length)		—	
	Trouser inseam		—	
	Waist to knee length		—	
	Crotch depth (sitting)		3/4"	
	Crotch depth (standing)		2-3"	

Table 2.1.
Measurement and
Ease Chart.

In the back of the pattern catalog you will find different figure types for men, women (Fig. 2.1), and children. Find the one most like yourself or the person you are sewing for. Then look at the pattern you have chosen in the pattern catalog and find the size that most closely fits your measurements. Other information to help you find the right size is in the descriptive paragraph found on the catalog page or on the back of the pattern (Fig. 2.2). This often tells you if the garment is "fitted," "loose fitting," or "very loose fitting," which indicates how much ease is allowed in the pattern.

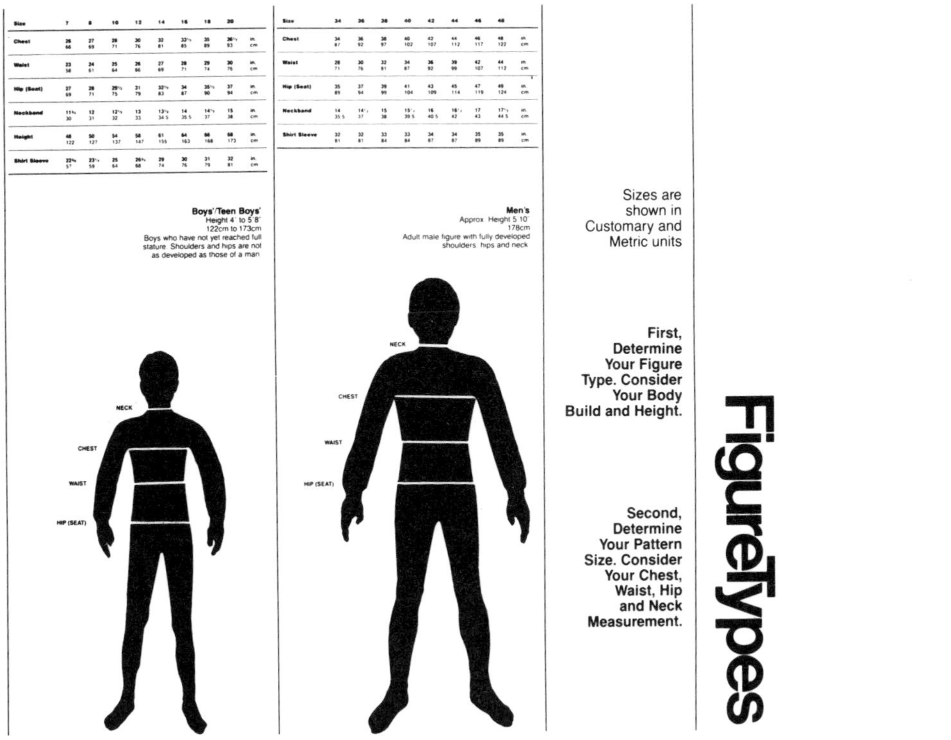

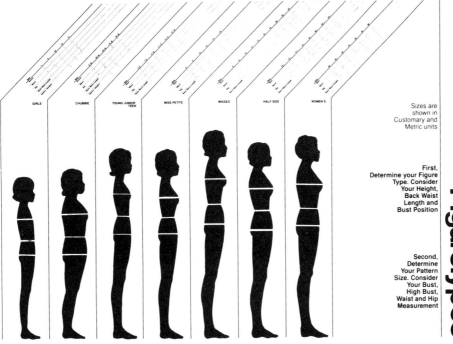

Fig. 2.1.
Figure types found in the back of pattern catalogs (courtesy of the McCall Pattern Company).

Fig. 2.2.
Descriptive paragraph found on the catalog page and back of pattern. Find the width on back of pattern to determine how much fabric to buy (courtesy of the McCall Pattern Company).

GIRLS' OR BOYS' CARDIGAN, TOP, PANTS AND SHORTS – CARDIGAN AND TOP – FOR STRETCH KNITS ONLY: Cardigan has extended shoulders, long sleeves, patch pockets and front button opening. Pullover top has extended shoulders, short sleeves and patch pocket. Pants with or without elasticized ankle and pull-on shorts in two lengths have elasticized waistline.

Sew-How: *Even a fitted garment has 2" (5cm) ease in its circumference. Loose fitting or very loose fitting garments usually have more than 2" (5cm) and up to 8" (40cm) of ease and are subject to your interpretation of the words "loose" and "very loose."*

FABRIC SELECTION

Which comes first, the pattern or the fabric? Judging from my personal stockpile, it must be the fabric. Besides, selecting the fabric is the part I like the best—it's like eating dessert first.

For the shorts, choose a medium-weight woven fabric, such as poplin, weaver's (kettle) cloth, or duck. For easy care and comfort, choose fabric that is a cotton and polyester blend (see bolt end for fiber content, fabric width, and care instructions). It won't shrink or wrinkle as much as 100% cotton, and it's easy to sew. Have fun while you're in the store; look at and feel a lot of fabric. Then choose one without nap (see New Sewer's Note). If you need help, the salespeople will gladly show you different fabrics.

New Sewer's Note: *Plaids, stripes, one-way prints, and pile fabrics such as corduroy and velvet all have a nap. They are laid out and cut so the pattern or design matches, or the pile or one-way design lies in one direction. This requires more yardage than fabrics without a nap. See back of pattern envelope for "with" and "without nap" yardage requirements.*

For the top, choose an all-cotton or cotton/polyester T-shirt knit to coordinate with your shorts fabric. Choose one that does not curl or run. To check for running and curling, pull the fabric across the grain at the cut end.

New Sewer's Note: *In a woven fabric, warp yarns are placed in the lengthwise direction on a loom. Filler or weft yarns are woven across the warp to create a piece of fabric. The lengthwise grain is parallel to the warp or lengthwise yarns, the crosswise grain is parallel to the weft or filler yarns.*

Grain lines indicate yarn direction; they are illustrated on the tissue pattern piece as a line with an arrowhead on either end (Fig. 2.3). Most pattern pieces are laid out so the length of the pattern piece follows the lengthwise grain. Lengthwise yarns are stronger than crosswise yarns, so the pattern piece is less likely to stretch out of shape or distort when laid out this way.

A knit fabric is made with a series of interconnecting loops. Although the fabric isn't stronger in the lengthwise direction, a knit is generally stable on the lengthwise grain and stretches across the grain.

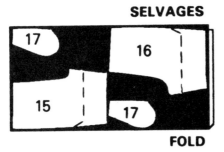

PRESHRINKING

Care and washing instructions should be written on the bolt end for most fabrics. Some stores include care labels with your purchase (ask when you pay). If not, copy the information from the bolt end. It is important to preshrink washable fabrics, trims, and elastics before cutting so they won't shrink and so the colors won't run after the project is completed. Preshrinking also removes the sizing or finish put on some fabrics. Sizing gives fabric body, but can cause skipped stitches if it is not washed out of the fabric before sewing.

Sew-How: *As soon as you walk in your door from the fabric store, preshrink your washable fabric, elastic, interfacing, zippers, and trims in the manner in which you intend to care for the project after construction. For example, if your fabric is a dark blue print and is a cotton/polyester blend, preshrink in cold water and dry on the permanent press setting in your dryer. Read your notes from the bolt end for care instructions.* **Note:** *If the interfacing is fusible, immerse it in warm water, wring it out by hand, then dry it on the line. Don't ever put fusible interfacing yardage in the dryer.*

When the fabric is dry, clip off a small square from a corner and tape or glue it to a piece of paper, along with its fiber content, cost, and where you bought it. Store the paper in your notebook.

How much fabric to buy? You'll find out next when selecting the pattern.

PATTERN SELECTION

For the shorts project, select a pattern recommended for woven fabrics, with elastic in a fold-over casing for the waistline, and a front or back patch pocket. For the top, select a pattern recommended for knits, with a crew neck, raglan or set-in sleeve, and a straight hem (Fig. 2.4).

Fig. 2.4.
Recommended
patterns for woven
shorts and knit top
(courtesy of The
McCall Pattern
Company).

New Sewer's Note: *For the top, select a pattern marked "for knits only." You may find an ease chart printed on the pattern back to help you determine how stretchy a knit is and whether the pattern is appropriate for your fabric. For this project, choose a knit in which, when stretched across the grain, 4" (10cm) stretches to 5" (12.5cm) but not more than 8" (20cm). For the top, select a pattern with either a raglan sleeve, set-in sleeve, or sleeve bands. You may find both top and shorts in one pattern—look in the pattern catalog under "coordinates" or "sportswear." If you are a new sewer, a pattern for a specific size rather than one that includes several sizes is easier to read and understand because there are fewer cutting lines to follow.*

Children and teens may enjoy using Kid Sew™ or Kids Can Sew™ patterns or To Sew kits (see Sources of Supply). The instructions are well written and easy to understand. The styling is also simple and fashionable, so young people enjoy immediate success and are proud to wear and display their creations.

To buy the correct yardage, you need to know the width of the fabric. Fabric width is printed on the bolt end and is commonly 45" (1.1m) or 60" (1.5m). Read the back of the pattern for the correct width to determine how much fabric to buy (Fig. 2.2). Also check the list of notions and other supplies you'll need, to save another trip to the store later.

To make the shorts, you'll need elastic and thread. The easiest elastic to use has a knitted construction. When stretched, the holes open up and the elastic doesn't narrow. Knit elastic is comfortable to wear and doesn't stretch out, even when stitched through.

How much elastic to buy? Enough to fit comfortably around your waist, with a little extra for experimenting. I usually buy enough at a time for two waistlines.

Select a thread color one shade darker than the fabric. If you are using a print, thread color should match the background or the most dominant color. See Table 1.1.

This knit top also requires ribbing. Ribbing is usually knitted in a tube and priced by the inch. See pattern back for yardage requirements. Sometimes fabric stores put ribbing bolts in a different place than regular knits. Ask for help finding it.

Sew-How: *If you can't find ribbing to match your knit fabric, you can often use the same knit fabric for bands. Cut and stitch as described on pages 65-67 for the knit ribbing neckband. If the fabric is a jacquard knit, the right and wrong sides look different but obviously are made with the same colored yarn. For a contrasting band, use the wrong side of the fabric. This trick also works with stretch terry cloth and velour.*

Step Two:

SEW WOVEN PULL-ON SHORTS

Sew-How: *Before starting, remove and unfold the pattern instructions from the pattern envelope. On the instruction sheet you should find a list of common pattern symbols as shown in Fig. 2.5. Besides the explanation on your instruction sheet, I will also explain what the symbols mean as we go along.*

LAYOUT AND CUTTING

Fig. 2.5.
Pattern symbols you
need to know to read
and understand a
pattern (courtesy of the
McCall Pattern
Company).

Place on fold
FOLD LINE: Lay and pin fold line directly on fabric fold. Never cut on fold line.

SEAM LINE: Broken line showing where to sew. Seam lines do not appear on multi-size patterns.

SEAM ALLOWANCE: Distance between sewing and cutting lines.

CUTTING LINE: Thickest black line around pattern tissue showing where to cut.

NOTCHES: Wedges cut outward, used to match one piece to another correctly.

CIRCLES: Also used for matching pattern pieces.

If a garment is cut off-grain, perfect sewing technique and all the pressing in the world will not correct the mistake, so let's start off on the right foot.

1. Unfold the pattern tissue. Find the correct layout for the width of your fabric on the pattern instructions and circle it for easy reference. Your pattern instructions also list the pattern pieces needed for a particular view. They are identified by name and a number or letter (e.g., Pants Back B). Cut the pattern tissue apart between the pieces. You can either cut on the black cutting lines or cut in the plain areas between the pieces. Put aside the pattern pieces you need. Put the rest in the pattern envelope. If you have selected a multisized pattern, trim away surrounding tissue to the proper size.

Sew-How: *Fold extra pattern pieces so the number and name of each is visible. This way, when you use a pattern piece again, you can find it easily. Since it's difficult to refold patterns small enough, you may want to store your pattern pieces in a larger envelope, pinning the original pattern to the outside.*

---

2. If the fabric needs it, iron it flat, then, if appropriate for the layout, fold it in half the long way, right sides together, so the selvages are even. If you need to straighten the grain, unfold your fabric and pull it on the bias to square it up (Fig. 2.6). Then, if necessary iron your **pattern** smooth with a hot, dry iron.

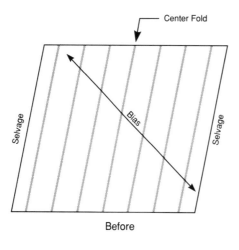
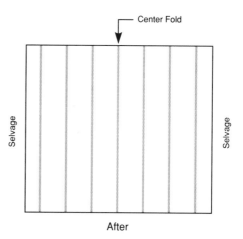

Fig. 2.6.
If the fabric is off grain, unfold it and pull on the bias to square it up.

New Sewer's Note: *Selvages are finished edges that run parallel to each other and with the lengthwise grain.*

■ *Teaching yourself to sew means more than making just garments. You can sew a hobby horse (Chapter 6) and practice machine quilting on a wall quilt (Chapter 5).*

■ Once you learn to construct a knit top and woven pull-on pants (Chapter 2), you can embellish the pants pocket with your machine (Chapter 3).

■ Make a fabric gameboard and pouch (Chapter 7) and a Compass Tote Bag (Chapter 2) for a day at the beach.

■ *Master buttonholes, mitered corners, and professional edge finishes on the Envelope Placemats and matching "Lapkins" (Chapter 4).*

Sew-How: *Even after preshrinking, the center crease may be difficult to press out on some fabrics. Either refold the fabric and lay out the pattern to avoid the crease or use a mixture of half white vinegar, half water on a press cloth to press out the crease. The vinegar/water mixture can also be used for setting creases in pants and pressed-in pleats.*

3. Follow the layout so pattern pieces are laid out on the straight of grain (Fig. 2.3). This means the grain line arrow on the pattern tissue runs parallel with the fold and/or selvage edge. When the distance from the printed grain line to one selvage is the same everywhere along the grain line, your layout is correct.

Sew-How: *Before pinning pattern to the fabric, push a pin straight through one arrow head of the grain line so pattern piece pivots around the pin. This way, you can pivot the pattern piece one way or the other so the grain line is parallel with the selvage edge or fold. Check that the entire grain line is parallel to the selvage or fold, measuring with your tape measure.*

4. Pin tissue pattern pieces to the fabric or use weights to hold pattern pieces in place. Cut fabric, following the black cutting line on the pattern tissue and using your shears or rotary cutter and mat.

Fig. 2.7.
Use the tips of your shears or scissors to snip notch 1/8 – 1/4" (3 – 6mm) at each notch on cutting line.

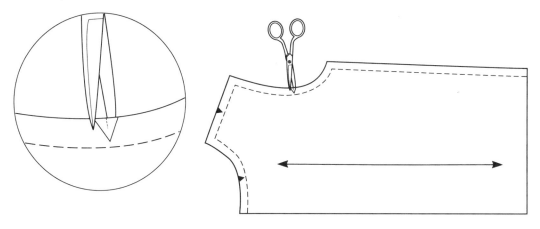

Sew-How: *Notches on the cutting line are usually numbered and indicate where the pattern pieces match up to one another during construction. Single notches are usually found on front pattern pieces; double notches on back pattern pieces; triple notches when front and back pieces are put together. Instead of cutting around every notch, cut across them. Then use the point of your shears and snip into the seam allowance 1/8" (3mm) to 1/4" (6mm) at each notch (Fig. 2.7).*

MARKING

The best time to mark your pattern is before removing the pattern tissue. An easy way to mark a light- to medium-colored fabric is with a water-erasable or a vanishing marker. If you plan to work on a project right away, use the vanishing marker; otherwise, use the water-erasable marker. We will mark the pocket position and the waistline casing line.

Hold the point of the marker over the pattern tissue at a dot. Let the ink from the marker bleed through the tissue pattern piece, through one layer of fabric, then to the other layer of fabric. In a few seconds, both fabric layers are accurately marked.

Mark darker fabrics this way: From the pattern side, use a fine head pin and push it through the dot. Turn fabric over and push another pin through to the other side. Carefully pull pattern tissue off the fabric, then pull pattern pieces apart and mark pin placement with a soap sliver or disappearing dressmaker's chalk (Clo-Chalk; see Sources of Supply).

If the fabric looks the same on both sides and the shape of the pattern pieces look similar, identify them before removing the pattern tissue. On the wrong side of the fabric, label each pattern piece with masking tape. It's easy to write on and won't melt if accidentally pressed over. **Note:** Before using masking tape, put tape on a scrap of your fabric to be sure it will not mark or damage the fabric when removed.

New Sewer's Note: *In addition to labeling the pattern pieces with masking tape, you may also want to indicate the top of each piece by drawing an arrow (Fig. 2.8).*

Fig. 2.8.
On the wrong side of the fabric, label pattern pieces with masking tape. The arrow indicates the top of each piece.

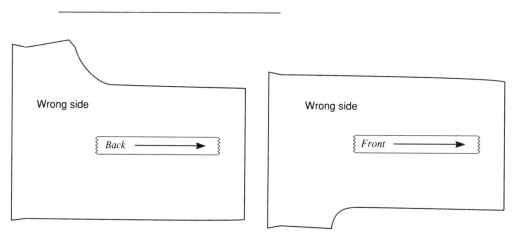

PRESS-AS-YOU-SEW

Pressing each seam as you go is as important as using the proper sewing techniques. Throughout this project and the others in this book, you will be directed to press as you sew.

The correct way to press a seam is first to press it flat and together to set or blend the stitches into the fabric. Then, from the wrong side, press seams open with steam, using an up-and-down **pressing** motion rather than a side-to-side **sliding** motion.

To prevent shine on the right side of the fabric, use a press cloth between the fabric and iron. This is called **top pressing**.

SEAMS AND SEAM FINISHES FOR WOVEN FABRIC

Seam allowances on patterns are usually 5/8" (1.5cm). Depending on the project and the fabric, I generally use 5/8" (1.5cm) seam allowances on a woven and 1/4" (6mm) seam allowances on a knit. On the knit seam allowances, I usually trim to 1/4" (6mm) after stitching, which I'll explain later in the chapter.

To give the inside of the shorts a finished look and to prevent the fabric from raveling, overcast the raw edges using the three-step zigzag (A19) (see Figs. 8.35 and 9.15). After finishing raw edges, steam press edges flat on the right side.

New Sewer's Note: *Overcast the inseam, out seam, and crotch of the shorts. The waistline and hem edge will be evened and finished later.*

POCKETS

Most of us who sew a lot don't follow the pattern instructions to the letter because we've learned easier, faster ways. I construct a project by using the Viking stitches and presser feet as well as shortcuts I've learned. Here are two ways to put on patch pockets, using your Viking to its fullest capability.

Machine Readiness Checklist	
Stitch:	straight (A2)
Length:	2.5
Width:	0
Foot:	standard A metal zigzag
Needle:	80/12 universal
Thread:	all-purpose sewing
Tension:	normal
Needle Position:	center

Patch Pocket (for New Sewer)

1. Fold down pocket hem of pattern tissue. Fold fabric right sides together perpendicular to the **lengthwise** grain; entire pocket is cut on a double layer. Lay out and cut pocket so the top is on the fold (Fig. 2.9).

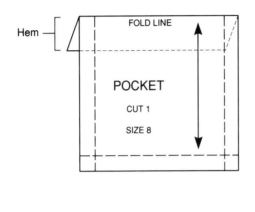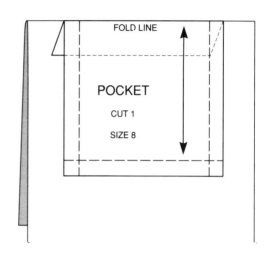

Fig. 2.9.
Fold down pocket hem.
Cut pocket on
lengthwise grain and
so top is on the fold.

2. With right sides together and the fold at the top, stitch around three sides of the pocket on the 5/8" (1.5cm) seam allowance, leaving a 1" (2.5cm) opening at the bottom.

Sew-How: *For sharp corners, take one stitch across the corner.*

---

3. Trim corners and seam allowance as shown (Fig. 2.10). Backstitch or tie off threads on either side of the opening on the bottom of the pocket. Turn pocket right side out. Gently push a point turner or the tip of blunt-nosed scissors into each corner of pocket. Once corners have been squared, top press the pocket, using a press cloth and steam.

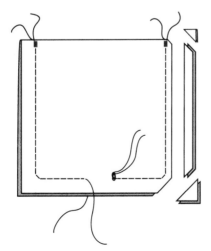

Fig. 2.10.
Stitch pocket leaving a
1" (2.5cm) opening at
the bottom. For sharp
corners, take one stitch
across the corner. Trim
and clip corners.

4. Pin pocket on shorts front or back. Align edge of pocket with the right edge of the standard A metal zigzag presser foot and topstitch with a 3-length straight stitch.

Sew-How: *When topstitching 1/4" (6mm) from the edge, the distance from the needle in the center position to the right edge of the foot is generally 1/4" (6mm) (see Fig. 8.9). To be sure, measure your foot by placing the needle on the 1" (2.5cm) mark of your tape measure with the end to your right. Lower the foot. Does the right side of the foot rest on the 3/4" (2cm) mark?*

Curved Patch Pocket (for Intermediate and Advanced Sewers)

1. Cut unlined pocket and lightweight fusible interfacing following the pattern instructions. Trim interfacing seam allowances to 1/8" (3mm) and fuse to the wrong side of pocket.

Sew-How: *Use heat, moisture, and pressure to bond interfacing permanently to the fashion fabric. Heat iron to cotton setting. Place rough side of interfacing to wrong side of pocket. Using a very damp press cloth over the pocket, press over interfacing and press cloth with even pressure for about 10 seconds. Let the steam escape, then press again until the fabric is dry (see Fig. 1.17).*

---

2. Overcast pocket hem edge. With right sides together, stitch sides of pocket hem at the 5/8" (1.5cm) seamline. Trim and clip corner. Turn hem right side out, and top-press pocket, using a press cloth.

3. Starting 1" (2.5cm) above each curve, easestitch "plus" 1/4" (6mm) from the raw edge (See Fig. 8.5).

4. Place pocket on shorts back so there is a little slack and topstitch 1/4" (6mm) from the edge. The slack enables wearer to put things in the pocket without putting stress on the stitches.

Sew-How: *Put on the transparent B (appliqué) foot and set your machine on a 0.5 length, 2 width zigzag. Satin stitch 1/4" (6mm) at each corner for extra reinforcement (Fig. 2.11). Pull threads to the wrong side and tie them off. If your Viking has an automatic tie-off, use it instead, then clip threads off at the fabric. If you have the 1100, use A37 instead.*

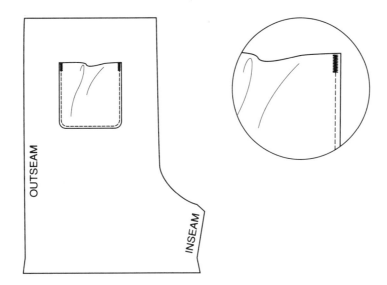

Fig. 2.11.
Place pocket on shorts
back so there is a little
slack, and topstitch.
Satin stitch 1/4"
(6mm) at each corner.

CONSTRUCT ONE LEG AT A TIME

New Sewer's Note: *To make the shorts fit, baste them together first (see explanation on page 163).*

You can construct a pair of shorts or pants in two ways. One way is to stitch the front of the pants, the back of the pants, then stitch the inside and outside leg seams. The other way is to construct each leg individually, then stitch legs together at the crotch seam. For pull-on garments, the one-leg-at-a-time method is easier to alter, and results in a better fit.

Machine Readiness Checklist

Stitch:	straight (A2)
Length:	2.5
Width:	0
Foot:	standard A metal zigzag
Needle:	80/12 universal
Thread:	all-purpose
Tension:	normal
Needle Position:	center

1. Find a front and back leg piece. Place and pin right sides together, matching notches so pins are perpendicular to the seam line. Stitch the inseam and outside seam at the 5/8" (1.5cm) seam line, removing pins before stitching over them. Repeat for other leg.

Sew-How: *You may have been told your machine can sew over pins. This is not a good practice. When the needle hits a pin, the broken ends may fall into the workings of your machine or hit you in the face. It also dulls the needle or creates burrs, which may snag on your fabric.*

Press seams flat and together, then press them open.

Sew-How: *Sometimes a seam that is pressed open leaves a ridge on either side of the seam line. To prevent this, press seams open over a seam roll—a stuffed cushion about the size and shape of a rolling pin, but without the handles. Seam rolls are available at fabric stores.*

---

2. Turn one leg right side out. Slip it inside the other leg, right sides together. Match notches, pin, and stitch the long front and back crotch seam at the 5/8" (1.5cm) seam line.

3. Press open center front and center back seam from notches to waistline. Turn shorts right side out, and try them on. Tie or pin a piece of elastic around the waist. Remember, the top of the shorts have a casing that folds down over elastic, so place elastic where the finished waistline will be. Adjust gathers and check the fit.

Sew-How: *If seams need to be adjusted, pin from the right side. If adjustments are made with the garment inside out, adjustments are made for the wrong side of the body (most of us are lopsided). After pinning, remove the garment and use a fabric marker to transfer pin marks on the wrong side by gently separating the fabric and marking where pin enters the fabric.*

---

4. Once shorts fit, trim crotch seam, notch to notch, to 3/8" (1mm) and overcast seam allowance with the three-step zigzag (A19 or 20) length 1, width 4 – 5.

ELASTIC APPLICATION

Do you use a large safety pin or bodkin to pull elastic through a casing? Did either one hang up in the seam allowances or pull off the end before the elastic was all the way through the casing?

This one-step method takes about the same amount of time as pulling elastic through a casing, but eliminates the frustration.

1. Cut elastic 3" (7.5cm) to 5" (12.5cm) shorter than waistline measurement. Before cutting it to length, check that elastic fits over your hips. (You wouldn't want to get the elastic stitched in, then be unable to pull your pants up over your hips.) Join elastic into a circle by overlapping the ends. Stitch using a three-step zigzag (A19 or 20) on a 1 length, 4 – 5 width. **Note:** Overlapping the join rather than seaming elastic ends eliminates bulk and evenly distributes stress on the stitches.

2. Overcast raw edge of fabric casing using the three-step zigzag (A19) on a 1 length and a 4 – 5 width. Fold down to the inside and press casing the width of elastic plus 5/8" (1.5cm). Edgestitch 1/8" (3mm) from fold (see Fig. 8.6).

3. Pin elastic circle inside casing, pinning under and parallel to the elastic (Fig. 2.12). Elastic should pull freely around the top of the shorts.

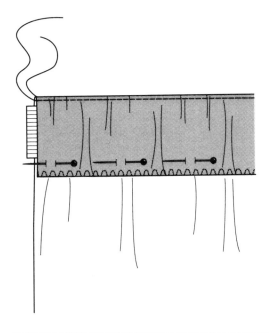

Fig. 2.12. Pin elastic in casing, at overcast edge, parallel to elastic. Elastic should pull freely around the top of shorts.

Machine Readiness Checklist

Stitch:	straight (A2)
Length:	2 – 2.5
Width:	0
Foot:	transparent B (appliqué)
Needle:	80/11-12 universal
Thread:	all-purpose or 100% cotton
Needle Position:	center

4. With wrong side up, place casing under the foot so the needle does not stitch through elastic. Smooth fabric casing in front and behind the needle so the elastic is relaxed and the fabric is flat.

Sew-How: *Use a mark on your needle plate to guide the edgestitched fold. For example, if your elastic is 1" (2.5cm) wide, the line of stitching under the elastic should measure 1-1/4" (3cm) from the top of the casing fold so that elastic moves freely within the casing. Therefore, guide the fold at the 1-1/4" (3cm) mark on the needle plate. If elastic is too wide to guide by a mark in the needle plate, use the edge guide (see Fig. 9.17) or put a piece of masking tape on the bed of your machine. (Remove tape after stitching or it will become gummy.)*

---

5. Stitch a short distance, stop with the needle in the fabric, raise the foot, then pull elastic toward you so the casing fabric in front of the foot is smoothed flat (Fig. 2.13). Stitch a short distance, then repeat. This way, the elastic is stitched flat and in one step ... no more pins or bodkins to pull through a casing.

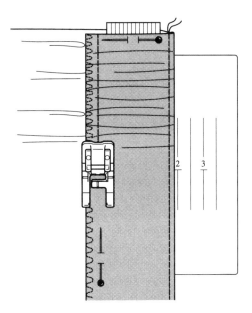

Fig. 2.13.
Stitch a short distance, stop with the needle in the fabric, raise the foot, then pull elastic toward you so the casing is smoothed flat in front of the foot.

6. Try on the shorts and adjust the fullness around the waist as desired. Then stitch-in-the-ditch at the center front, center back, and side seams through the casing and width of elastic, to prevent elastic from rolling (see Fig. 8.8).

HEMMING

1. Even raw hem edge, and overcast with the three-step zigzag (A19) on a 1 length and a 4 – 5 width (see Fig. 8.35).

2. Pin up leg hem desired depth, with pins perpendicular to the hem edge. Press hem without pressing over the pins.

3. Blind hem each leg hem using the woven blind hem stitch (A30) and blind hem D foot (see Figs. 8.49, 8.50, and 9.10).

Step Three:

SEW A KNIT TOP WITH RIBBING

Layout, cutting, and marking are similar to the shorts—let's review.

• Lay out top pattern so the center front and center back are cut on the fold. The lengthwise grainline will be parallel to fold and selvage edge. When laid out this way, the stretch goes around the body—necessary for proper fit and ease (Fig. 2.14).

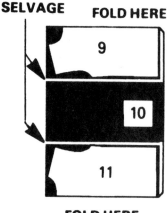

SELVAGE FOLD HERE

9

10

11

FOLD HERE

Fig. 2.14.
Lay out top pattern so center front and center back are cut on the fold and with the most stretch around the body (courtesy of the McCall Pattern Company).

• Cut pattern and fabric on black cutting line using a pair of shears or rotary cutter and mat.

Sew-How: *Do not cut a knit with pinking shears. The notched blades snag the fabric.*

• Snip 1/8" (3mm) into seam allowance to mark notches, as you did for the shorts.

• Mark dots on pattern pieces with vanishing or water-erasable marker.

• Label pattern pieces with masking tape (optional).

As with the pull-on shorts, the following construction and stitching sequence better uses your Viking.

SEAMS AND SEAM FINISHES FOR KNIT FABRICS

It's difficult to press open a 5/8" (1.5cm) seam on most knits. Therefore, we will use 1/4" (6mm) seams, and press them to one side. Rather than trimming the seam allowance to 1/4" (6mm) before stitching, however, leave the 5/8" (1.5cm) seam allowance to allow for fitting. In most cases, the seam also looks better when trimmed to 1/4" (6mm) after stitching. Exceptions are those areas where ribbing is applied at a neck edge or at a cuff and when making lingerie with nylon tricot. In these cases, it is generally easier to trim the seam allowance to 1/4" (6mm) and stitch.

Shoulder Seams

Because Trimotion™ "stretch" stitches are tough to rip out, speed-baste knit projects together to check fit (see Fig. 8.25). Here are two ways to stitch a 1/4" (6mm) seam, depending on the stitches available for your Viking. If your pattern calls for 5/8" (1.5cm) seams, trim them to 1/4" (6mm) after stitching is complete.

1/4" (6mm) Seam, One-Step Method Using Trimotion Stitches

Test for the appropriate Trimotion stitch on a double layer of knit (for suggestions, see Figs. 8.41, 8.42, 8.43, and stitches A21 – A26). Place test samples in your notebook. Identify the stitch and stitch setting on each sample.

Sew-How: *When testing for the right stitch, remember this principle. If the fabric waves out of shape, lengthen the stitch. If the fabric puckers, shorten the stitch length.*

New Sewer's Note: *If your shirt has raglan sleeves, pin each sleeve, right sides together, to front and back shirt pieces, matching notches. Double notches indicate the back of the shirt; single notches, the front of the shirt. You may find it helpful to lay shirt on a large table to do this (Fig. 2.15).*

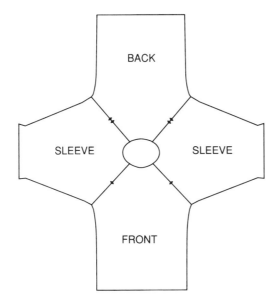

Fig. 2.15. Pin shirt right sides together, matching notches. You may find it helpful to lay shirt on a large table to do this.

Intermediate and Advanced Sewer's Note: *To prevent cross-grain shoulder seams from stretching out of shape, place a double strand of elastic thread or a length of preshrunk twill tape under the foot. Sew across the grain without pulling elastic thread or tape (see Fig. 8.43).*

1. For all seams, pin right sides together so pins are perpendicular to the seam line. Guiding by the 5/8" (1.5cm) seam line, stitch seam with the best Trimotion stitch tested above.

2. Trim excess seam allowances up to the stitch. Press seam to one side.

Sew-How: *If seam is trimmed to 1/4" (6mm) before seaming, guide fabric so the stitch falls over the raw edge on the right (see Fig. 8.41).*

1/4" (6mm) Seam, Two-Step Method

If you don't have one of the Trimotion stitches mentioned above, stitch 1/4" (6mm) seams in two steps. If your pattern calls for 5/8" (1.5cm) seams, trim them to 1/4" (6mm) after stitching is complete.

Machine Readiness Checklist	
Stitch:	tricot (A6) or tiny zigzag
Length:	1.5 – 2
Width:	1
Foot:	transparent B (appliqué)
Needle:	75/11 stretch
Thread:	all-purpose
Needle Position:	center

1. For all seams, pin right sides together so pins are perpendicular to the seam line. Sew the tricot stitch or tiny zigzag 5/8" (1.5cm) from raw edge, removing pins before sewing over them.

2. Using the three-step zigzag (A19) on a 1 length and a 4 – 5 width, stitch to the immediate right of the tiny zigzag. Trim excess seam allowance up to the stitch (Fig. 2.16).

Set-in Sleeves and Side Seams

Set-in sleeves generally must be eased into each armhole—some sleeves more than others. The flatter the curve of a sleeve, the less fabric is eased into the armhole. If the knit you are working with will not stretch enough for the sleeve to fit into the armhole, use this method. This technique also works on woven fabrics.

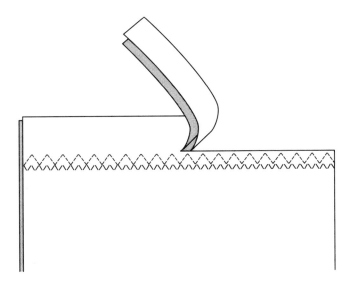

1. Snip the notch at the top of the sleeve cap. Easestitch "plus" each sleeve from back notches to front notches, stitching 1/2" (1.3mm) from the raw edge (see Fig. 8.5).

Sew-How: *If the sleeve hasn't eased in enough, rip out first stitches and this time tighten upper tension as you easestitch "plus."*

---

2. Open shirt flat and pin sleeve into armhole, right sides together, matching notches and with the garment body on top. The snipped notch at the sleeve cap should match the shoulder seam of the top. Speed-baste sleeve in place so sleeve is down against the feed dogs (see Fig. 8.25). The action of the feed dogs helps ease in the fullness of the sleeve cap. After sleeve is basted so the seam is smooth, and without tucks, final stitch each sleeve using one of the two methods described above for a 1/4" (6mm) seam finish.

3. For the side seams, start at the bottom of the sleeve and use a 1/4" (6mm) seam finish. Press side seams toward the front. At the break of the hem, twist the seam allowance and press the rest of the seam toward the back. This way, when the hem is turned up, there is less bulk at the seam and it is easier to stitch over without distorting the stitch.

Neck Band

Neck band or ribbing patterns are often the wrong length for the openings. The following measuring and stitching techniques have never failed me. **Remember, cut bands with the most stretch around the body.**

1. To determine the proper band **length** for a crew neck or waistband, cut band two-thirds the circumference of the opening so the stretch goes around the body. To determine the proper band **width,** double the finished width and add 1/2" (1.3cm) (which allows for 1/4" [6mm] seam allowances). Therefore, a finished 1" (2.5cm) wide band starts out 2-1/2" (6.4cm) wide because it is folded in half and stitched with a 1/4" (6mm) seam allowance.

Sew-How: *For a crew neck, sleeve band, cuff, or ankle band, cut band two-thirds the circumference of the opening. For a V-neck or U-neck, cut band three-fourths the circumference of the neckline opening.*

2. Trim neckline seam allowance to 1/4" (6mm). Pin band into a circle so narrow ends are right sides together. Stitch a 1/4" (6mm) seam using the tricot (A6) or tiny zigzag stitch (1.5 length, 1 width). Gently steam-press seam open.

3. Fold band in half the long way so the seam is on the inside of band. If ribbing is difficult to handle, speed-baste raw edges together using the longest 4 width zigzag stitch (A12) and a loosened upper tension (see Fig. 8.25). Carefully steam-press band.

4. Quarter and mark bands with pins.

New Sewer's Note: *You may find it easier to mark band and neckline into eight, rather than four, equal parts. If your shirt has a crew or turtle neck, pin band into neckline, raw edges even, matching quarter marks to center front, center back, and shoulder seams (Fig. 2.17).*

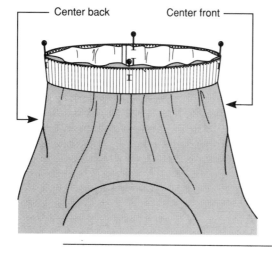

Fig. 2.17.
Pin band into neckline opening at center front, center back, and shoulder seams.

Sew-How: *For a V-neck or U-neck, quarter and mark the neckline in the shirt. The quarter marks will fall on the center front and center back and will be slightly forward of the shoulder seams.*

5. With the band side up, stitch a 1/4" (6mm) seam, using either method described above. **Note:** If you have a free-arm on your machine, slip the neckline around it and stitch.

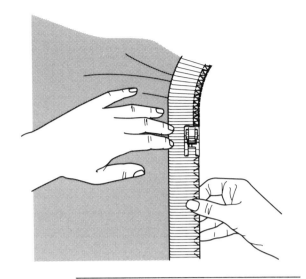

Fig. 2.18.
Pull band with your
right hand while
guiding the neckline
with your left.

Sew-How: *To stretch band to fit opening, pull the band with your right hand while guiding the neckline with the left (Fig. 2.18).*

Hemming

The fastest, easiest, and most secure way to hem a knit is with twin needles. Two needles, positioned on a crossbar and shank, are threaded on the top. The bobbin thread shares itself between the two top threads, creating a zigzag stitch on the underside (see Fig. 8.10). The shirt found in the color pages was hemmed with a size 3.0/75(11) twin needle. This means the needles are 3mm (1/8") apart, and the needles are a size 75/11.

For a ready-to-wear look to the neckline ribbing, use your twin needle to topstitch under the neckband through the seam allowance 1/8" (3mm) from seamline.

Sew-How: *Twin-needle hemming is possible only if your machine has a top- or front-loading bobbin. If your bobbin loads from the side, twin needles sit in the machine sideways and will not work.*

If your machine has a side-loading bobbin, blind hem knits as shown in Figs. 8.49, 8.50, and 9.10.

Step Four:

PROJECT VARIATIONS

INSTANT T-SHIRTS

For an "instant" coordinate to your shorts, try purchasing a ready-made T-shirt or sweatshirt and adding custom touches. You can also add embellished pockets like the ones made in Chapter 3, Sew Embellishments—Machine Appliqué and Embroider.

Many households have a "button jar" or an odd collection of buttons that can be stitched to a T-shirt or sweatshirt. If you don't have such a collection, find interesting buttons at garage sales, flea markets, or in the bargain bin at your favorite discount or fabric store.

If this project is for a child, use a variety of buttons identifying a special interest—dinosaurs, hearts, or animal shapes, for instance.

BUTTON SEWING WITH YOUR VIKING

The fastest and easiest way to stitch on a lot of buttons is by machine. **Note:** In this project, buttons sewn on the T-shirt or sweatshirt are for decoration only. They will never be buttoned through another layer of fabric. Therefore, it's not necessary to create a shank between the fabric and button. See Figs. 8.17, 9.18 and stitch A31 in Chapter 8 for machine settings.

ATTACHING RIBBONS AND BOWS

Sandra Betzina, newspaper columnist and author of *Power Sewing,* said her daughter tied and stitched bows all over a ready-made T-shirt and was out the door wearing it in 45 minutes. Here's how she did it:

1. Preshrink T-shirt and ribbon. Mark bow or ribbon placement with a vanishing marker.

2. If you have spool pins spaced 1-1/2" (3.8cm) to 2" (5cm) apart you can make bows using your spool pins. Put ribbon around spool pins, crossing ends in the front. This creates the loop ends of the bow. Holding left end stationary, take right end over bow at the center and tie a knot (Fig. 2.19). Remove bow from spool pins. This way, all bows are the same size and are tied tight enough that they won't come undone in the wash.

Sew-How: *If you don't have vertical spool pins on your Viking, find a willing volunteer and tie bows as described above using their index fingers instead of spool pins.*

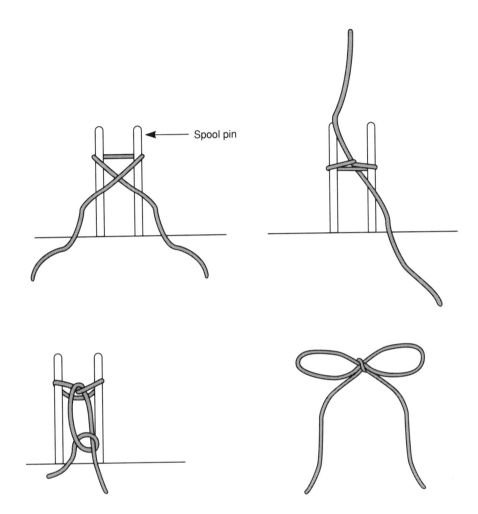

Spool pin

Fig. 2.19.
Put ribbon around
spool pins, crossing
ends in the front. This
creates the loop ends
of the bow. Holding
left end stationary,
take right end over
bow at the center and
tie a knot.

3. Thread machine with nylon monofilament thread. This way you don't have to rethread your machine and bobbin case for each color ribbon. Pin bows over marks on T-shirt.

4. Position T-shirt under the presser foot so bow is under the foot. Lower foot, remove pin, and tack across the knot in the bow (see Fig. 8.26). Repeat for other colors.

For a boy, add a fabric stripe, fabric paint, custom patches, or woven labels to a ready-made T-shirt or jacket. For adults, remove ribbing and hems from T-shirt. Then add a pocket, knitted collar, and contrasting sleeve, neck, and waistbands.

TRANSFERABLE LEARNINGS

The information and techniques you have learned by making the woven shorts and knit top have given you the skills necessary to sew many other projects. You have learned how to:

• Read a pattern envelope and buy the correct type and amount of fabric and appropriate notions.

• Understand pattern layout and cutting.
  ❖ Lengthwise grain is parallel to selvage edge and/or fold.
  ❖ Knits are laid out and cut with the most stretch around the body.
  ❖ Patterns are cut on the black cutting line.
  ❖ Notches are snip-marked using scissor tips for speed and accuracy.

• Mark pattern pieces.
  ❖ Mark light-colored fabrics with vanishing or water-erasable marker.
  ❖ Mark dark fabrics with soap sliver or disappearing dressmakers' chalk (Clo-Chalk, see Sources of Supply).

• Stitch and finish 5/8" (1.5cm) or 1/4" (6mm) seam allowances on knit and woven fabric.

• Topstitch 1/4" (6mm) from a finished edge using center needle position and guiding the edge of the standard A metal zigzag foot by the finished edge of the fabric.

• Permanently bond a fusible interfacing to fashion fabric using heat, moisture, and pressure.

• Stitch elastic in a casing in one step. This technique can be used for elastic insertion at a waistline, wrist, or ankle.

• Use an up-and-down pressing motion to press seams open or to one side.

• Blind hem woven fabrics with the blind hem foot and blind hem stitch. Hem knits with twin needles.

• Easestitch "plus" the sleeve before it is stitched into the armhole. Final stitch sleeve into the arm hole with the sleeve side against the feed dogs to ease in the fullness.

• Measure and cut knit bands to fit various parts of a garment.

You have learned a lot in this chapter about sewing woven and knit fabrics. I hope this approach encourages you to think through a project to make the best use of your tools, accessories, and Viking.

Next, you will "Sew Embellishments" and decorate a tote bag. The design you see in the tote can also be translated to a pocket on the pair of shorts or T-shirt you just made (see color pages).

SEW EMBELLISHMENTS— MACHINE APPLIQUÉ AND EMBROIDER

- *Step One: Plan Your Project*

- *Step Two: Compass Tote Bag*

- *Step Three: Project Variations—Pocket and T-Shirt Embellishment*

- *Transferable Learnings*

---

ma·chine (me shEn') *noun*, a structure consisting of a framework and various fixed and moving parts, for doing some kind of work; mechanism [a sewing machine]

ap·pli·qué (ap'le ka') *noun*, a decoration or trimming made of one material attached by sewing, gluing, etc., to another. *adj.*, applied as such a decoration. *verb* -quéd', qué'ing, *1.* to decorate with appliqué *2.* to put on as appliqué

em·broi·der (im broi'der) *verb*, *1.* to ornament (fabric) with a design in needlework *2.* to make (a design, etc.) on fabric with needlework *3.* to embellish (a story, etc.); add fanciful details to

This chapter will investigate machine appliqué and machine embroidery as ways to embellish a base fabric. We will work the design on a base fabric that can be put in your notebook or turned into a pocket for the Compass Tote Bag. Once you have mastered the compass design, you can embellish a ready-to-wear T-shirt with it, or a pocket for a pair of shorts (see color pages). If your appetite for machine embellishment has been whetted, see the Bibliography for more on machine appliqué and machine embroidery.

Step One:

PLAN YOUR PROJECT

The compass design teaches you how to turn corners as well as how to use some closed decorative stitches or Satin Elements to create Pictograms on your Viking. If you have an older model, or one not capable of making Pictograms, this is a good opportunity to practice your manual embroidery skills.

In the Machine Readiness Checklists, note that each stitch is described by name and corresponding cassette number for both the Viking 1100 and 990 models. For example, on the Viking 990 cassette the Tulips are 2-10, the Train Engine, 2-21, etc. On the Viking 1100, the Hearts are stitch D24, the Clover is D14. I keep Fig. 3.1 in front of me while sewing for easy reference. But before stitching your compass embroidery, you need to know about fabrics, threads, and other embroidery supplies (Fig. 3.2).

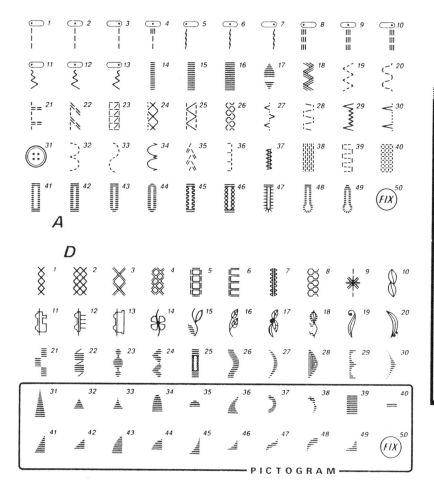

Fig. 3.1.
Viking 1100 utility and
decorative cassettes;
Viking 990 decorative
cassette.

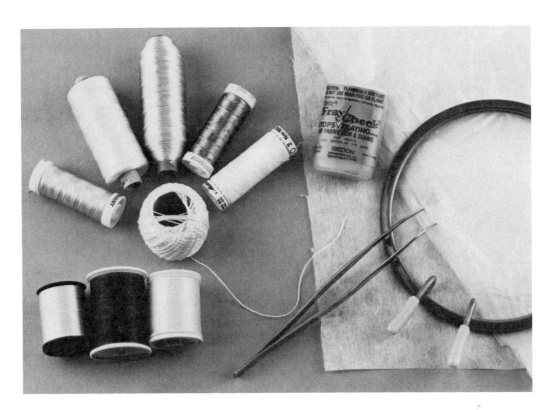

Fig. 3.2.
Threads, fabrics, and
other embroidery
supplies.

FABRICS AND THREADS

All-natural fabrics are easiest to use for machine appliqué and embroidery because they are more forgiving than their synthetic counterparts. If puckering occurs, pressing usually removes the worst of it. Wool felt and woven fabrics are also easier to work with than knits because they don't distort in a hoop. Cut wool felt, all-cotton duck or kettle cloth, and organza into 9" (23 cm) practice squares. Use them as "doodle cloths" and for stitch testing, then put them in your notebook for future reference.

The best threads for machine appliqué and embroidery are all-cotton or rayon embroidery thread. Both have a nice sheen and cause little or no tension problems. They are also generally finer than thread used for clothing construction. Look for brand names such as DMC, J. & P. Coats, Madeira Mettler, Sulky, and Zwicky in your local sewing machine dealership or in better fabric stores.

Sew-How: *If you have old thread that shreds, splits, or breaks when you are using it, put it in the refrigerator overnight. The moisture in the refrigerator is absorbed by the thread so that it regains its original tensile strength. If you don't have time to wait, accomplish the same thing by dribbling a line of Needle-Lube™ (a thread moisturizer) on the thread along the length of the spool.*

Other threads used for machine embroidery are cotton **darning thread** and nylon monofilament thread. Because darning thread is very fine—a size 70 or 120—it does not create bulk, even in heavily stitched areas. This makes it a good bobbin thread for embroidery. Since darning thread is available only in black and white, it is necessary to loosen top thread tension so stitches lock under the fabric. This way, bobbin thread will not pull up to the surface and show. This method saves time because a single bobbin of darning thread can be used with a variety of colors. Also, because darning thread is so fine, a bobbin holds more of it than other threads.

Sew-How: *The Viking 1100 and 900 series machines loosen the upper tension automatically for embroidery stitches, Satin Elements, and Pictograms.*

Sew-How: *Darning thread (sometimes called basting thread) is too fine to use for clothing construction; however, when it's on the bobbin, it looks like any other white or black thread. To prevent confusion, mark bobbins wound with darning thread with fingernail polish.*

Nylon monofilament thread is transparent and has many of the same advantages as cotton darning thread—you can get a lot on a bobbin, and you don't need to wind and thread new bobbins when changing the top thread color. However, some brands are stiff and wiry and won't hold a knot. The best type I've used is called "Invisible Wonder Nylon Thread." It's as fine as hair, breaks like regular sewing thread, and is available through mail-order sources.

Other Embroidery Supplies

To ensure a smooth finish, you need a way to stabilize the fabric so the embroidery does not pucker while you are stitching. This can be accomplished by using an embroidery hoop; by backing the fabric with a stabilizer such as iron-on freezer wrap, tear-away, or fusible interfacing; or by using a combination of the above.

The easiest type of embroidery hoop to use for machine embroidery is a **spring hoop.** It's narrow enough to fit under the presser foot and needle, and it's easy to move when your work is in the machine. Spring hoops are available in 3" (7.5cm), 5-3/8" (13.5cm) and 7" (18cm) sizes. I use the 5-3/8" (13.5cm) the most. Purchase a spring hoop through your local sewing machine dealer or mail-order source.

Plastic-coated freezer wrap, used as an iron-on stabilizer, helps prevent skipped stitches and puckering. It is also easily removed after stitching and available at your local grocery store. Iron the shiny side to the underside of your fabric.

Tear-Away™ or Stitch-n-Tear™ are other fabric stabilizers. These do not iron on and are easily removed after stitching.

Fusible interfacing supports a limp fabric and can stabilize a knit fabric when the interfacing is fused to the back. This makes pucker-free embroidering on a knit possible.

Other supplies you will see listed in this chapter are:

- **Wonder-Under™ Transfer Web**—fusible web on one side, paper on the other; makes any fabric fusible without "gunking up" the iron (see instructions below).

- **Water-erasable or vanishing markers**—the mark is removed with clear water or disappears after 24 to 48 hours.

- **Liquid seam sealant**—put a drop on thread ends so they don't have to be tied off or to prevent a knot from coming untied. A brand to look for is Dritz Fray Check.

Step Two:

COMPASS TOTE BAG

We tote our possessions to school, to the beach, to class, and back. We tote things on vacation and tote notes to a lecture. We tote things home from the mall, so we can tote the same things elsewhere. So why not make something large and attractive to do the toting? The finished dimensions of the Compass Tote are 14 X 17-1/2 X 5" (35cm X 44cm X 12.5cm), and it has a 7" (18cm) square embroidered pocket on the front.

The embroidery on the pocket will be done with the feed dogs up. This means that your Viking will move the fabric under the presser foot while the needle moves from side to side creating a decorative stitch or Pictogram.

After making the pocket, you will freely embroider a label or name tag to stitch to the inside of the tote. For this step the feed dogs are lowered; the fabric is stretched in a hoop, then moved manually under the needle.

New Sewer's Note: *It takes practice to perfect your embroidery skills so you may want to practice the embroidery techniques on squares to go in your notebook. If you find one of your practice squares acceptable, turn it into a pocket to stitch to your tote as instructed. If you aren't happy with your embroidery sample, and if you need more practice, either make a plain pocket, or stitch a purchased crest or woven label on the pocket in lieu of the embroidery.*

In addition to the embroidery supplies mentioned above, to make the tote you will need:

Supplies

- 1/2 yard (45.5cm) Wonder-Under (or paper-backed fusible web)
- 2/3 yard (61cm) of 5/8" (1.5cm)-wide white grosgrain ribbon
- 1/4 yard (23cm) of 1-1/2" (3.8cm)-wide white grosgrain ribbon

- water-soluble stabilizer, double layer to fit into embroidery hoop
- white canvas cut 24" wide X 16-1/2" long (60cm wide X 41cm long)
- yellow canvas cut 24" wide X 20" long (60cm wide X 50cm long)
- yellow canvas cut 16" wide X 3-3/4" long (40.6cm X 9.5cm) for stripes
- 9" (23cm) squares: two of fusible interfacing, three of black woven cotton, two of cotton woven for practice squares
- 9" (23cm) tear-away stabilizer
- 48" (1.2m) 1" (2.5cm) webbing cut in half for the handles
- black and yellow fabric paint to match tote fabrics

Sew-How: *The handles are black on one side and yellow on the other. Rather than buying twice the amount of webbing specified to get the two-toned effect, buy white webbing and paint one side black, the other side yellow to match the canvas.*

- Sulky rayon embroidery thread in white and yellow to match canvas; white darning thread for bobbin; black, white, and yellow all-purpose thread for bag construction
- white or gray dressmaker's carbon paper and empty ballpoint
- vanishing marker
- ruler
- rotary cutter, mat, and see-through cutting ruler to cut everything square
- spring hoop
- heavy cardboard cut to fit the bottom of the bag
- small fusible letters (N, S, E, W)—optional if your Viking cannot stitch letters

TRACE AND TRANSFER THE DESIGN

1. Fuse the square of interfacing to the wrong side of a 9" (23cm) black square. Iron a square of freezer wrap to the wrong side of the interfaced square. The freezer wrap stabilizes the fabric so an embroidery hoop is not necessary.

Sew-How: *Prepare two squares as described in Step 1. Use one for experimentation to properly adjust the stitch length, width, and tension; use the other as your finished square.*

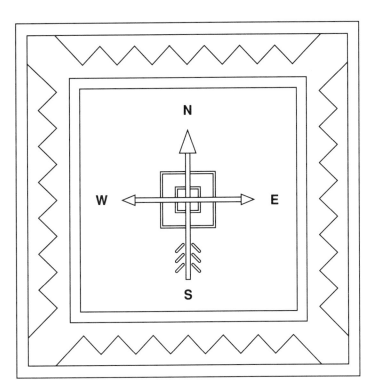

Fig. 3.3.
Compass embroidery
design. Pattern is 1/2
size.

2. Enlarge the design in Fig. 3.3 to twice the size on a photocopier at your local copy center.

3. Find the exact center of the black fabric square. To mark the center, fold the square into quarters and finger-press. Stick a straight pin through the back of the fabric square where the pressed lines intersect, so the point of the pin is up. Place the black fabric square on a table, right side up, so the point of the pin is up. Stack the dressmaker's carbon and the pattern over the fabric, pushing the pin through the center of the design. Pin pattern and carbon paper to the fabric so they won't shift. Remove the straight pin from the center.

4. Using the empty ballpoint pen and ruler, trace the compass design and border on the fabric. Remove the pattern. Can you see the lines clearly? If not, fill in the lines using marking chalk.

EMBROIDER THE POCKET

1. Stitch compass center squares.

Machine Readiness Checklist	
Stitch:	zigzag (A15)
Length:	0.3 – 0.5
Width:	2 – 2.5
Foot:	transparent B (appliqué)
Needle:	90/14 stretch
Thread:	top, white rayon embroidery; bobbin, white darning
Tension:	top, loosened slightly; bobbin, normal or tightened slightly
Fabric:	9" (23cm) black interfaced woven cotton backed with iron-on freezer wrap

---

Sew-How: *Test and practice each technique on your practice square before stitching on the pocket square.*

Starting in the center of the right side of the smaller square, stitch to the corner, stopping with the needle in the left side of the stitch. Lift the presser foot and pivot the fabric slightly. Put the foot down and zigzag so the needle stitches over and back into the pivot hole in the corner (hold the fabric firmly to keep it from feeding). Lift the presser foot, pivot fabric slightly, stitch, and so on, so the stitches fan out from the same point around the corner (Fig. 3.4).

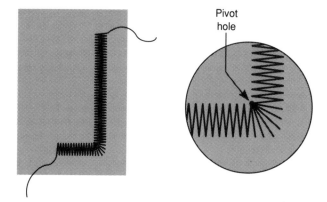

Pivot
hole

Fig. 3.4.
Lift the presser foot, pivot fabric slightly, and stitch again so the stitches fan out from the same point around the corner.

Stitch the rest of the small square, and around the larger square, fanning stitches at each corner as described above.

2. Stitch compass crossbars. Use the same needle, thread, and tension settings as described in Step 1.

Machine Readiness Checklist

Stitch:	zigzag (A15)
Length:	0.3 – 0.5
Width:	2.5 – 3
Foot:	transparent B (appliqué)

Center the line of the vertical crossbar in the center of your transparent B foot. Satin stitch the length of the crossbar. Repeat for the horizontal crossbar. Stitch over crossbars a second time with a slightly longer satin stitch. This gives the embroidery a high, rounded appearance.

3. Stitch the small arrowheads. If you have a decorative stitch available that looks like the small arrowhead pictured at the end of the horizontal crossbar in Fig. 3.3, set your Viking as follows. (If you don't have an arrowhead design on your Viking, you can create one by manually tapering a satin stitch. Before you proceed to Step 4, skip to the Warm-Up Exercise below.) Use the same needle, thread, and tension settings as described in Step 1.

Machine Readiness Checklist

Stitch:	arrowhead (990, 2-36; 1100, D32)
Length:	0.3 – 0.5
Width:	6
Foot:	transparent B (appliqué)

Sew-How: *The easiest way to stitch the arrowhead is to start sewing it at the end of the crossbar and stitch from the widest part of the arrowhead to the point. If the arrowhead on your Viking starts stitching at the point end, see if you have an end-to-end mirror image feature, so you can flip the pattern over.*

If you can't start the arrowhead at the wide end, stitch a few individual arrowheads on your test square and measure them. On your pocket square, mark where to start the arrowhead so the wide part meets the end of the crossbar. Then stitch.

Warm-Up Exercise: Tapered Satin Stitch

The needle, thread, and tension settings are the same as described in Step 1.

Machine Readiness Checklist

Stitch:	zigzag
Length:	0.3 – 0.5
Width:	widest tapering to 0
Foot:	transparent B (appliqué)
Needle position:	center

On your practice square, satin stitch while you slowly move the width control from wide to narrow. Once you gain some confidence, run the machine at the fastest speed. You should find that tapered satin stitch shapes are smoother and more uniform when you run the machine quickly and the width control slowly.

Now practice the arrowhead shape. When you have perfected it, stitch an arrowhead on each end of the horizontal crossbar.

4. Stitch the large arrowhead. Use the same needle, thread, and tension settings as described in Step 1.

Machine Readiness Checklist

Stitch:	half-arrow (990: 2-37, 39; 1100: D41) or tapered satin stitch
Length:	0.3 – 0.5
Width:	6 for 900 and 1100 series; 0 – widest
Foot:	transparent B (appliqué)
Needle position:	left; right (for manual taper only)

To create the large arrowhead, use two Satin Element half-arrow designs. One should taper out from the left; the other should taper out from the right (Fig. 3.5).

On your practice square, make an arrowhead, stitching one side; then turn the fabric around and make the other side. The straight side of the stitch should meet in the middle of the arrowhead. Each Viking model varies, so you may have to experiment with some of the settings and the mirror image to get the arrowhead effect you want.

Fig. 3.5. Create the large arrow by using two half-arrow Satin Elements. One should taper out from the left, and one should taper out from the right.

1100 Note: *Create the right side of the arrow by using D41. (Remember to push the stop display to stop sewing at the end of the arrow.) Stop with the needle in the fabric at the bottom of the first side of the arrow, then pivot, lower the foot, and raise the needle. Create the second side of the arrow by pushing the end-to-end mirror image.*

990 Note: *Create the right side of the arrow by using 2-37. (Push the finishing button to stop at the end of the arrow.) Create the left side of the arrow with 2-37 on mirror image.*

If you don't have an arrowhead design, create the same effect by tapering a satin stitch. See the Warm-Up Exercise in Step 3 above, and set your machine in left needle position as described. Notice that the straight side of the stitch is on the left, while the stitch tapers out to the right.

Next, decenter the needle to the right and satin stitch. Now the straight part of the pattern is on the right while the stitch tapers out the the left. Practice satin stitching in right and left needle positions until you get a smooth, even taper. Practice until you perfect your arrowhead, tapering from left and right needle positions. Stitch the large arrowhead at the top of the vertical crossbar.

5. Stitch the bartack feathers at the bottom of the vertical crossbar. Use the same needle, thread, and tension settings as described in Step 1.

Machine Readiness Checklist

Stitch:	zigzag (A11)
Length:	0 or drop feed dogs
Width:	widest; 0
Foot:	transparent B (appliqué)
Needle Position:	left

Place the transparent B (appliqué) foot over the mark for feather placement, and stitch five or six stitches in place. Move the width to 0 and take a few stitches in place. Remove the work. Cut the threads, leaving them long enough to tie off, and stitch another bartack feather. Repeat until all feathers are stitched. Pull threads to the back and tie them off. Remember to raise the feed dogs for normal sewing.

1100 Note: *To program the same number of stitches for each bartack feather, push **Select Function** until you see PROG (meaning "program") come up on the Infodisplay. Find an empty program by pushing the 1 – 9 Memory button. Push stitch A11, width 6, then the cursor button. Repeat two more times, then push the STOP display. The program has been entered. Push **Select Function** until you see REP (meaning "repeat") on the Infodisplay and stitch. The bartack feather has six stitches and locks off in left needle positon automatically. This can be done for stitch A31 to program the same number of stitches when sewing on a button with your Viking 1100.*

6. Stitch the yellow border.

Machine Readiness Checklist

Stitch:	zigzag (A15)
Length:	0.3 – 0.5
Width:	widest
Foot:	transparent B (appliqué)

Start sewing in the middle of one of the borders and stitch to the end. To turn the corner, remove the fabric. Cut the threads, leaving them long enough to tie off, and turn the fabric 90 degrees. Start the next row of stitching at the edge of the first row; then stitch to the end of the next border (Fig. 3.3). Repeat for the other sides.

7. If your Viking can embroider the alphabet, stitch the letters N, E, S, W as shown. Do this by stitching a test swatch for proper positioning. If you don't have the lettering option on your Viking, purchase small white fusible letters at the fabric store and fuse them in place.

Stitch the Ribbon Work

This tote pocket features a sawtooth ribbon point border using white grosgrain ribbon appliquéd to the pocket.

Sew-How: *This same technique is used to decorate the top of the pocket for the shorts, using black ribbon (see color pages).*

1. Cut four 6" (15cm) lengths of 5/8" (1.5cm)-wide white grosgrain ribbon. Place the strip of ribbon over your enlarged pocket pattern copied from Fig. 3.3, and mark the points of each sawtooth with a vanishing marker.

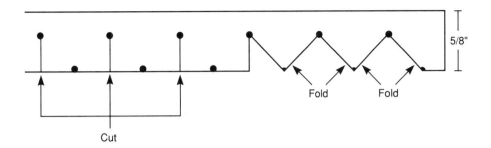

Fig. 3.6.
Clip ribbon from the
bottom edge to the dot
close to the top edge
of the ribbon. Fold
under ribbon edges to
create the sawtooth
design, and press.

2. Using a sharp pair of embroidery scissors, clip ribbon from the bottom edge to the dot close to the top edge of ribbon as shown (Fig. 3.6).

3. Pin top edge of ribbon to the ironing board. Fold under the edges of the cut ribbon to create the sawtooth design and press (Fig. 3.6).

Sew-How: *To prevent the ribbon from fraying, put a drop of seam sealant at the inside edge of each sawtooth.*

---

4. Pin and stitch sawtooth ribbon points around the pocket square, guiding as close to the edge as possible.

Machine Readiness Checklist

Stitch:	straight (A2)
Length:	2.5
Width:	0
Foot:	transparent B (appliqué) or standard A metal zigzag
Needle:	80/12 universal
Thread:	white all-purpose
Tension:	normal

Finish the Pocket

1. Pull off freezer wrap from the wrong side of embroidered pocket. Press the embroidery from the wrong side.

Sew-How: *With the right side down, press embroidery over a lofty terry cloth towel. The embroidery embeds itself into the terry cloth while the rest of the fabric can be pressed smoothly around the stitches.*

---

2. Pin a plain black square to the embroidered pocket square, right sides together.

Machine Readiness Checklist

Stitch:	straight (A2)
Length:	2.5
Foot:	standard A metal zigzag
Needle:	80/12 universal
Thread:	black all-purpose
Tension:	normal

To finish the pocket, use a 1/2" (1.3cm) seam allowance. Starting at the bottom of the pocket, sew all the way around, leaving 2" (5cm) open at the bottom to turn the pocket through.

3. Clip each corner and trim seam allowance all the way around as shown (Fig. 3.7), and turn pocket through the opening at the bottom. To square a corner, push it out with a point turner or the point of a pair of curved-blade scissors. Top-press pocket with steam and a press cloth.

Fig. 3.7.
Trim and clip pocket corners and turn it, right side out, through the opening at the bottom.

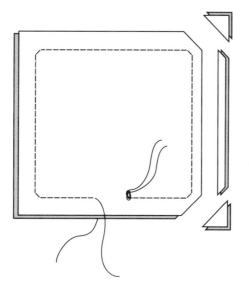

New Sewer's Note: *To top-press, place pocket on the ironing board with the right side up. Cover pocket with a press cloth and press pocket with steam.*

Press the opening closed at the bottom of pocket. Set pocket aside and admire your work. This will become the focal point of the tote bag. **Note:** The opening will be stitched closed when you topstitch the pocket on the tote bag.

Embroider the Label

Another way to embroider is freely by machine, which means moving the fabric freely under the moving needle as if you were moving a piece of paper under a stationary pen or pencil. If you have never tried this technique, try the following Warm-Up Exercise on a 9" (23cm) practice square.

Warm-Up Exercise: Sewing Machine Spaghetti

Machine Readiness Checklist

Stitch:	straight (A2); zigzag (A12)
Length:	0
Width:	0, 2, 3, 4 – widest
Foot:	darning foot or none
Needle:	90/14 stretch
Thread:	top: dark-colored rayon embroidery; bobbin: darning
Feed dogs:	down
Pressure:	released to 0
Tension:	top: loosened slightly; bobbin: normal or tightened slightly
Fabric:	9" (23cm) square of light-colored woven cotton
Accessories:	tear-away stabilizer, spring hoop, vanishing marker

1. Place the fabric in the spring hoop, and pull it taut. Then place the piece of tear-away stabilizer under the fabric. The tear-away prevents the fabric from puckering.

Sew-How: *When stretching fabric in a hoop for free-machine embroidery, it looks upside-down from hand embroidery because the flat side must be against the bed of the machine. The fabric should also be taut enough that, when you tap it with your finger, it sounds like a drum beat.*

---

2. Put your practice "doodle cloth" under the sewing machine needle. (You may want to try this technique with and without the darning foot to find out what is most comfortable [see Fig. 9.28].) Although you may prefer not using a foot on the machine, you must lower the presser foot (presser bar lever) before sewing. This engages the upper tension—important for proper stitch formation. If you forget this step, your machine usually tells you by making a lot of noise or tangling the thread so you have to start over.

3. Lower the needle into the fabric and pull bobbin thread to the surface of the fabric. With stitch width at 0, take a couple of stitches in one place to lock off the threads. Trim thread tails off at the surface of the fabric being careful not to cut the thread from the spool.

4. With the needle up, set stitch width to 2. Running the machine at a moderate to fast speed, begin moving the fabric smoothly to the left, then to the right. The faster you run the machine and the slower you move your work, the closer together the zigzag stitches become. Practice moving the fabric smoothly from side to side, creating a spaghetti-like row of stitching (Fig. 3.8). Do not pivot the hoop at a curve so the stitches taper as you change direction. (The resulting stitches look as if the line was created by a calligrapher's pen.) Try this exercise with varying zigzag widths so you are comfortable. Then practice writing your name or initials. Remove tear-away stabilizer after stitching. When you have perfected your name or initials, you are ready to embroider your label.

Fig. 3.8.
Practice moving the
fabric smoothly from
side to side, creating a
spaghetti-like row of
stitching.

Sew-How: *To cross the letter "t" or dot the letter "i", extend the stem of the last letter and bring it around as shown in Fig. 3.9. If you are having difficulty perfecting your lettering, you may choose to embroider a design instead. To do this, practice filling in a design on your doodle cloth as below.*

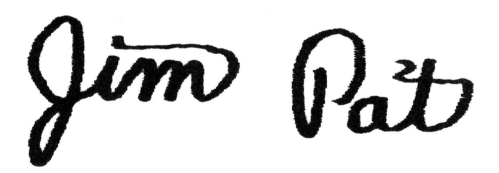

Fig. 3.9.
To cross the letter "t",
or dot the letter "i",
extend the stem of the
last letter.

5. Draw a sailboat on your doodle cloth with the vanishing marker as shown in Fig. 3.10. Place the right sail so it is sideways under the needle. With stitch width at 0 and starting at the left side, bring the bobbin thread up, take a few stitches in one place, and then cut off thread tails at the fabric. With a stitch width of 2 or 3, begin filling in the sail by moving your work to the left and right, in a long side to side motion. When you get to the straight edge of a sail, change direction, filling in the shape of the sail and moving your work smoothly, side to side to the right. This is called a fill-in stitch.

Repeat this for the other sail and the boat. **Note:** Use the fill-in stitch and move the fabric side to side the length of the boat. For smaller areas, reduce the width of your zigzag.

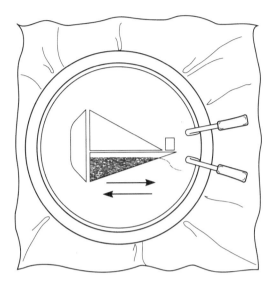

Fig. 3.10. Draw sailboat design on your doodle cloth with a vanishing marker.

Sew-How: *If you don't know which direction to move the fabric to fill in a design, test it on a scrap. If you are stitching an animal, follow the way the fur grows. If you are stitching a flower petal or leaf, fan stitches out from the center by moving the fabric side to side the length of the leaf or petal, in the same way as you stitched the length of the sail. For a totally different texture, move the fabric up and down to create a "corn-row" effect.*

---

6. To make the label, set your machine as follows:

Machine Readiness Checklist	
Stitch:	zigzag (A12)
Length:	0
Foot:	darning foot or none
Width:	2 – 4
Needle:	90/14 stretch
Thread:	top: black rayon embroidery; bobbin: black darning
Feed dogs:	down
Pressure:	0
Tension:	top, loosened slightly; bobbin, normal or tightened slightly
Fabric:	1/4 yard (23cm) of 1-1/2" (4cm)-wide white grosgrain ribbon
Accessories:	vanishing marker, water-soluble stabilizer, spring hoop

Baste ribbon on a double layer of water-soluble stabilizer then stretch it in the spring hoop so stabilizer is underneath. Draw your initials, name, or design on the ribbon, and freely embroider as you did on your doodle cloth. Remove the ribbon and wash away the stabilizer. Cut label beyond the lettering or design so you can fold 1/4" (6mm) hems at the raw edges. The label will be stitched onto the tote at the center back.

CONSTRUCT THE COMPASS TOTE

1. Cut the white and yellow canvas as described in the supply list above (page 76) using the rotary cutter, mat and see-through cutting ruler.

2. Fuse Wonder-Under on the wrong side of the yellow canvas scraps. From these scraps, cut 5 stripes, 3/4 X 16" (2 X 40.5cm). Then cut each stripe in half so you have ten 8" (20.5cm) stripes. The stripes will be appliquéd to the front of the bag on either side of the pocket.

3. Finger-press a crease down the center of the white canvas by folding it in half on the lengthwise grain.

New Sewer's Note: *To finger-press a fold, crease or press the fabric by hand without using an iron. In this case the crease temporarily marks the center of the tote to help with the pocket placement.*

---

4. Position the pocket 5-1/2" (14cm) down from the cut edge of the white canvas, centering pocket over finger-pressed crease. Using a vanishing marker, put a dot on the canvas at each corner of the pocket to mark pocket placement. Remove pocket.

5. Remove the paper backing from the stripes.

Sew-How: *After the Wonder-Under paper backing has been peeled away from larger pieces of fabric, use it as a "paper press cloth" on top of and underneath other appliqués so the adhesive won't "gunk up" your iron or ironing board.*

Place top stripes so the top of each stripe is even with the top of the pocket. Place the bottom stripes so the bottom of each stripe is even with the bottom of the pocket (Fig. 3.11). Position the other stripes equidistant from each other. Once stripes are positioned, fuse them in place, following the manufacturer's instructions.

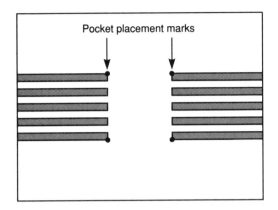

Pocket placement marks

Fig. 3.11.
Place top stripes and
bottom stripes so they
are even with the top
and bottom of the
pocket. Position the
rest of the stripes
equidistant in between.

Sew-How: *The following are the manufacturer's instructions for the proper use of Pellon's Wonder-Under (paper backed fusible web).*

Place the rough side of Wonder-Under against wrong side of fabric. Press for 3 seconds with a hot, dry iron. Let fabric cool. Cut this new fusible fabric into desired shapes (shapes can be traced directly onto paper backing before cutting). When ready to use, gently peel off paper backing.

Position fusible fabric, coated side down, on base fabric. Cover with a damp press cloth. With iron on "wool" setting, press for 10 seconds. For a large area, repeat fusing process, overlapping iron until all fabric is fused.

Machine Appliqué

Appliqué the yellow stripes to the white canvas by satin stitching along the straight edges of the stripes (see Fig. 8.27).

Machine Readiness Checklist	
Stitch:	zigzag (satin stitch) (990, 2-43; 1100, A14)
Length:	0.5 – 0.8
Width:	2 – 3
Foot:	transparent B (appliqué)
Needle:	80/12 universal or 90/14 stretch
Thread:	top, yellow rayon embroidery thread; bobbin, white darning thread
Tension:	top, loosened slightly; bobbin, normal or tightened slightly

Practice the following technique on a scrap to become comfortable with guiding the appliqué.

1. Starting with the bottom stripe, satin stitch over the cut edge so the needle enters the stripe on the left and swings over the raw edge on the right. Repeat for both edges of each stripe. Pull threads to the back and tie them off.

2. Attach the pocket. Rethread your Viking with all-purpose black thread, top and bobbin. Use a straight stitch length 2.5, the blind hem D foot, and topstitch around the pocket, stitching 1/8" (3mm) from the edge (see Fig. 8.6).

Finish the Tote

Machine Readiness Checklist	
Stitch:	straight (A2)
Length:	3 – 3.5
Width:	0
Foot:	standard A metal zigzag
Needle:	90/14 jeans
Thread:	white all-purpose
Tension:	normal

1. To make the body of the tote, place the 24" (60cm) end of the yellow canvas to the bottom edge of tote front, right sides together. Stitch a 1/4" (6mm) seam allowance (Fig. 3.12). Press the seam allowance toward the front of the tote and understitch (see Fig. 8.12).

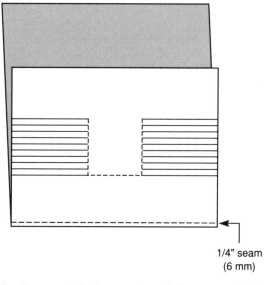

Fig. 3.12. Place the narrow end of the yellow canvas on the bottom edge of the tote front, right sides together, and stitch a 1/4" (6mm) seam.

1/4" seam (6 mm)

2. Overcast the long sides of the tote with the three-step zigzag (A19) (see Fig. 8.35). To stitch the side seams, fold the bag in half and use a 1/4" (6mm) seam allowance. Press this seam allowance open (Fig. 3.13).

3. To finish the top of the bag, fold a double hem. To do this, fold down the top edge of the tote 1" (2.5cm) and press. Fold hem down again and press.

Fig. 3.13.
Fold bag in half and seam edges together using a 1/4" (6mm) seam allowance. Position webbing handles and stitch around the top of the bag, catching the handles in the stitching.

4. Draw a line 1-1/2" (4cm) from each end of webbing handle. Make an arch with one length of webbing and position it on the front, centering ends over the pocket. The lines on each end of the webbing should be even with the top of the bag. Pin handle in place. Repeat for the back of the bag (Fig. 3.13).

5. Topstitch around the top of the bag, guiding 1/8" (3mm) from the fold.

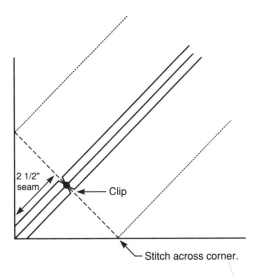

2 1/2" seam

Clip

Stitch across corner.

Fig. 3.14.
Fold one side seam so it lies along the bottom fold in the fabric.

Sew-How: *For even topstitching, use the blind hem D foot, decenter the needle to the left, and snug the fold against the inside edge of the right toe (see Figs. 9.10 and 9.11).*

Stitch the hem again, guiding slightly less than 1" (2.5cm) from the fold, catching the bottom edge of the hem in the stitching.

6. Position your embroidered label between the webbing handles on the back of the bag, and straight stitch it to the bag at the narrow ends using the standard A metal zigzag foot.

7. To box the bottom corners of the bag, at the side seams measure up from the bottom fold 2-1/2" (6.4cm) and mark a dot in the seam allowance with the vanishing marker. Fold one side seam so it lies along the bottom fold in the fabric (Fig. 3.14). Draw a line on either side of the dot in the side seam, perpendicular to the side seam, and stitch along this line. Repeat for the other side. Turn tote inside out and push the triangles against the bottom of the bag.

8. Cut a piece of cardboard to fit snugly into the bottom of the bag to give it shape, hold the triangles against the bottom, and add stability at the base.

Step Three:

PROJECT VARIATIONS— POCKET AND T-SHIRT EMBELLISHMENT

POCKET EMBELLISHMENT

Embellish a pocket to stitch to the back of the shorts you made in Chapter 2, or to give an old pair of shorts, pants, or skirt a new look.

1. Using a white piece of woven cotton, cut a pocket 7 X 6-1/2" (18 X 16.5cm).

2. Interface the pocket with fusible interfacing. Back pocket with iron-on freezer wrap. Prepare another piece of fabric the same way for practice. Transfer the enlarged compass design from Fig. 3.3. onto the pocket, using dressmaker's carbon and an empty ballpoint pen.

3. Follow the embroidery instructions for the compass embroidery above, using white rayon embroidery thread. (The shininess of the rayon makes this white-on-white embroidery visible—and elegant.)

4. Using black 5/8" (1.5cm)-wide grosgrain ribbon, trace, clip, fold, and press the ribbon points as described above. Place the straight edge of the ribbon points, 5/8" (1.5cm) down from the top edge of pocket, centering ribbon over compass embroidery.

5. Rethread your machine with yellow rayon embroidery thread on the top and white darning thread in the bobbin. Sew a row of 3 – 4 width satin stitches (see Fig. 8.27), guiding 1/4" (6mm) under ribbon points (see color pages).

6. Remove freezer wrap from the wrong side of embellished pocket. Cut another pocket piece, 7 X 6-1/2" (18 X 16.5 cm). Place pocket pieces, right sides together. Stitch, trim, turn, as described above for tote bag pocket using a 1/2" (1.3cm) seam allowance. Topstitch pocket to shorts, pants, or skirt (see Fig. 8.9).

T-SHIRT EMBELLISHMENT

Embellish a ready-to-wear T-shirt or the T-shirt you made in Chapter 2 with the compass embroidery.

1. Using a water-erasable or vanishing marker, trace the enlarged design in Fig. 3.3 on a piece of tear-away stabilizer.

Sew-How: *Use a water-erasable or vanishing marker to trace the design on the tear-away stabilizer. If you use a pen or pencil, the mark may show and be difficult to wash out.*

2. To stabilize the knit so the embroidery will not distort the fabric, place a 4 – 5" (10 – 12cm) square of tear-away stabilizer under where the embroidery will be stitched. Place decorated tear-away on top of where the embroidery will be stitched. Pin through all three layers so the design and fabric will not shift.

Sew-How: *Find a similar piece of knit fabric to the T-shirt knit and test stitch before embroidering on your T-shirt.*

3. Using white rayon embroidery thread, stitch the compass design as described above for the tote bag.

4. Remove the tear-away from the right and wrong sides of the shirt.

Sew-How: *Because you are embroidering a white design on a white piece of fabric, the color from the marker may show through the thread. Rinse the shirt with clear cold water before pressing.*

5. Press embroidery, face side down, on a clean white terry cloth towel. Press it from the wrong side to set the piece. The stitches nestle into the soft terry cloth, while the fabric between the stitches presses flat.

TRANSFERABLE LEARNINGS

The information and techniques you have learned by embellishing the tote bag pocket and the pocket for the shorts, embellishing the T-shirt, and constructing the tote bag give you the skills necessary to sew many other projects. You have learned how to:

• Loosen the top thread tension when embroidering, so stitches lock on the underside of the fabric. This also applies when satin stitching an edge and free-machine monogramming.

• Use iron-on, tear-away, or water-soluble stabilizer or freezer wrap under your work when using decorative stitches, Satin Elements, or Pictograms, and when free-machine embroidering to eliminate skipped stitches and puckering.

• Use the decorative stitches and Satin Elements on your Viking to create a design. Not only can you create a compass, but a crest, flower, and other shapes, utilizing the decorative stitches available.

• Program your Viking 1100 to save a stitch setting for future use.

• Taper a satin stitch from left, center, and right needle position. Use a tapered satin stitch to monogram, create a stem or narrow leaf, or as a way of giving a straight line of stitching some dimension.

• Satin stitch around a corner. This technique is also used when turning a corner on an appliqué.

• Interface and line a pocket. Trim seam allowance to 1/4" (6mm) and clip fabric across each corner so corners are sharp. Leave an opening to turn the pocket through before topstitching it.

• Press embroidery right side down on a lofty terrycloth towel so stitches bury themselves in the loft and the fabric between the stitches can be pressed flat.

• Topstitch a pocket close to and even from the edge using your blind hem D foot. This technique is used to topstitch collars, cuffs, front tabs, yokes, and other parts of a garment.

• Fuse and use Wonder-Under. Besides using it for appliqué, cut it in into small pieces or strips and use to fuse-tack facings or to press up a hem.

Move the fabric under the needle as you would move a piece of paper under a stationary pen or pencil for free-machine embroidery. Use this technique for freehand monogramming, free-machine quilting, and other free-machine techniques (see bibliography for Know Your Sewing Machine book series by Jackie Dodson, Chilton Book Company).

Next, we will "Sew for Your Home." Besides the personal gratification, sewing for your home is a great way to stretch your decorating budget and to give a new look to an old room—in this case, to your kitchen or dining area. We will make placemats and matching "lapkins" while practicing edge finishes, buttonholes, and topstitching at the same time.

SEW FOR YOUR HOME

● *Step One: Plan Your Project*

● *Step Two: Envelope Placemats*

● *Step Three: Project Variation—Envelope "Lapkins"*

● *Transferable Learnings*

Step One:

PLAN YOUR PROJECT

Although a lot of us sew for the pleasure of it rather than to save money, one of the best places to economize is by sewing for your home. A lot of it is straight sewing, so the challenge is finding fabrics to work effectively with your color scheme.

Unlike a piece of clothing you can hang in the back of your closet if you don't like it, projects you stitch for your home require careful planning, because you may have to live with your decisions until you can afford to change them. For that reason, many people consult an interior designer. However, if you keep some basic principles of color in mind, you can gain the confidence and train your eye well enough to do it yourself.

COLOR SELECTION

Color has either a blue or yellow base. If you have had your personal colors done, you may know that winter and summer colors are cool, blue-based colors. Spring and autumn colors are warm, yellow-based colors. Color for your home works the same way.

When selecting colors for your home, work with the large surface areas first—the floors and counter tops. Once these colors have been chosen, everything else is planned around them. If you are not going to change the floor covering or counter tops, then take a closer look at what you have.

Is it bright and clear or grayed earth tones? To determine if your colors have a cool or warm base, take carpet swatches with you when you go shopping and compare them with other fabrics and colors in natural light. If you have to, take fabric and carpet swatches outside in the shade for a better look. The shade best duplicates a room in natural light. When you put a fabric next to your carpet, does the fabric look dirty? If so, chances are one of them is a cool blue-base and the other a warm yellow-base—neither one enhancing the other. After some comparison, you should begin to see the difference.

Another principle of color selection is to work with an odd number of colors in one room—three or five colors are more interesting than two or four. For example, if you've chosen three colors, two dominate, the third is an accent and used sparingly in a room. For example, you could have a white carpet, black bedspread, black and white draperies, and use red as an accent color in a pillow or flower arrangement. If a bathroom or sitting room adjoins, the accent color (in this case red) can dominate with black or white. The third color becomes the accent.

Once you have trained your eye, you'll begin to notice what works well together and what doesn't. If you have to study something a while or aren't sure your choices compliment each other, they probably don't.

Now, let's start with something small and spruce up your dining area with a new table setting. In this chapter we'll make four placemats and matching "lapkins"—a napkin that has slots to hold the silverware, then unrolls to be used on your lap.

FABRICS, THREADS, AND OTHER SUPPLIES

Once you have decided on the color scheme, let's select the fabric. A woven cotton or cotton blend is your best bet for easy care and trouble-free sewing—poplin, kettle cloth, and lightweight duck are good choices. If you choose to make a contrasting appliqué, as we did here (see color pages), be sure the fiber contents of both fabrics are similar. As always, preshrink the fabric before cutting (see page 49 for preshrinking instructions).

Threads used in this project are:

- cotton or rayon embroidery thread in the appliqué color
- white or black darning thread wound on a bobbin
- nylon monofilament thread wound on a bobbin
- size #5 pearl cotton in the contrasting appliqué color
- all-purpose sewing thread in the prominent color of the placemat

You also need some Wonder-Under for the appliqués, a straight edge (preferably a see-through cutting ruler), a vanishing marker, and, for easy cutting, a rotary cutter and mat.

Step Two:

ENVELOPE PLACEMATS

The placemat looks like the back of an envelope with a button closure (see color pages). Each mat has a contrasting appliqué and a topstitched flap with a buttonhole for a machine-stitched button. The corners of each mat are mitered, then satin stitched with a narrow border.

The techniques used in this project apply to many aspects of sewing, and, because you will stitch each technique four times (by making four placemats and four lapkins), you will master each one. Here's what you'll need:

Supplies

- 1-1/2 yards Wonder-Under (paper-backed fusible web)
- 3 yards of 45" (1.1m) white poplin, weaver's (kettle) cloth, or lightweight duck
- 3/4 yard (23cm) fabric contrasting to poplin
- four 1/2 – 5/8" buttons (two- or four-hole)
- black cotton or rayon embroidery thread
- transparent tape (optional)

Sew-How: *Yardage requirements are for four placemats and four lapkins. Instructions below are written for one placemat and one lapkin.*

CUT

1. Cut one piece of white poplin 16 X 12" (41 X 30.5cm). This we'll call the "base mat." Cut another piece of white poplin 18 X 14" (46 X 35.5cm). This we'll call the "back mat." Note that the lengthwise grain is parallel to the short sides of each mat piece.

2. Cut two pieces of white poplin 10 X 12" (25 X 30.5cm). **Note:** Lengthwise grain is parallel to the 12" (25cm) side. In the upper left corner, mark the lengthwise grain on all poplin pieces using the vanishing or water-soluble marker.

3. Cut one piece of the contrasting appliqué fabric 10 X 12" (25 X 30.5cm) long. Mark lengthwise grain in upper right corner with a marker.

Sew-How: *If contrasting fabric is dark, mark grain line on a piece of transparent tape and stick tape in the upper right corner.*

---

4. Cut one piece of Wonder-Under 10 X 12" (25 X 30.5cm) and fuse it to the back of the contrasting 10 X 12" (25 X 30.5cm) fabric.

Sew-How: *See instructions for use of Wonder-Under in Chapter 3, page 89.*

---

5. Mark a dot along the edge of longer side 6" (15cm) down from the top of the all three 10 X 12" (25 X 30.5cm) fabric pieces.   Cut a triangle from each piece as shown (Fig. 4.1). On the contrasting triangle, trim angled edges 1/4" (6mm).

Fig. 4.1.
Mark a dot 6"
(15cm) in from the
side, and cut a
triangle. On the
contrasting fabric, trim
bias-cut edges 1/4"
(6mm).

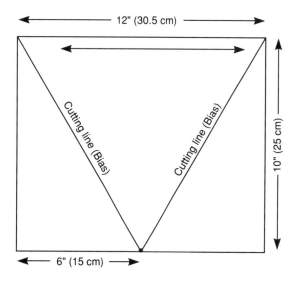

Sew-How: *This triangle has two bias-cut edges and one edge cut on the lengthwise grain. Notice the bias-cut edge hardly ravels compared to the edge cut on the lengthwise grain. Because of this, the bias-cut edge of the appliqué is finished differently than other raw edges are finished.*

APPLIQUÉ

1. Remove the paper backing. Center contrasting triangle on the 16 X 12" (41 X 30.5cm) poplin so the lengthwise grain of the appliqué and the lengthwise grain of the base mat are in the same direction (Fig. 4.2). Fuse contrasting triangle to the base mat.

2. Appliqué the contrasting triangle to base mat.

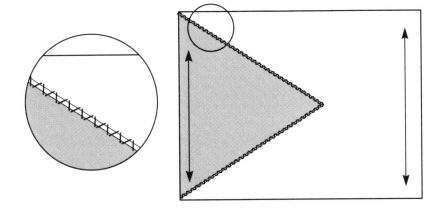

Fig. 4.2.
Center triangle so the
lengthwise grain of the
appliqué is positioned
on the lengthwise
grain of the base mat.

Machine Readiness Checklist

Stitch:	zigzag (A12)
Length:	2
Width:	2.5
Foot:	transparent B (appliqué) or narrow braiding
Needle:	90/14 stretch
Thread:	top, rayon embroidery to match contrasting fabric; bobbin, darning thread
Tension:	top, loosened slightly; bobbin, normal
Accessories:	double strand of #5 pearl cotton

Place a double strand of pearl cotton under the transparent B foot or in the clip of the narrow braiding foot. Place bias-cut edge of triangle appliqué under the foot so the pearl cotton is stitched on the edge of it, then sew. The needle will stitch over the cord, attaching it to the fabric. This technique is called couching (see Figs. 8.20, 9.22, 9.23).

At the corner, stop with the needle on the inside of the corner, lift the presser foot, pivot the work, and pull the pearl cotton under the foot so it will follow the other edge of the appliqué. Lower presser foot, and couch over the pearl cotton along the other edge of the appliqué (see Figs. 9.22, 9.23).

MAKE THE TRIANGLE FLAP

1. Using the standard A metal zigzag foot, place two poplin triangles right sides together, and straight stitch (length 2.5 – 3) a 1/4" (6mm) seam on the two bias-cut edges. Shorten the stitch length, and take one or two stitches across the corner (Fig. 4.3). This insures a sharp corner when the flap is turned and pressed.

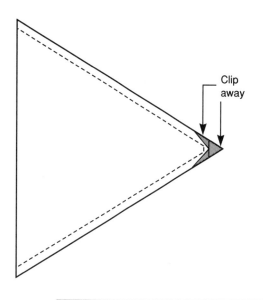

Fig. 4.3.
Shorten the stitch
length and take one
or two stitches across
the corner.

Clip
away

Sew-How: *Use this technique on collar points, cuffs, or when lining a square-cornered pocket.*

---

2. Clip away the fabric at the corner as shown (Fig. 4.3), and turn the flap right side out. Using a point turner or the rounded end of a pair of scissors, gently push the corner out to a nice point without pushing the points through the fabric.

3. For a straight, crisp edge, pin flap around the edge so the seamline is on the edge of the flap. Press flap *without* pressing over the pins.

4. Using a straight edge and vanishing marker, draw a line to mark the center of the flap. Measure 5/8" (1.5cm) in from the point and draw a line perpendicular to the center line. The buttonhole starts where the lines intersect (Fig. 4.4).

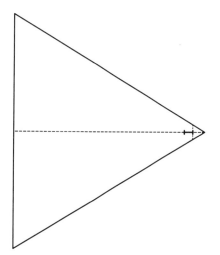

Fig. 4.4.
Start the buttonhole
where the lines
intersect.

5. Set your machine for a buttonhole, and stitch a sample buttonhole on a double layer of scrap poplin to determine what size is needed for your button.

Sew-How: *To determine what size buttonhole you need for a particular button, cut a narrow strip of paper about 2-1/2 times longer than your button is in diameter. Fold the paper strip in half, and slip the button into it as shown, snugging one edge of the button in the fold of the strip (Fig. 4.5A). Hold the paper firmly and crease it at the opposite edge of the fold with your fingernail. Remove the button and flatten the paper strip. The length of the buttonhole needed is the distance from the fold to the fingernail crease in the strip of paper (Fig. 4.5B).*

Fig. 4.5A.
Snug one edge of the button into the folded paper strip.

Fig. 4.5B.
The length of the buttonhole needed for this button is the distance from the fold to the fingernail crease in the paper strip.

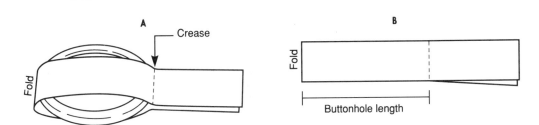

6. Make the buttonhole starting at the mark 5/8" (1.5cm) from the point of the flap. Cut the buttonhole open (see Figs. 8.55, 8.56, and 8.57).

7. Pin poplin triangle flap on base mat and mark the button placement. To do this, find the middle of the buttonhole, and push a pin straight through the buttonhole and base mat. Using a fabric marker, put a dot on the base mat where the pin enters the fabric. Remove the pin.

8. Remove the flap and machine stitch the button in place (see Figs. 8.17, 9.18).

9. Button flap over button and pin flap on base mat for topstitching. Topstitch flap in place.

Machine Readiness Checklist	
Stitch:	straight (A2)
Length:	3.5 – 4
Width:	0
Foot:	standard A metal zigzag or Teflon H
Needle:	90/14 stretch
Thread:	2 all-purpose threads through the same needle in a thread color to match appliqué
Tension:	normal
Needle Position:	left

Topstitch around flap, guiding 1/4" (6mm) from the edge. Note that sewing in left needle position allows you to avoid hitting the button. Two threads through the same needle gives the topstitch a bolder appearance (see Fig. 8.9).

Sew-How: *Heavier topstitching threads are available in a rainbow of colors at your local fabric store. Most are 100% polyester and must be used with a heavy needle. Although a size 14/90 needle is usually large enough, there is a special topstitching needle with an elongated eye designed to accommodate the heavier thread. See Table 1.1.*

ATTACH BASE MAT TO BACK MAT

Rather than stitching on a separate border, which is tricky and cumbersome, the back mat is cut larger than the base mat so it can be folded over the base mat to create the border. The corners are mitered, then the border is topstitched all the way around both to finish the border and to frame the placemat.

1. Center the base mat on the back mat, wrong sides together. Fold the edges of the back mat over the base mat to create a 1" (2.5cm) border. Use an iron and steam to crease a border all the way around on the right side. Remove the base mat.

2. To miter a corner, press one border edge toward the right side. Fold a triangle at the corner the depth of the border (Fig. 4.6A).

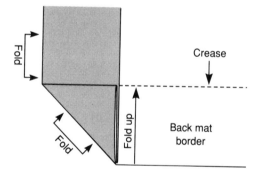

Fig. 4.6A.
Fold a triangle at the corner the depth of the border.

3. Fold edge perpendicular to the border over the triangle made in Step 2. Crease and press (Fig. 4.6B).

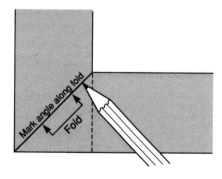

Fig. 4.6B.
Fold edge perpendicular to the border over the triangle. Crease and press. Mark the angle of the miter on the border, and along the side of the fold.

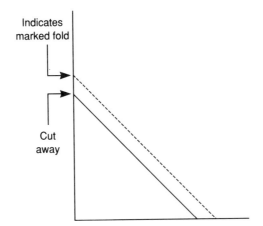

Fig. 4.6C. Unfold corner. The line makes a large triangle which becomes the stitching line.

4. With a water-erasable or vanishing marker, mark the angle of the miter on the border, so that the marker touches both fabric edges on the angle.

5. Unfold the corner. When connected, your lines make a large triangle in the corner which becomes the stitching line (Fig. 4.6C). Set the base mat aside. You will be stitching just the back mat.

6. Fold triangle in half, placing right sides together, and straight stitch on the line marked in Step 5. Trim seam allowance to 1/4" (6mm) and finger-press seam open. Turn mitered corner to the right side, and press corner with an iron and steam.

Sew-How: *For a sharp point at the corner of each miter, clip excess seam allowance at the corner close to the stitching line as you did at the point of the flap.*

FINISH THE ENVELOPE PLACEMAT

1. Slip the base mat into the back mat, snugly fitting corners of base mat into the mitered corners of the back mat. If the base mat ripples a little or does not lie flat, remove from back mat and slightly trim around the outside edge.

2. Using one or two strands of pearl cotton, couch the cord around the edge of the border as you did for the appliqué, guiding 1/8" (3mm) from the raw border edge.

3. Using cotton or rayon embroidery thread on the top and darning thread on the bobbin, stitch over the cord with a 3 width satin stitch to create a narrow border (see Figs. 8.20, 8.27). The cording gives the stitch a higher, rounded appearance.

4. Steam press the envelope mat with the right side against the ironing board.

Step Three:

PROJECT VARIATION—ENVELOPE LAPKINS

The lapkin is also appliquéd like the placemats. The edge is finished with a corded satin stitch, to emulate a serged rolled hem.

1. Cut a 16" (41cm) square out of white poplin.

2. Cut a 9-1/2" (24cm) square out of contrasting fabric and of Wonder-Under.

3. Fuse Wonder-Under on the wrong side of contrasting fabric square. Cut square in half diagonally so you have two triangles.

4. Remove paper backing and fuse contrasting triangles on opposite corners of the poplin square (Fig. 4.7).

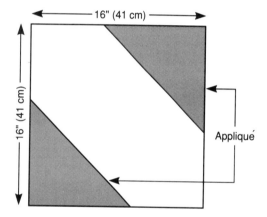

Fig. 4.7.
Fuse contrasting
triangles on
opposite corners
of the poplin
square.

5. Appliqué the triangles (on the bias edges only) as described above for the contrasting appliqué on the placemat, using monofilament thread on the bobbin. This way the bobbin thread will not show when the lapkin is loaded with silverware, and rolled up next to the placemat.

6. Cord the edge of the lapkin.

Stitch:	zigzag (A12)
Length:	2
Width:	1.5 – 2
Foot:	transparent B (appliqué) or narrow braiding
Needle:	90/14 stretch
Thread:	top, cotton or rayon embroidery to match contrasting fabric; bobbin, darning
Tension:	top, loosened slightly; bobbin, normal
Accessories:	#5 pearl cotton

Place a strand of pearl cotton under the foot and couch over it, guiding 1/4" (6mm) from the raw edge. When you come to the corner, leave the needle on the inside corner, lift the presser foot, and pivot the work, pulling the cord so it will follow the second edge of the lapkin. Lower foot, then continue sewing. This gives the corner a slight curve.

7. Trim the excess fabric up to the stitching, being careful not to cut the stitches (Fig. 4.8). Satin stitch around the outside edge of the lapkin with a 4 width satin stitch (see Fig. 8.27). Guide the fabric halfway under the foot, so the needle stitches just over the cord on the left and swings off the raw edge on the right. Satin stitch around the lapkin. Pull threads to the back and tie them off.

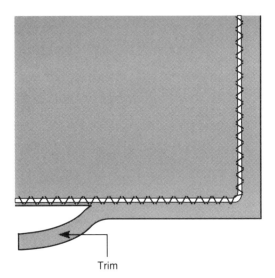

Fig. 4.8.
Trim excess fabric up to the corded stitching being careful not to cut the stitches.

Trim

Sew-How: *For a professional-looking satin-stitched corner, stop with the needle on the inside, lift the presser foot, pivot the fabric slightly, lower the foot, take a stitch over the cord and back, stopping with the needle on the inside corner in the same pivot hole as before. Continue so the stitches fan out to form the corner (Fig. 4.9).*

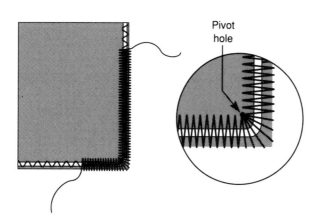

Pivot hole

Fig. 4.9.
To turn a corner with a satin stitch, stop the needle at inside corner. Lift foot, pivot fabric slightly. Lower foot, stitch, and pivot from same pivot hole so stitches fan out around the corner.

8. Stitch the silverware slots. Fold lapkin in half to make a triangle, so the appliquéd corners are at the top and appliqués are on the inside. On the bottom of the triangle, measure 9" (23cm) in from the left corner, and mark a dot. Mark three more dots along the fold to the right, spacing them 1-1/2" (4cm) apart. Fold down top appliquéd corner, creasing it 6" (15cm) above the first fold. Unfold corner, and draw a straight line on the crease, using a vanishing marker.

9. Draw four lines perpendicular to the bottom fold, up to the line drawn on the crease, as shown (Fig. 4.10).

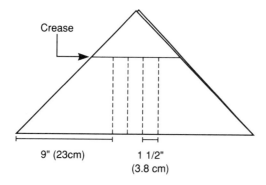

Crease

9" (23cm)   1 1/2" (3.8 cm)

Fig. 4.10.
Draw four lines perpendicular to the bottom fold, up to the line drawn on the crease. Straight stitch over the lines to create the slots for the silverware to slip into.

10. Using all-purpose thread to match the poplin, run four rows of straight stitching from the fold to the line marked in Step 9, backstitching at the top and bottom of each row. Fold the appliquéd corner down and press. Slide a knife, fork, and spoon in each slot. Then roll up the lapkin and put it beside the placemat so the appliquéd corner shows (see color pages).

Lapkins can be made from scratch, or from purchased fabric napkins to match your favorite table setting. For a formal occasion, make them out of linen; for backyard picnics and barbecues, use print bandanas. Play with different color schemes to learn how colors interact.

TRANSFERABLE LEARNINGS

The information and techniques you have learned by making this table setting have given you skills necessary to sew other projects. You have learned to:

• Build a color scheme in a room around the large surface areas—counter tops and floors.

• Identify the difference between blue-based and yellow-based colors.

• Use an odd number of colors in a room for interest.

• Identify the difference in a piece of fabric cut on the bias and one cut on the straight of grain.

• Stitch, clip, turn, and topstitch a facing to create the flap on the placemat. These techniques are used when sewing a collar or cuff or when lining a pocket.

• Make machine-stitched buttonholes to fit a button. Use this on other projects.

• Sew a button on by machine. Now you can sew buttons on to stay.

• Topstitch using two threads through the same needle for a bolder look to any area you want to topstitch.

• Miter corners—handy for creating a fabric border on a quilt, mitering a corner with ribbon or trim, mitering a placket on a sleeve or kick pleat.

• Couch a strand or two of pearl cotton to a base fabric. Use this method as a decorative topstitch, or to edge appliqués.

• Cord a satin-stitched edge. This edge finish can be used to edge placemats, appliqués, or cut work, or to narrow-hem the edge of chiffon.

• Turn a satin-stitched corner so the stitches fan out from a pivot point. This technique is used around the corner of an appliqué, or any time you turn a corner with a satin stitch.

Next, try some machine quilting techniques by making a small wall hanging. In Chapter 5, you'll try enough to find out whether you like machine quilting. If so, you can make a larger lap blanket or a full-sized quilt.

SEW A QUILT

● *Step One: Plan Your Project*

● *Step Two: Quilted Wall Hanging*

● *Transferable Learnings*

What is a quilt? Robbie and Tony Fanning define it in *The Complete Book of Machine Quilting* (Chilton, 1980) as "a sandwich of three distinct layers: a *top*, some *filler* (usually called batting, regardless of the material used), and a *backing* (sometimes called a lining). The top is secured to the backing through the filler with thread to keep the three layers from shifting around."

Some quilts are stitched entirely by hand; others, entirely by machine; still others are a combination of both. As much as I would like to try hand quilting, like many people these days, I don't have the time to perfect it, so let's quilt with our Vikings.

The small quilted wall hanging we'll make in this chapter is designed to help you explore and practice the following machine-quilting techniques:

- free-machine quilting
- piecing and 1/4" seam allowances
- quilt-as-you-go
- stitch-in-the-ditch quilting
- adding borders
- straight-stitch quilting
- machine tying

As you gain experience in each of these techniques, you can decide whether you want to tackle bigger and more complex quilting projects.

Step One:

PLAN YOUR PROJECT

FABRIC SELECTION

The most exciting part of making a quilt is selecting the fabric. It's also the most confusing. I used primary colors in this, as well as in other projects in this book. They work well together and are a way of preserving scraps from the other projects in my quilt. After all, isn't that what some quilts used to be—a collection of fabric scraps from "Susie's dress," "Johnny's shirt," "Grandma's wedding dress"?

Fabrics best for quilting are light- to medium-weight woven cottons or cotton/polyester blends. Many fabric stores have a special section devoted to quilting fabrics and supplies. Before leaving the store choose a batting.

Sew-How: *For larger, more complex quilts, read* **Speed-Cut Quilts—1200 Speed-Cut Quilt Blocks** *by Donna Poster (Chilton, 1989). In her book, Donna not only presents principles of good color selection, talking about hue, value, and intensity of color; she also illustrates 400 quilt blocks in three sizes. She has devised an ingenious plan for selecting the yardage for each part of the block, lattice strips, and borders—what a timesaver!*

Batting

Bonded polyester batting is the easiest batting to work with for machine quilting. It keeps its loft, is easy to handle, washes well, holds up well over years of use, and doesn't have to be quilted as closely as cotton batting. It also comes in a variety of sizes and weights. Use lighter-weight batting for clothing and table coverings; use medium to heavy for quilts.

Preshrinking

- Preshrink your fabric the way you intend to care for your quilt after construction.

- Wash light and dark fabrics separately, to prevent dark colors from running on light-colored fabrics. Trim off all selvage edges *after* washing.

- It is not necessary to preshrink the bonded polyester batting.

Sew-How: *To cut down on raveling and tangling, snip a 1/4" triangle off the four corners of your fabric before washing.*

OTHER MACHINE QUILTING SUPPLIES

Machine quilters find the following items helpful. Each one is described in Chapter 1, Step Two: Assemble Your Tools.

- Rotary cutter and mat—if you become a serious machine quilter, purchase the largest cutter and mat available.

- See-through cutting ruler—for accuracy, use the same ruler throughout a quilting project.

- Glass-head quilting pins—they're extra long and sharp, and pin easily through the quilt sandwich. I love to use them for most other sewing, too.

- Nickel-plated safety pins, 1" (2.5cm) long, to baste your quilt together.

- Water-erasable marking pen or disappearing dress-maker's chalk (for Clo-Chalk, see Sources of Supply).

- 8" spring or screw-type embroidery hoop—necessary for free-machine quilting.

Needles, Threads, Bobbins, and Presser Feet

Needles

As with any new project, your machine must be lint-free and outfitted with a new needle. For piecing, a 70/10 or 80/12 universal needle is recommended. For machine quilting, use a needle with a larger eye so the thread will not shred, wear, or break when you stitch through the quilt sandwich. A 90/14 universal or stretch needle works well. A curved hand needle is also helpful for hand basting the quilt sandwich (optional).

Threads

The rule of thumb for almost all sewing projects is to select a thread made of the same fiber or blend of fibers as the fabric. Because it's easier to repair stitches than shredded fabric after the quilt has been washed a few times, use a thread less strong than the fabric. Therefore, if top and backing are 100% cotton, use 100% cotton thread. If fabrics are a cotton/poly blend, a cotton-wrapped polyester (all-purpose) thread works well. If your fabric is lightweight, use a machine-embroidery thread to piece the top, so the fabric won't pucker. When free-machine quilting, use a lighter-weight cotton machine-embroidery thread if possible. Choose colors to blend with the most predominant colors of the top and backing fabrics.

Extra Bobbins

Before starting a quilting project, decide on the colors you'll be using and wind bobbins of each. This saves time and encourages more testing and experimentation because you don't have to take time to wind a bobbin.

Presser Feet

The presser feet used the most in machine quilting are:

- The darning foot for free-machine quilting. It provides support around the needle and promotes better stitch formation when you stitch through the quilt sandwich (see Fig. 9.28).

- The standard A metal zigzag foot for precise 1/4" seams (see Figs. 9.4, 9.5).

- The dual feed foot is for straight quilting and quilt-as you-go techniques. It prevents the quilt sandwich from shifting and minimizes puckering (see Fig. 9.29).

Step Two:

QUILTED WALL HANGING

This wall hanging is constructed from the center out. Let's preview how we'll make it together. First, the center "medallion," or focal point, is free-machine quilted. Look for light- to midweight fabric with an allover print of big shapes, or a print panel. I used a child's print for my project. Note that yardage requirements and the size of the pieced border are based on a 10" center medallion square (see color pages).

Sew-How: *If you can't find a medallion print you like, create your own: find an allover print and cut out shapes to appliqué to a solid color background fabric.*

After quilting the center medallion, a pieced border is constructed. The most important principle to practice with machine quilting is accuracy—accuracy in measuring, cutting, and sewing which you will perfect in piecing this border.

Sew-How: *Notice that there are no metric conversions in this chapter. Machine quilting requires such precision and accuracy, I couldn't convert inches to centimeters closely enough to guarantee that each piece would fit.*

Next, the backing is attached. A lattice border and the pieced border are added in separate steps to frame the medallion. Each is attached to the batting and backing to learn the quilt-as-you-go and stitch-in-the-ditch quilting techniques.

The last border is created by bringing the backing over the front. Corners are mitered; edges are turned under, then topstitched. This last "frame," created by the backing, is straight-stitch machine-quilted for depth and dimension.

Got the picture? Let's begin. Here's what you'll need:

Supplies

10" square light- to midweight allover print or print panel for center medallion

1/8 yd. each of black, white, and yellow solid-colored, and red mini-print cotton fabric or colors to match your center medallion fabric

5/8 yd. blue print

5/8 yd. medium-weight bonded batting

Three 3/4" plastic drapery rings

Optional: curved hand needle, masking tape, nickel-plated safety pins

---

Sew-How: *Before starting on your finished project, practice each technique on a scrap until you are comfortable with it. Put stitch samples in your notebook.*

FREE-MACHINE QUILT THE MEDALLION

1. Because you're using bonded batting, you don't need a fabric backing to quilt to it. Lay batting on a large flat table and cut into a 20" square. Center and pin medallion on batting. Baste in place around four sides using the dual feed foot (see Fig. 9.29) and a 4 – 5 length straight stitch.

Machine Readiness Checklist	
Stitch:	straight (A2)
Length:	0
Width:	0
Foot:	darning
Needle:	80/12 universal or 90/14 stretch
Thread:	cotton embroidery thread in predominant color of print background
Feed dogs:	down
Pressure:	0
Tension:	top, loosened slightly; bobbin, normal
Fabric:	center medallion print, batting
Accessories:	8" spring or screw-type embroidery hoop, extension table to cover the free-arm

2. Put outer hoop of embroidery hoop on a flat surface. Loosen the screw of inner hoop or squeeze the clamp. Place medallion, basted to the batting over the outer hoop with the right side up. Press in the inner hoop so the fabric is taut. Place project under the needle by tipping the hoop. Put presser bar lever down to engage the upper thread tension. Turn the flywheel one stitch and pull bobbin thread through the surface of the fabric. Take a few up-and-down locking stitches, then cut threads off at the fabric.

Sew-How: *A small pair of curved-blade scissors come with some Viking sewing machines. The blades are curved so they won't accidentally snip into the fabric while clipping off threads. If you have a different model, purchase a pair through your local Viking dealer.*

---

3. Begin stitching at medium speed while moving the fabric freely under the needle, following the outline of the print medallion. Slowly stitch around each shape. If shapes are not connected, stitch around to where you started, take a few locking stitches, lift the presser foot to release the upper tension, and move the fabric to the next shape. Put the presser foot down, take a few locking stitches, then proceed as described above for all shapes (Fig. 5.1). Clip connecting threads and pull them to the wrong side.

Fig. 5.1. With project under needle and darning foot, lower presser bar lever, turn flywheel one stitch, and pull bobbin thread to the surface of the fabric. Lock a few stitches and clip threads off at the fabric. Then free-machine quilt around shapes on your medallion fabric.

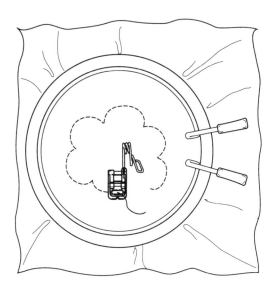

ADD THE BACKING

Cut backing fabric 23" square. Lay backing, **wrong** side up, on a large, flat surface. Center quilted medallion, right side up, on backing so the lengthwise grain is parallel to the sides. Starting from the center and working out, baste the quilt sandwich together with safety pins, pinning safety pins every 3 – 4" through all layers across the medallion. After each pin, straighten backing by pulling on all four sides to avoid pinning in wrinkles.

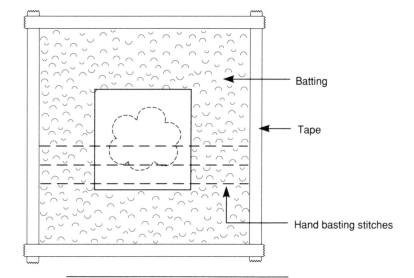

Batting

Tape

Hand basting stitches

Fig. 5.2.
Hand baste quilted
medallion to backing
with a curved needle
and stitch 1" basting
stiches, working from
the center out.

Sew-How: *For this small project, you may want to hand baste using a long running stitch. To do this, tape the backing, wrong side up, to a table top smoothing out all the wrinkles. Center quilted medallion, right side up, over the backing. Using a curved needle, hand baste a row of 1" basting stitches in a thread color contrasting the backing. Stitch a center row, then successive rows about 1-1/2" apart on either side, working from the center out (Fig. 5.2).*

PIECE A BORDER

1. Using the rotary cutter, mat, and see-through cutting ruler, cut two each 2 x 12" strips of black, white, yellow, red print, and blue print so the 12" length is cut across the grain.

2. Cut one each 3" square of black, yellow, red print, and blue print.

Machine Readiness Checklist

Stitch:	straight (A2)
Length:	2 – 2.5
Width:	0
Foot:	standard A metal zigzag
Needle:	70/10 or 80/12 universal
Thread:	all-purpose
Feed dogs:	up
Pressure:	normal
Tension:	normal
Needle position:	variable
Fabric:	a couple of strips cut as described in Step 1 above for practice stitching
Accessories:	sewing gauge, iron, and ironing board

3. Using two of your test strips, place right sides together and stitch an exact 1/4" seam. Check it for accuracy against the 1/4" mark on your sewing gauge.

Sew-How: *If there is not a clear-cut place on your presser foot or needle plate to guide for 1/4" seams, move your needle position slightly to the right or left as needed (see your Operating Manual to find out how to adjust your needle position). Accuracy is important. If you're off only a 1/16", when it is multiplied by eight cut edges, the difference measures 1/2", which can throw off piecing and overall finished quilt dimensions.*

To make a pieced border, pin and stitch strips together in the order shown in Fig. 5.3, piecing with perfect 1/4" seams.

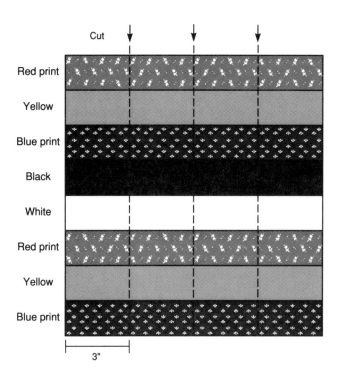

Fig. 5.3.
Cut pieced border
into four 3" widths.

Cut

Red print

Yellow

Blue print

Black

White

Red print

Yellow

Blue print

3"

4. From the wrong side, press seam allowances flat and together to set the stitches. Then, using the tip of your iron, press seams open. Cut pieced border into four 3" widths (Fig. 5.3).

5. On one of the pieced border strips, stitch the yellow square so it is above the red print strip using a 1/4" seam allowance. On the other end of that strip, stitch the black square to the blue print strip (Fig. 5.4).

Fig. 5.4.
On one strip stitch
yellow square next to
red print, and stitch
black square next to
blue print. On
another strip stitch
red print square
next to blue print, and
stitch blue print square
next to red print.

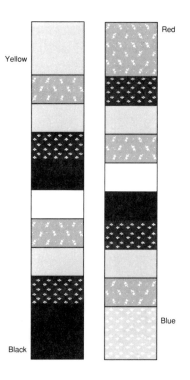

Yellow

Red

Black

Blue

6. On another pieced border strip, stitch the red print square to the blue print strip. On the other end of that strip, stitch the blue print square to the red print strip (Fig. 5.4). Press seams open and set these pieced border strips aside.

ADD LATTICE BORDER AND QUILT-AS-YOU-SEW

1. Cut two black border strips 1-1/2 X 10". Cut two more black border strips 1-1/2 X 12".

Machine Readiness Checklist	
Stitch:	straight (A2)
Length:	3 – 3.5
Width:	0
Foot:	dual feed
Needle:	80/12 universal or 14/90 stretch
Thread:	all-purpose top, to match border strips; bobbin, to match backing fabric

2. Remove any safety pins that may be in the way and pin short black border pieces, centering them on either side of quilted medallion. Stitch a 1/4" seam allowance starting and stopping at the ends of each border piece. Lock threads by pushing the finishing button or STOP display, or by putting the stitch length to 0 and taking three to four stitches in one place; or pull threads to the front and tie them off. Press side border pieces so the seam allowance is to the inside (Fig. 5.5).

Fig. 5.5.
Press side border pieces so the seam allowance is to the inside.

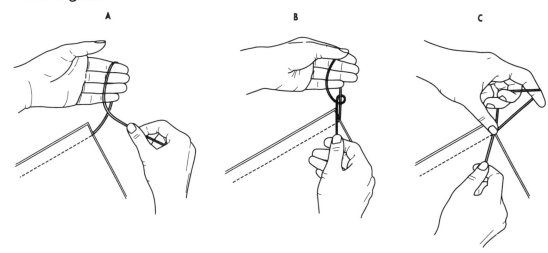

A   B   C

Fig. 5.6A.
Form a loop.

Fig. 5.6B.
Bring thread
end around and
through loop.

Fig. 5.6C.
Work loop down to
the base of the stitch
with your thumb.

Sew-How: *To tie a secure knot, give yourself thread tails at least 7" long. Hold threads together in your left hand and form a loop (Fig. 5.6A). Bring the thread end around and through the loop (Fig. 5.6B). Holding the loop in your left hand, work the loop down to the base and hold it in place with your left thumb (Fig. 5.6C). Pull thread taut with your right hand so the loop forms a knot at the base of the fabric.*

---

3. Place longer border pieces across the top and bottom of quilted medallion, right sides together, so ends are even with side border pieces. Pin and stitch, using 1/4" seams, starting and stopping 1/4" from the end of each strip. Pull threads to the back side and leave them free. Press longer border pieces so seam allowance is to the inside (Fig. 5.7).

Fig. 5.7.
Press longer border
pieces so seam
allowances are
to the inside.

ADD PIECED BORDERS AND QUILT-AS-YOU-GO

The pieced border is stitched in the same sequence as the frame border described above—the sides first, then the top and bottom strips. If you have pin-basted, remove safety pins that may get in the way of stitching.

1. Center short pieced borders made in "Piece a Border" on each side, aligning cut edges, right sides together, against the frame border. Position the red print at the top for the shorter right pieced strip. Position the blue print at the top for the shorter left pieced strip (see color pages). This way contrasting fabric will be on either side of the squares in each corner.

2. Pin and stitch a 1/4" seam. Pull threads to the right side and tie them off as before. Press seam flat then open. Repeat for the other side.

3. Place longer pieced border strips so the red square is in the upper left corner, the yellow square in the upper right, the black square is in the lower right corner, and the blue square in the lower left (see color pages). Pin top and bottom strips so the square, piecing, and frame border match perfectly in each corner (Fig. 5.8 A). Stitch a 1/4" seam. Pull threads to the right side of your work and tie them off.

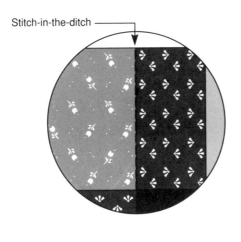

Stitch-in-the-ditch

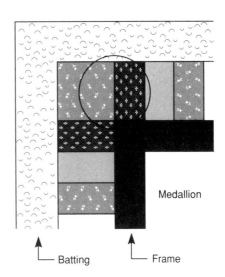

Medallion

Batting   Frame

Fig. 5.8.
Pin top and bottom strips so the square, piecing, and frame border match perfectly in each corner. Stitch-in-the-ditch on one side of the square in each corner.

4. Press pieced border so seam allowance is to the inside. Stitch-in-the-ditch on one side of each corner square so the squares have been quilted around the two inside edges (Fig. 5.8B; see Fig. 8.8).

Sew-How: *To stitch-in-the-ditch means to sew from the right side in the indentation between two seamed fabrics. See above or Fig. 8.7.*

FINISH BACKING AND LAST BORDER

Instead of adding another border, the backing is brought over the front, encasing the batting and covering the raw edge of the pieced border.

You have handled your quilt a lot during its construction, so you may have to square up the batting and backing. Measure and trim where necessary so batting and backing are square.

1. Press a 1/2" hem to the wrong side all the way around the backing square.

Sew-How: *Instead of measuring, pinning, and pressing a narrow hem, take your sewing gauge to the ironing board and move the guide the desired distance required for the hem. Fold the fabric edge over the end of the gauge so the raw edge is even with the guide and press (Fig. 5.9). Continue down the length of the edge, folding and pressing as you go.*

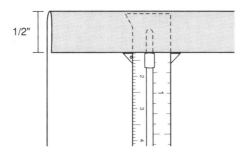

Fig. 5.9.
Fold fabric edge over end of gauge so raw edge is even with the guide. Press.

For longer hems, use this same pressing technique with a metal Dritz EZY-HEM™ Gauge, available in sewing stores.

2. Miter each corner as described in Chapter 4 (Fig. 4.6). Note that once the stitching line is established, the miter in your quilt is made by stitching through the 1/2" pressed hem in Step 1 above.

3. Trim a 1/2" square out of each corner of the batting to reduce bulk. Turn batting under 1/2" all the way around. This extra loft gives a fuller look to the outside edge of the border.

Fig. 5.10.
Using the dual feed foot, straight quilt two rows inside backing border, 5/8" apart.

4. Turn miter right side out. Pin backing so the hem edge covers raw edges of pieced border. Stitch 1/16" inside the folded edge (Fig. 5.10).

Sew-How: *For precise stitching, guide the folded edge by the inside of the presser foot. Then move the needle position so stitching is 1/16" from the fold.*

STRAIGHT-STITCH QUILTING

1. Using the dual feed foot, and top and bobbin thread to match backing, straight stitch quilt 5/8" inside the backing border. Quilt another row, 5/8" next to the first (Fig. 5.10). Either guide it by a line on your needle plate or put masking tape on it to use as a guide.

2. Turn your quilt over. You should see a square quilted in each corner and two concentric squares quilted in the middle around the medallion. Look at the threads you have not tied off yet. Are they even with the outside concentric square? If not, loosen a couple of stitches so the rows meet. Then tie off free threads.

Three rows of straight quilting should be around the edge to create a border.

3. Hand stitch plastic drapery rings on the top back of wall hanging.

TIE A QUILT

Another option to quilting-as-you-go or stitch-in-the-ditch quilting as you did at the squares in each corner, is to tie a quilt together. Use the three-step zigzag (A19) and tack a triple strand of a 3 – 4" length of pearl cotton in the center of the strand, through the quilt sandwich (see Fig. 8.37). Lock and tie off the stitches; then tie the pearl cotton into a square knot. Clip ends to 1/2".

TRANSFERABLE LEARNINGS

The information and techniques you have learned and practiced by constructing the quilted wall hanging have given you skills necessary to sew other projects. You have learned how to:

• Preshrink woven fabrics by snipping a triangle off each corner to cut down on raveling. This is helpful when preshrinking any woven fabric.

• Measure, mark, and cut accurately—necessary for tailoring and more complicated quilting projects.

• Move the fabric freely under a stitching needle. The movement and technique for free-machine quilting is similar to free-machine embroidery.

• Use a larger-eyed needle when stitching through quilt sandwich or other heavy fabric so thread won't shred or break.

• Quilt using the stitch-in-the-ditch technique. The same technique is used to tack down facings and waistbands.

• Quilt with a straight stitch (A2) to create a textured border. This technique is done with the dual feed foot to stitch yardage that is cut for jacket or tote bag linings. Using a lighter-weight batting and the edge guide, straight-stitch quilt table coverings and other lighter-weight projects.

• Create a border for a quilt or any wall hanging by turning the backing over the front and mitering the corners.

• Adjust your needle position, rather than move the fabric, for precise seam allowances and topstitching.

• Press a narrow hem, using your sewing gauge and iron, to save a lot of hand pinning.

• Tie a quilt using the three-step zigzag (A19) . This technique is also a way to tack down facings, small appliqués, and embroideries.

In the next chapter, Sew Toys, we'll make stuffed fabric blocks and a stuffed hobbyhorse, whimsical projects that help us discover what fun it is to use the special marking foot and weaver's reed.

SEW TOYS

- *Step One: Plan Your Project*

- *Step Two: Sew Jumbo Fabric Blocks*

- *Step Three: Make a Hobbyhorse*

- *Transferable Learnings*

Step One:

PLAN YOUR PROJECT

Fabric lends itself beautifully to making toys. It's pliable, washable, and, when stuffed, irresistibly cuddly. In this chapter, new sewers start by making fabric blocks. If you don't have a little person in your life, the principles learned here will be helpful in making other stuffed fabric structures. Decorate the blocks and make them smaller for Christmas ornaments. Make them much larger and use canvas or Naugahyde for a hassock or a bean bag chair.

The hobbyhorse is made of both straight and curved shapes—so you'll clip and notch seam allowances to make smooth, continuous curves. You'll also use the special marking foot to make eyelashes and the weaver's reed to make the mane—these accessories help you add texture and dimension to projects.

FABRIC AND THREAD

The fabrics and supplies used in both projects are easy to work with—woven cotton/polyester blends, felt, and polyester fiberfill.

Make both projects washable by preshrinking the fabric in the same way you plan to take care of the finished project. Although you may find wool felt, look for washable polyester felt, available in a rainbow of colors at your local fabric or craft store. Make the mane of the hobbyhorse out of a washable nylon or cotton yarn.

Because both the blocks and the hobbyhorse are constructed of different colored fabrics, use nylon monofilament thread, top and bobbin, unless directed otherwise. This way, you don't have to rethread with each fabric color change.

Step Two:

SEW JUMBO FABRIC BLOCKS

The following instructions are for making three fabric blocks at a time.

Supplies

- 1/4 yd. (23cm) each of woven cotton/polyester in a red print and green print; blue, black, white, and yellow solids
- 2 black polyester felt squares
- 1/2 bag of polyester fiberfill (save remainder for hobbyhorse)
- nylon monofilament thread
- red, blue, green, white, and yellow all-purpose, rayon, or 100% cotton embroidery thread
- 5" wide (12.5cm) strip of Wonder-Under (if you are making the game board later in this book, buy a yard [meter])
- rotary cutter, mat, and see-through ruler
- tracing paper and vanishing marker
- iron-on freezer wrap
- print motif fabric to cut appliqués from (e.g., trucks,airplanes, flowers, etc.)
- woven fusible interfacing
- blunt-nosed scissors, point turner, or wooden spoon

DECORATE THE SQUARES

1. Cut three 6" (15cm) squares each in white, black, blue, and yellow solids; green and red prints.

2. At your local copy center, enlarge letters to twice the size in Fig. 6.1. Using the tracing paper and marker, trace letters from the photocopy to make your pattern.

3. Fuse Wonder-Under on the wrong side of black felt squares, and the appliqué fabric, following manufacturer's instructions (see Chapter 3).

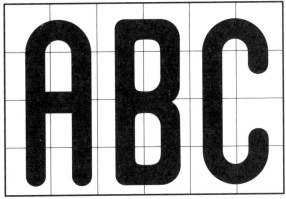

Fig. 6.1.
Trace letters to make
the pattern for the
fabric blocks. Pattern
is 1/2 size.

One square = one inch.

4. Cut out three each of the letters from the black felt and remove the paper backing.
   - Center and fuse the letter A to two red squares and one yellow square.
   - Center and fuse the letter B to two blue squares and one green square.
   - Center and fuse the letter C to two green squares and one yellow square.
   - Center and fuse the appliqués cut from printed fabric to the three white squares.

5. Stitch black felt letters to the squares.

Machine Readiness Checklist

Stitch:	straight (A2)
Length:	2
Width:	0
Foot:	standard A metal zigzag, buttonhole C, or blind hem D
Needle:	80/12 universal
Thread:	nylon monofilament
Tension:	top, loosened halfway between normal and loose; bobbin, normal

Straight stitch around each letter guiding 1/8" (3mm) from cut edge.

Sew-How: *If you use the blind hem D or buttonhole C foot, guide the edge of the letter along the inside right toe. You may have to decenter the needle slightly to stitch 1/8" (3mm) from the edge (see your Operating Manual). (See Figs. 9.8, 9.11.)*

Backstitch or push the finishing button or STOP display to lockstitch at beginning and end of each letter. Press each lettered square with the right side down using a hot iron and steam.

6. Stitch around the appliqué with a 2 width satin stitch (990: 2-43; 1100: A14) (see Fig. 8.27).

7. Iron freezer wrap to the wrong side of each decorated square. Fuse woven interfacing to the wrong side of each undecorated square. Top thread your machine with red thread. Stack the decorated squares and set to one side of your machine. Set the undecorated squares aside.

Machine Readiness Checklist

Stitch:	zigzag or satin (990: 2-43; 1100 A14)
Length:	0.5
Width:	2
Foot:	transparent B (appliqué)
Thread:	top: red, blue, yellow, and green rayon, or 100% cotton embroidery; bobbin: darning or nylon monofilament
Tension:	top, loosened slightly; bobbin, normal

8. Top thread your machine with red thread. With the right side up, stitch a row of satin stitches, guiding 1/2" (1.3cm) from the raw edge of one side of each decorated square.

9. Using yellow thread on one side, blue thread on one side, and green thread on one side of each square, rethread and satin stitch 1/2" (1.3mm) from the raw edge (Fig. 6.2). On those sides where the thread color matches the fabric, satin stitch with white thread.

Fig. 6.2.
With red thread, stitch a row of satin stitches, guiding 1/2" (1.3cm) from the raw edge on one side of each square. Rethread and repeat for the other three sides, using yellow thread on one side, blue thread on one side, and green thread on one side.

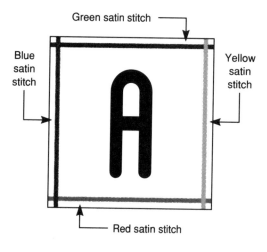

Sew-How: *To satin stitch each square quickly, butt one square up to the next, and satin stitch one side, stitching one color at a time. When stitched, the squares resemble a kite tail. Clip threads between the squares to separate them, then restack for the next satin-stitched color. (See Fig. 8.35.)*

ASSEMBLE JUMBO BLOCKS

1. Separate squares so each block is made of one appliqué square, three letter squares (A, B, and C), and two plain squares. Using the vanishing marker, mark dots 1/4" (6mm) from each corner on each square. Remove freezer wrap from decorated squares.

2. With right sides together, pin lettered A, B, and C squares next to each other. Then, pin appliquéd square next to the letter C square as shown. Straight stitch squares together using exact 1/4" (6mm) seam allowances starting and stopping seams at each dot (Fig. 6.3). Press seams flat and together, then press seams open. Press 1/4" (6mm) seam allowances on the two short ends of the row of stitched squares.

Fig. 6.3.
Mark a dot 1/4" (6mm) from the corner in each square. Pin A, B, C, and appliquéd squares together, and stitch 1/4" (6mm) seams, starting and stopping at the dots in each corner.

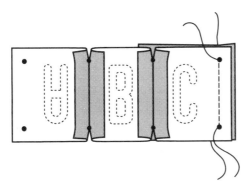

Sew-How: *To save a lot of time hand tying threads at the beginning and end of each seam, start and stop each seam with the finishing button or push the STOP display button. (This feature is not on all Vikings, so check your Operating Manual or call your dealer and ask.)*

---

3. With right sides together, align the bottom of the A square to one side of the plain bottom square, matching dots. Place block under the standard A metal or Teflon H presser foot so the plain square that makes the bottom of the block is against the feed

Fig. 6.4A.
Align the bottom of A square to one side of plain bottom square, and stitch a 1/4" (6mm) seam, starting and stopping at the dots in the corner.

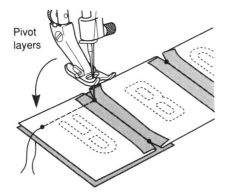

dogs. Starting at the dot and 1/4" (6mm) from the corner, sew the first side, stopping with your needle in the fabric at the dot in the opposite corner (Fig. 6.4A).

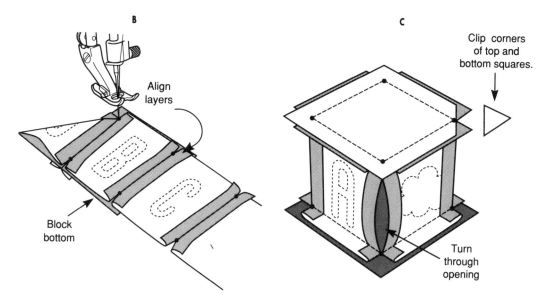

Lift the presser foot and pivot work 90 degrees. Align the bottom of the B square with the corresponding side of the bottom square. Lower presser foot and stitch the bottom of the B square to the second side of the plain square, stopping with the needle in the dot at the corner (Fig. 6.4B). Repeat for the other two sides of the bottom square to create the block.

4. Repeat Step 3 to stitch the top square to the block (Fig. 6.4C).

5. Turn block right side out, through the opening. Using a pair of blunt-nosed scissors or a point turner, gently push out each corner of the block, so it's sharp and square.

6. Using a handful of fiberfill, begin stuffing the block until it is comfortably full. Use scissor points, wooden spoon handle, or point turner to push fiberfill into each corner.

7. Turn seam allowance of opening toward inside of block, and pin it shut.

8. Decenter your needle to the far left (see your Operating Manual), and straight stitch the opening closed guiding 1/8" (3mm) from the edge. Tie off thread ends.

Aren't the blocks cute? and so easy to make. Are you ready for something more challenging? Let's make the hobbyhorse.

Step Three:

MAKE A HOBBYHORSE

Supplies

- 1/2 yd. (.5m) red cotton print
- 1/8 yd. (12cm) blue and white cotton print
- 1 black polyester felt scrap for eyes and nostrils
- 1 white polyester felt scrap for eyes
- 1 oz. (28g) ball of cotton or nylon yarn for mane

- two 1" (2.5cm) red or blue buttons for the bridle
- nylon monofilament thread
- black cotton embroidery thread
- all-purpose thread to coordinate with other fabrics (optional)
- Wonder-Under (paper-backed fusible web)
- 1/2 bag of polyester fiberfill (remainder used for Jumbo Fabric Blocks)
- graph paper (1" [2.5cm] square preferred), tracing paper, pencil
- French curve (optional)
- 2 yd. (2m) blue 1" (2.5) grosgrain ribbon for bridle and reins
- #3 pearl cotton
- hand needle
- 1 broom handle
- weaver's reed
- adding-machine tape
- seam sealant (e.g., Fray Check)
- dressmaker's chalk

MAKE THE PATTERN

1. If you have access to a photocopy machine, enlarge the pattern to twice the size in Fig. 6.5A, B, and C. Note that gusset must be joined at the arrows as shown.

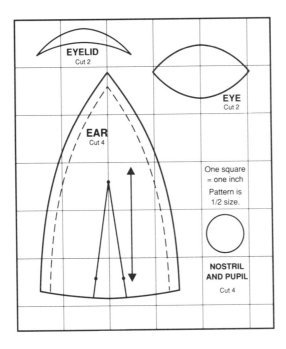

Fig. 6.5A.
Hobbyhorse pattern
ear and eye pieces.
Pattern is 1/2 size.

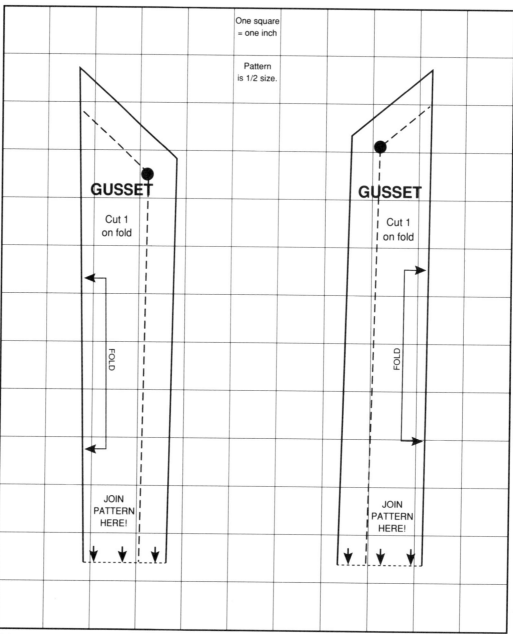

One square
= one inch

Pattern
is 1/2 size.

GUSSET

Cut 1
on fold

FOLD

JOIN
PATTERN
HERE!

GUSSET

Cut 1
on fold

FOLD

JOIN
PATTERN
HERE!

Fig. 6.5B.
Hobbyhorse pattern
gusset piece.
Pattern is 1/2 size.

Join two pieces to form one pattern

To enlarge the pattern freehand, each square on the pattern represents a square inch (2.5cm) on your graph paper. Begin counting blocks and plot dots in each square of your graph paper where the direction of the line changes.

2. Use the French curve, moving and pivoting between the dots marked, to approximate the curves. Note that each pattern piece includes the seam allowance. The ear pattern uses 1/4" (6mm) seam allowances; other pattern pieces have   5/8" (1.5cm) seam allowances.

3. On each pattern piece, mark the grain line, dots, and ear and eye placement; then label each piece and mark how many of each one to cut.

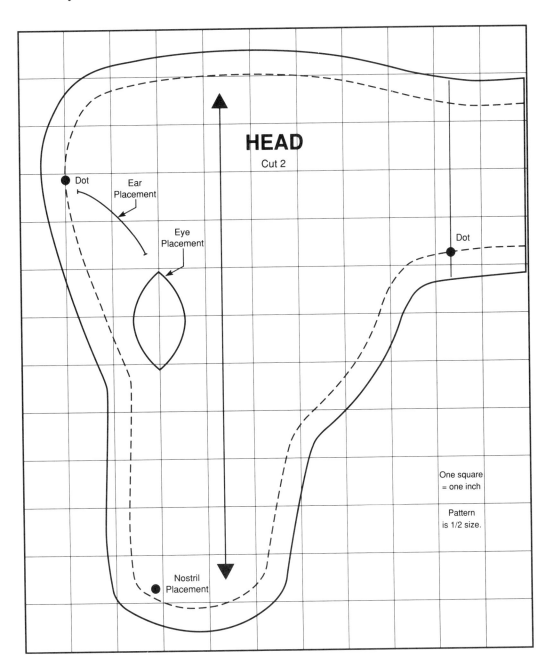

HEAD

Cut 2

Dot

Ear
Placement

Eye
Placement

Dot

One square
= one inch

Pattern
is 1/2 size.

Nostril
Placement

Fig. 6.5C.
Hobbyhorse pattern
head piece.
Pattern is 1/2 size.

MAKE THE HORSE

1. Fuse a piece of Wonder-Under to the underside of the black and white felt pieces. Cut out eye pieces and nostrils. Remove paper backing from the black pupils. Center and fuse them to the white eye pieces. Fuse eyelid aligning the outside curve with the top of white eye piece.

2. Lay out and cut horse pattern pieces, following the grain lines marked on each piece. Cut gusset and ear pieces from blue and white print. Cut face pieces from red print.

3. Mark darts on ear pieces by pushing pins straight through the dots then mark with chalk as shown (Fig. 6.6).

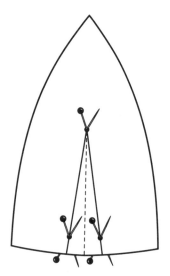

Fig. 6.6.
Mark darts on ear pieces by pushing pins straight through the dots.

Ears

Machine Readiness Checklist

Stitch:	straight (A2)
Length:	2 – 2.5
Width:	0
Foot:	standard A metal zigzag or Teflon H
Needle:	80/12 universal
Thread:	all-purpose to match fabric or nylon monofilament
Tension:	normal

1. Fold and stitch darts; then press dart to one side.

New Sewer's Note: *Start stitching a dart at the wide end, stitching to the point. Do not backstitch at the point—you may end up with a pouch that will not press out. Tie off threads at the point of dart.*

---

2. Place two ear pieces, right sides together, and sew a 1/4" (6mm) seam with a 2 length straight stitch, leaving the straight side open. Clip across point at the top, close to the stitching line (Fig. 6.7). Press ear flat. Repeat for other ear.

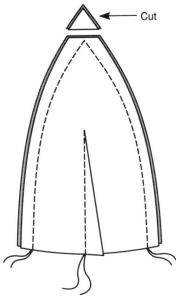

← Cut

Fig. 6.7.
Place two ear pieces right sides together, and sew a 1/4" (6mm) seam with a 2 length straight stitch. Clip across point, and press seams flat and together.

3. Trim seam allowance to 1/8" (3mm). Turn ears right side out. Gently push point out with blunt end of scissors or a point turner. Turn under raw edge 1/4" (6mm) at the base of each ear and press.

4. Stuff a little fiberfill in each ear, pushing it to the point with blunt end scissors or point turner. Do not overstuff.

5. Turn under raw edge 1/4" (6mm) and pin.

Head

1. Remove Wonder-Under paper from eye piece and fuse to the head as marked.

Machine Readiness Checklist

Stitch:	straight (A2); zigzag (A12)
Length:	2 – 2.5
Width:	0; 4
Foot:	transparent B (appliqué); special marking
Thread:	nylon monofilament; black cotton embroidery
Tension:	top, loosened slightly; bobbin, normal

Topstitch 1/8" (3mm) from cut edge first on white eye piece, then on pupil.

2. Rethread top and bobbin with black thread. Using the special marking foot, stitch the eyelashes on each eye guiding the middle of the foot where eyelid and white pieces overlap (see Fig. 9.39).

3. Position and pin ears on each side of the head. Whipstitch ears to head pieces.

New Sewer's Note: *A whipstitch is a catching stitch done with a hand needle and thread. Thread needle and tie a knot. Insert needle at right angles and close to the folded edge, picking up a few threads from the ear and head fabrics. Stitches should be close together and slightly angled so ears are stitched securely to the head piece (Fig. 6.8).*

Fig. 6.8. Whipstitch ears to head piece by inserting the hand needle at right angles and close to the folded edge, picking up a few threads from the ear and head fabrics. Stitch close together and at a slight angle so ears are stitched securely to the head.

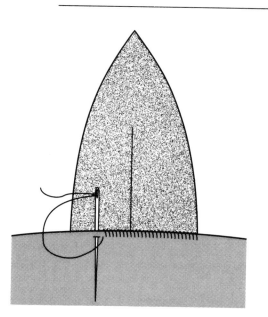

4. Clip 1/2" (1.3cm) into gusset and head piece seam allowance when it turns each corner. (Fig. 6.9.)

New Sewer's Note: *A clip is a short, 1/2" (1.3cm) cut in a seam allowance. When stitching a straight piece to a curved or angled piece of fabric, clipping allows a curve or corner to open and lie flat so the fabric pieces fit together easily. Use your scissor tips to clip, so you don't cut too far into the seam allowance.*

Starting at the dot on the wide end of gusset, place right sides together, pinning one head piece to one side of gusset, following down and around the head piece to the dot at the neck.

5. Straight stitch on the 5/8" (1.5cm) seam allowance, stitching from the dot at the top of the head stopping at the dot at the neck. Repeat pinning, clipping, and stitching procedure for the other side of head piece. Seams should come together at the point of each gusset. Clip seam allowance at each curve as shown (Fig. 6.9). Turn right side out.

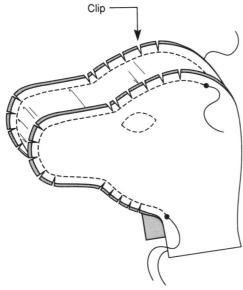

Fig. 6.9.
Clip 1/2" (1.3cm)
into gusset seam
allowance each time it
turns a corner. Also
clip into the seam
allowance at each
curve as shown so the
fabric smoothly follows
the curve of the seam.

6. Place nostrils at the end of the nose and fuse in place. Zigzag tack in the center of each nostril (see Fig. 8.26). It is easier to stitch this with the head turned inside out.

Mane and Bangs

1. Cut a piece of adding-machine tape 24" (61cm) long. Wrap weaver's reed with yarn and straight stitch yarn to adding-machine tape to make fringe for the mane (see Fig. 9.41).

2. Cut off about 4-1/2" (11.5cm) of fringe. Pull off the adding-machine tape and pin fringe across the widest part of the gusset (forehead) to make bangs, positioning the long loops toward the nose.

Sew-How: *After adding-machine tape has been removed, the fringe grows in length a little bit.*

Machine Readiness Checklist	
Stitch:	straight (A2)
Length:	3
Width:	0
Foot:	transparent B (appliqué)
Thread:	all-purpose to match fringe or nylon monofilament
Tension:	normal

Stitch fringe to gusset, centering the foot over the original stitching line. Cut another length of fringe, shorter than the first. Pin and straight stitch it above the first row of fringe, overlapping it slightly so the long loops hide the previous row of stitching. Repeat until the crown is covered with fringe, stitching one row of fringe above the next. Cut loops after fringe is secured to the crown.

3. Turn head inside out. Carefully remove adding-machine tape from the unused fringe. Pin back head pieces, right sides together, sandwiching the short loops of fringe in the seam allowance. Stop fringe 1-1/2" (3.8cm) from the neck opening (Fig. 6.10). Stitch seam. Finish stitching other side of neck from dot at the bottom of gusset to raw edge.

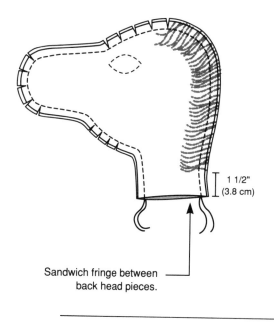

Fig. 6.10. Sandwich fringe between the two head pieces. Stop fringe 1-1/2" (3.8cm) from the neck opening and stitch.

1 1/2" (3.8 cm)

Sandwich fringe between back head pieces.

Sew-How: *You may have some fringe left. It will be used to thicken the top of the mane.*

---

4. Turn up raw neck edge 1/2" (1.3cm) and press. With the head inside out, gather over a 10" (25.5cm) length of pearl cotton around the right side of neck opening (see Fig. 8.22) guiding 1/8" (3mm) from fold.

Sew-How: *The pearl cotton is used to draw up the neck once it is attached to the broom handle, so it has to be strong. Therefore, use at least a #3 pearl cotton or fine string so it won't break when pulled.*

---

5. Turn head right side out. Take remainder of fringe and fold it in half on the stitching line. Starting at the top of the mane, sandwich loose fringe around the fringe stitched in the seam. Straight stitch loose fringe to mane, backstitching at beginning and end. Cut yarn loops. **Note:** If machine stitching is too cumbersome, use a double thread, and hand stitch this extra fringe to the mane.

6. Stuff head with fiberfill. The neck opening should be large enough to reach your hand in to stuff fill into the corners. If it isn't, use a ruler or a wooden spoon to push fill in place.

Bridle

1. Put ribbon around the end of the nose so it fits snuggly. Cut and seam it into a circle. Put the larger length of ribbon at right angles to create the reins. Seam it into a circle. Pin bridle together where ribbons intersect, long ribbon beneath short ribbon circle, so the seam on the small ribbon in under the chin, and the seam of large ribbon is under the intersection (Fig. 6.11). (You may have to put the bridle on the horse for proper positioning.)

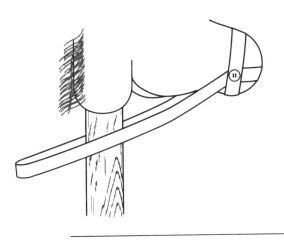

Fig. 6.11.
To make the bridle, put a circle of ribbon around the end of the nose and seam it together. Put a smaller length of ribbon at right angles to the first. Pin where ribbons intersect, so the seam on the first ribbon is under the chin, and the seam of the large ribbon is under the intersect. Machine stitch buttons at each intersect.

Sew-How: *Put a drop of seam sealant on ribbon ends to prevent raveling.*

2. In order to stitch the buttons in place, remove bridle and machine stitch a button on each side where ribbons intersect (see Fig. 8.17).

3. Hand tack bridle at each seamline so it won't slip off when hobbyhorse is played with.

4. Put broom handle up in the head. You may have to stuff extra fiberfill around broom handle to secure it.

5. Draw up pearl cotton, gathering the neck around broom handle and tie securely.

TRANSFERABLE LEARNINGS

The information and techniques you have learned by making the fabric blocks and hobbyhorse have given you the skills necessary to sew many other projects. You have learned to:

• Enlarge and draw a pattern from a reduced version using graph paper and a curve—helpful for enlarging other patterns. Using a curve is also helpful when making some pattern alterations.

• Stitch, turn, stuff, and close three-dimensional shapes. Techniques are the same for stuffed toys, some pillows, a hassock, or a beanbag chair.

• Insert a gusset. Use this technique in garment construction, as well as for slipcovers, pillows, and cushions.

• Use Wonder-Under to make any fabric fusible.

• Properly fuse one fabric to the other with heat, moisture, and pressure.

• Appliqué using a straight stitch on a nonraveling fabric. Use this technique with leather, vinyl, or suede.

• Sew a dart. Darts are used in other projects to create shape so that a pattern piece conforms to the shape of the body.

• Use the special marking foot to make eyelashes.

• Make yarn fringe using the weaver's reed. Make fringe trim this way to match any fabric, rather than searching for fringe trim by the yard.

• Gather over a cord for even gathers. This also adds strength to the gathering stitch so thread won't break. This technique is used to gather almost any medium to heavy fabric.

I hope that, in addition to your exploring another spoke in our World of Sewing, your family members will enjoy playing with the blocks and hobbyhorse you made as you stitched your way through this chapter.

Next you will further your knowledge by sewing gifts. The key rings make great gifts for anyone and take as long to make as it would to shop for something, and each is personalized for the recipient. The fabric game board also makes a welcome gift for peaceful travel time in a car or plane, or on family vacations.

SEW GIFTS

- *Step One: Plan Your Projects*

- *Step Two: Sew Three Key Rings*

- *Step Three: Sew a Fabric Game Board and Pouch*

- *Transferable Learnings*

When people know you sew, even if it's only once in a while, friends and family sometimes expect a handmade gift. In this chapter, we'll make a few quick gifts using a little ribbon or fabric scraps—you probably have most of the supplies on hand. We will also make a fabric game board and game piece pouch, a welcome gift for family or friends.

Step One:

PLAN YOUR PROJECTS

Everyone needs a set of keys so let's stitch some decorative key rings. I bought a simple metal key ring from the hardware store; the others are kits from a cross-stitch shop. The rest of the supplies are listed under each project.

These small embroideries showcase your stitchery, so use rayon embroidery thread because it has a lot of shine and fills in better than all-purpose thread.

The game board is made of cotton-blend prints and solids, cotton/polyester hem facing (available in 2-1/2 yard [2.3m] packages at your local fabric store), felt, grosgrain ribbon, yarn, and Wonder-Under. The game pouch is made from a red cotton-blend, a black-and-white checked fabric, a zipper, and scraps of turquoise and yellow solids.

Sew-How: *For a perfect color match to the game board, I had to make this pouch out of knit fabrics. If you, too, have difficulty finding woven fabrics for your pouch, stabilize the knit by fusing a piece of interfacing to the wrong side of each fabric. Then it behaves like a woven fabric.*

To make your game board washable, preshrink all the fabrics, except the Wonder-Under and the washable polyester felt (washable polyester felt is available at most fabric stores.)

To preshrink hem facing tape without uncreasing the prefolded edges, immerse the tape in very hot tap water leaving it wrapped around the cardboard core; then roll it in a towel to remove most of the moisture. Remove cardboard, then line dry or press with a hot iron.

You will also use nylon monofilament thread in both key ring and game board projects. This way, you don't have to rethread the top and bobbin each time you change the fabric color.

Step Two:

SEW THREE KEY RINGS

My Viking can stitch letters and numbers—a feature I thought I would use only rarely but which I have come to appreciate. If your machine has the same capacity, make a script **monogrammed key ring** (Fig. 7.1).

Fig. 7.1.
Key ring projects.

MAKE THE MONOGRAMMED KEY RING

I subscribe to a lot of needlecraft magazines to see how stitchery of all kinds is stitched and displayed. Although I don't hand cross-stich, I found many great gift ideas for small stitchery in one of the cross-stitch magazines, which inspired me to seek out a cross-stitch shop in my area. Once there, I found kits of all kinds for bookmarks, paperweights, trivets, and the key rings kits described below—an easy way to frame small embroideries stitched on the sewing machine, then to give away as gifts. Take the opportunity to stop into a cross-stitch shop in your area or subscribe to needlecraft magazines for these and other ingenious gift ideas. **Note:** If you can't find key ring kits in your area, skip ahead to the "Fob" key ring instructions.

Machine Readiness Checklist

Stitch:	block or script lettering
Length:	varies
Width:	widest
Foot:	transparent B (appliqué)
Needle:	90/14 stretch
Thread:	rayon embroidery
Tension:	top, loosened slightly; bobbin, normal
Fabric:	1-1/2 X 1-1/2" (3.8 X 3.8cm) grosgrain ribbon or felt
Accessories:	key ring kit, iron-on freezer wrap, vanishing marker

1. Iron freezer wrap to the wrong side of ribbon or felt. (Make a test swatch to determine letter spacing.) Mark where to start the lettering and draw a line with the vanishing marker so lettering is straight.

2. Program initials and stitch. Remove the freezer wrap. Press top and bottom up desired amount to fit in acrylic key ring frame. (The key ring kit is similar to a watch. The stitchery fits into a small frame, then a crystal snaps in place over the top.)

MAKE THE ROUND KEY RING

The round key ring is satin stitched with an off-center plaid design and embroidered initials in one corner.

Stitch:	zigzag (satin stitch) (990: 2-43; 1100: A16)
Length:	0.4 – 0.6
Width:	widest
Foot:	transparent B (appliqué)
Needle:	14/90 stretch
Thread:	red and blue rayon embroidery
Tension:	top, slightly loosened; bobbin, normal
Fabric:	closely woven kettle (weaver's) cloth
Accessories:	key ring kit, iron-on freezer wrap, vanishing marker, seam sealant (optional)

1. Iron freezer wrap to wrong side of your fabric. Remove crystal from key ring and trace the circle on your fabric. Mark a straight line to follow for the first row of satin stitching.

2. Thread top and bobbin with red thread. Satin stitch one row, starting and stopping just inside the circle. Remove work from the machine and draw another line perpendicular to the first. Satin stitch following that line.

3. Rethread top and bobbin with blue thread. Satin stitch next to the first row of red satin stitches, starting and stopping just inside the circle. Turn your work perpendicular and repeat.

4. Rethread top and bobbin with red thread. Program the appropriate initials. Test for spacing on a scrap. Mark where to start lettering with the vanishing marker. Stitch initials. Remove freezer wrap. Pull threads to the wrong side and tie them off.

Sew-How: *Put a drop of seam sealant on each knot so they won't pull out.*

---

5. Cut embroidery to fit inside the frame. Snap crystal over the top.

MAKE THE "FOB" KEY RING

If you can't find a kit like those shown above, buy a simple key ring at the hardware store and embroider a "fob."

Machine Readiness Checklist

Stitch:	Satin Element diamond (990: 2-36 + 2-36;1100: D32 + D32)
Length:	0.3 – 0.5
Width:	widest
Foot:	utility B
Needle:	90/14 stretch
Thread:	rayon embroidery; nylon monofilament
Tension:	top, loosened slightly; bobbin, normal
Fabric:	Ultrasuede™, Ultraleather™ or felt, fusible interfacing, Wonder-Under
Accessories:	key ring, tracing paper, vanishing marker

1. Fuse interfacing to the wrong side of fob fabric. Trace fob pattern in Fig. 7.2.

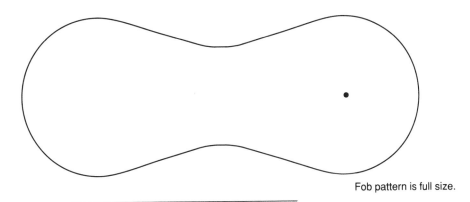

Fig. 7.2.
Key ring fob pattern.

Fob pattern is full size.

New Sewer's Note: *Set iron on cotton setting. Place interfacing so the rough side is against the wrong side of fob fabric. Dampen a press cloth and fuse interfacing with firm pressure for about 10 seconds. Remove iron, let steam escape, then press again until the fabric and press cloth are dry.*

2. Cut out Ultrasuede, Ultraleather, or felt using the pattern. Cut Wonder-Under slightly smaller than the pattern.

3. On the right side of the fabric, mark the center of one side of fob with a dot, using the vanishing marker (Fig. 7.2).

Sew-How: *The design in the center of the fob is a snowflake created by decorative stitches. Before stitching your fob, practice and perfect your technique on a fabric scrap backed with interfacing.*

4. Program your machine for the Satin Element diamond stitch. You will have to use the mirror image function to create it.

Sew-How: *This diamond flower can be made on many Vikings because the diamond is a common stitch. However, experiment with other decorative stitches to invent your own motifs.*

---

5. Starting in the center, stitch one diamond and stop. Remove the fabric, cut the threads, and turn fob 180 degrees. Stitch another diamond across from the first. Remove fabric, cut threads, and pivot 90 degrees. Starting in the center again, stitch another diamond shape. Repeat for the last diamond (Fig 7.3). Pull threads to the wrong side and tie them off.

Fig. 7.3.
Starting in the center, stitch one diamond and stop. Remove the fabric, cut the threads, and turn the fabric 180 degrees. Stitch another diamond across from the first. Remove the fabric, cut the threads, turn the fabric 90 degrees, and stitch another diamond. Repeat for the last diamond.

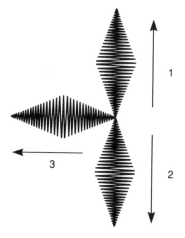

6. Press Wonder-Under to the wrong side of fob, following manufacturer's instructions. After fabric is cool, remove the paper and pull fob through key ring. Line up cut edges and fuse fob together.

7. Rethread top and bobbin with nylon monofilament thread. Put the Teflon H presser foot on your Viking (see Fig. 9.16). Decenter the needle to the far left and topstitch 1/8" (3mm) from cut edges. Lock stitches at the end of the stitching.

Wasn't that fun? Let's try something more challenging.

Step Three:

SEW A FABRIC GAME BOARD AND POUCH

The fabric game board is easy to pack, travels well in a car or on a plane, and can stave off back-seat wars during the family vacation. Both backgammon and checkerboard are combined in one travel game you make yourself.

Supplies

- 2 packages black 1-3/4" (4.5cm) wide hem facing (cotton/polyester blend)
- 2 packages red 1-3/4" (4.5cm) wide hem facing (cotton/polyester blend)
- 1 yard (meter) of 1" (2.5cm) grosgrain ribbon
- 1/2 yard (45.5cm) Wonder-Under (paper-backed fusible web)
- 16" (40.5cm) square of cotton/polyester red print fabric
- 1 yellow washable felt square
- 1 blue washable felt square
- 1 white strip and 1 black strip of woven cotton-blend fabric each at least 1-1/2 X 16"   (3.8 X 40.5cm)
- nylon monofilament thread
- all-purpose thread in black and white
- 4 yards (3.6m) black yarn, #3 or #5 pearl cotton
- tracing paper and water-erasable marker

MAKE THE BACKGAMMON BOARD

1. Enlarge pattern to twice the size of Fig. 7.4 at your photocopy center. Trace patterns for triangles and bars.

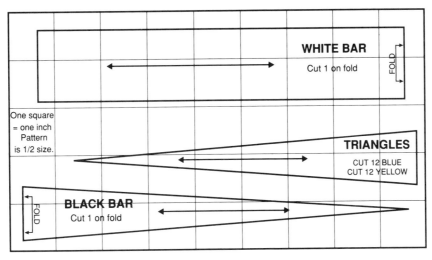

Fig. 7.4.
Backgammon triangles
and bar patterns.
Pattern is 1/2 size.

2. Fuse a piece of Wonder-Under on the back of the yellow and the back of the blue felt squares, and the wrong side of black and white cotton strips, following manufacturer's instructions.

3. Using the pattern traced in Step 1, cut twelve triangles from yellow felt square and twelve triangles from blue felt square.

Sew-How: *To cut both colored triangles at the same time, place yellow and blue felt squares, one on top of the other. Use your sharp rotary cutter and see-through ruler to cut through both layers.*

---

4. Cut out black and white bars.

5. Fold 16" (40.5cm) print square in half and press a crease. Open square. Remove Wonder-Under paper from white strip. Center and fuse white bar over crease on the right side of print square.

Machine Readiness Checklist	
Stitch:	zigzag (satin stitch) (990: 2-43; 1100: A14)
Length:	0.4 – 0.6
Width:	2
Foot:	transparent B (appliqué)
Needle:	80/12 universal
Thread:	white all-purpose or cotton or rayon embroidery
Tension:	top, loosened slightly; bobbin, normal

Satin stitch both raw edges of the white bar, centering the raw edge under the foot.

6. Fold square in half again in the other direction, and press a crease. Open square. Remove Wonder-Under paper from the black bar, center and fuse it over crease on the right side of print square. Rethread top and bobbin with black thread and satin stitch both sides of bar.

7. Starting on either side of the black bar, remove paper backing and position blue and yellow triangles, alternating colors as shown in Fig. 7.5. Be sure triangle points are exactly opposite one another across the board. Carefully fuse triangles on print square using a damp press cloth and steam.

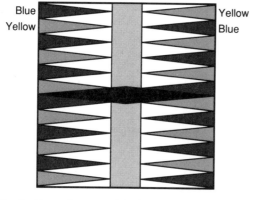

Fig. 7.5.
Position blue and yellow triangles, alternating colors so the points are exactly opposite one another across the board.

8. Rethread top and bobbin with nylon monofilament thread.

Machine Readiness Checklist

Stitch:	straight (A2)
Length:	2
Width:	0
Foot:	standard A metal zigzag or blind hem D
Needle:	80/12 universal
Thread:	nylon monofilament
Tension:	top, loosened halfway between normal and very loose; bobbin, normal

Topstitch around each triangle, stitching 1/8" (3mm) from the cut edge. Don't cut threads between triangles. Simply lift the presser foot, turn the fabric around, and continue stitching.

Sew-How: *When using the blind hem D foot, guide the straight edge of appliqué to the inside of the right toe. If necessary, move the needle position slightly to the left so stitching is 1/8" (3mm) from cut edge of felt (see Figs. 9.10, 9.11).*

---

9. With the wrong side up, press backgammon board with steam.

10. Cut a 16" (40.5cm) square of Wonder-Under, and fuse it to the wrong side of backgammon board. After cooling, remove the paper backing. This enables you to fuse the checkerboard to the back of the backgammon board.

Sew-How: *Save Wonder-Under paper to use as a paper press cloth. Put the paper over your work to prevent fusible web from gumming up the sole plate of your iron.*

MAKE THE CHECKERBOARD

1. Cut eight 16" (40.5cm) strips of black hem facing and eight 16" (40.5cm) strips of red hem facing.

2. Starting in the center of the board and working out, pin black hem facing strips next to each other on one side of the board so the wrong side of the tape is against the wrong side of the backgammon board. **Note:** Leave the hems in hem facing strips.

3. Pin red hem facing strips next to each other on a side adjacent to the first, weaving them in and out of black strips as shown (Fig. 7.6).

Fig. 7.6.
Pin black strips next to each other on one side of the board. Pin red strips next to each other on a side adjacent to the first, weaving them in and out of black strips.

4. Set iron on the hottest setting. Thoroughly dampen a press cloth and place it over the checkerboard.

5. Fuse checkerboard to the back of backgammon board. For a permanent bond, apply a lot of pressure, and press work until it is dry.

FINISH THE EDGE

1. Straighten the edges of your board using the rotary cutter, mat, and cutting ruler.

2. Starting in the middle of a straight edge, couch over yarn or double strand of pearl cotton.

Machine Readiness Checklist	
Stitch:	zigzag (A12)
Length:	2
Width:	4
Foot:	narrow braiding or transparent B (appliqué)
Needle:	80/12 universal
Thread:	all-purpose black
Tension:	normal
Accessories:	black yarn or pearl cotton

Guide the yarn so the needle stitches into the fabric on the left and swings off the edge at the right (see Figures 8.20, 9.22, 9.23). Stitch a gentle curve at the corners (with the needle on the inside corner, pivot fabric around it). At the join, cut yarn off, overlap the ends, and zigzag couch over them.

3. Satin stitch over couched yarn or pearl cotton using a 0.6 – 0.8 length, 4 – 5 width zigzag stitch, and slightly loosened upper tension (see Fig. 8.27). Flair stitches out at the corners using the inside of the corner as a pivot point (see Fig. 3.4).

4. Satin stitch around the edge again, using a slightly longer stitch length and the widest stitch width. This second row of satin stitches over the first helps to firm up and finish the edge of the board.

5. To smooth out the satin-stitched edge, couch over another piece of yarn around the outside edge of game board.

Machine Readiness Checklist	
Stitch:	zigzag (A12)
Length:	1.5 – 2
Width:	3
Foot:	narrow braiding
Thread:	all-purpose black, top and bobbin
Tension:	normal

Guide so the needle stitches just into the satin stitches on the left and swings over the yarn and off the edge on the right. As before, overlap yarn ends and couch over them.

6. Cut a length of grosgrain ribbon, 27" (68.5cm) long, and stitch it onto one end of the board by stitching-in-the-ditch along the satin stitched edge. Roll the board up and tie the ribbon into a bow.

MAKE THE GAME PIECE POUCH

Supplies

- Wonder-Under scraps
- two 9" (23cm) squares of red cotton or cotton-blend fabric
- 3 X 9" (7.5 X 23cm) strip of black-and-white checked fabric
- 2-1/4" (5.7cm) square of yellow fabric
- 1-5/8" (4cm) square of turquoise fabric (Lycra spandex swim wear fabric works well)
- fusible interfacing
- 10 – 12" (25.5 – 30.5cm) zipper
- red all-purpose thread; yellow and turquoise rayon embroidery thread

1. Fuse Wonder-Under to the back of the yellow and turquoise fabrics before cutting them out. If the red and checked fabrics are knits, fuse interfacing to the wrong side of each piece.

2. Center and fuse yellow square on checked fabric as shown (Fig. 7.7). Satin stitch around it with a 2.5 – 3 width zigzag (see Fig. 8.27).

3. Turn turquoise square on end, position and fuse over yellow square as shown (Fig. 7.7). If this fabric is a knit, straight stitch around it guiding 1/8" (3mm) from the raw edge. If it is a woven fabric, satin stitch around it as you did for the yellow square.

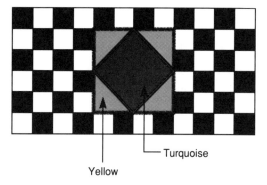

Turquoise

Yellow

Fig. 7.7.
Center and fuse
yellow square on
checked fabric, then
satin stitch around the
edge. Turn turquoise
square on end,
position and fuse over
the yellow square, then
straight stitch 1/8"
(3mm) from the edge.

4. Fold back a 1/2" (1.3cm) seam allowance on the two long edges of the checked fabric and press toward the wrong side. Center the checked strip on the right side of a red square, and position it so it goes across the grain. Topstitch along the two folded edges with a 3 length straight stitch and red thread (Fig. 7.8).

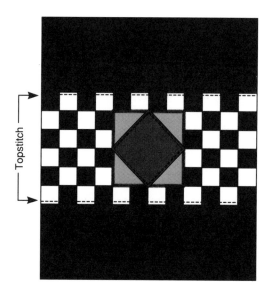

Topstitch

Fig. 7.8.
Topstitch along the two
folded edges with a
3 length straight stitch.

INSERT THE ZIPPER

1. Place zipped zipper along one 9" (23cm) edge of decorated square, right sides together, so the zipper is parallel to the checkered strip and aligning the edge of zipper tape with the cut edge. Note that the pull should be at one end of zipper, out of the way (Fig. 7.9A).

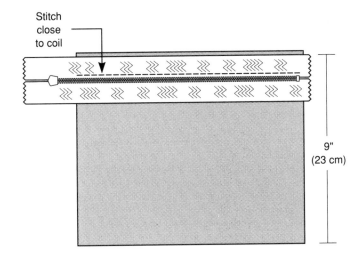

Fig. 7.9A.
Place decorated pouch
piece and zipper right
sides together, aligning
edge of zipper and
fabric edge. Pull
should be to one end,
out of the way. Stitch
close to coil.

2. Using your zipper E foot and a 3 length straight stitch, stitch zipper to fabric, sewing next to the zipper coil. Press seam away from the coil (Fig. 7.9B). (See Fig. 9.12.)

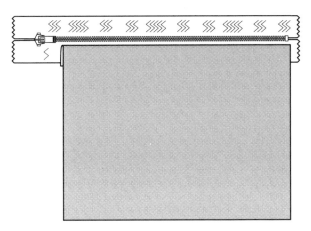

Fig. 7.9B.
Press seam away
from coil.

3. Repeat for the other edge of zipper on plain fabric square, being sure the cut edge is aligned with the edge of zipper tape and is across the grain and even with the first red square (Fig. 7.9C). This is called an exposed zipper application because the zipper coil is exposed.

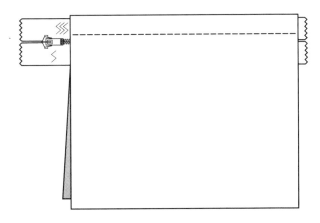

Fig. 7.9C.
Repeat to stitch the
other side of zipper
to other side of
pouch piece.

4. Unzip zipper slightly. Tack top of zipper so the two sides of the coil are together 1/2" (1.3mm) inside the cut edge of pouch (Figs. 7.9D, 8.26). Cut excess zipper tape off, even with the edge of the fabric.

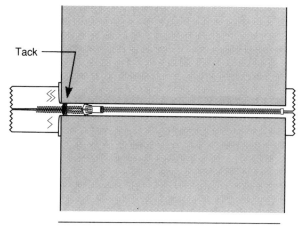

Tack

Fig. 7.9D.
Tack top of zipper coil so the pull will not come off track. Cut excess tape off, even with fabric.

Sew-How: *If you should accidentally slide the pull off the coil before tacking over it, remove the metal stop at the bottom of zipper. Then slide the pull back on track from the bottom up. Remember to replace the metal stop or tack across the bottom of the zipper.*

5. With the zipper still unzipped about 3" (7.6cm), place pouch, right sides together, and straight stitch around the remaining three sides of the pouch using a 1/2" (1.3mm) seam allowance. Backstitch over zipper coil a few times to secure both ends of the seam. Open zipper all the way, then turn the pouch right side out and press.

Sew-How: *To make the zipper easier to work, loop a couple of stands of #3 pearl cotton through the hole in the pull (see color pages).*

MAKE GAME PIECES

If you don't have an extra set of game pieces, make your own out of red and black felt. Each player needs fifteen game pieces for backgammon (only twelve for checkers), so make thirty pieces.

Machine Readiness Checklist

Stitch:	scallop (990: 2-32; 1100: D29); satin stitch (990: 2-43; 1100: A14)
Length:	0.5
Width:	widest for scallop; 2 for satin stitch
Foot:	transparent B (appliqué)
Needle:	80/12 universal
Thread:	yellow and white cotton embroidery
Tension:	top, loosened slightly; bobbin, normal
Fabric:	2 felt squares each of black and red
Accessories:	Wonder-Under, diappearing dressmaker's chalk, or soap sliver

1. Fuse a piece of Wonder-Under on one black felt square and one red felt square.

2. Mark fifteen 1-1/4" (3.2cm) squares on remaining black and red felt squares using a soap sliver or disappearing dressmaker's chalk.

3. On twelve squares of each color, sew a decorative stitch to create the crowns for the checkers (optional). I used a partial scallop stitch and yellow thread for the top, and a 2 width satin stitch and white thread for the bottom of each crown.

Sew-How: *To center the crown in each square, use the quilting guide along the edge of each square (Fig. 7.10).*

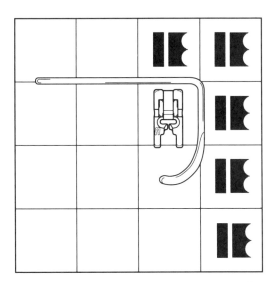

Fig. 7.10. Center crown on each square, using the quilting guide along the edge of each square.

4. Remove Wonder-Under paper, then fuse a plain black piece of felt on the back of black decorated pieces. Repeat stitching and fusing procedure for red felt piece. Cut 1-1/4" (3.2cm) squares apart. Trim each square into a circle to finish each game piece.

Put game pieces in the pouch, roll pouch in the game board, and tie ribbons into a bow.

TRANSFERABLE LEARNINGS

The information and techniques you have learned and practiced by making the gifts in this chapter have given you the skills necessary to sew many other projects. You have learned how to:

• Stitch and center lettering on a project.

• Use nylon monofilament thread top and bobbin so you don't have to rethread for different color fabrics in the same project.

• Appliqué using a straight stitch on fabrics that don't ravel, such as felt, leather, knits, suede, or synthetic leather or suede. Appliqué using a satin stitch on fabrics that ravel.

• Use Wonder-Under to make any fabric fusible.

• Use the blind hem D foot to topstitch evenly from a cut or finished edge—helpful when topstitching a pocket, lapel, front tab, belt loop, waistband, tote bag strap—the list goes on.

• Move needle position rather than the fabric to stitch precisely where you want to.

• Couch over a piece of yarn or pearl cotton using the narrow braiding foot and zigzag stitch as a way to add dimension under a satin stitch.

• Satin stitch an edge twice, with a progressively wider and longer zigzag stitch to create a better finish to an edge.

• Couch over a piece of yarn or pearl cotton on the outer edge of satin stitching to clean-finish an uneven edge. This technique is often used on European table linens, napkin edges, and cut work. It's also a way to finish an edge on a fabric too thick to seam and turn to the right side in the conventional way such as denim, leather, canvas, heavy duck cloth.

• Use an exposed zipper in a pocket or a seam.

• Use the quilting guide to guide fabric evenly, when you can't guide using the lines on the needle plate. This is helpful when stitching even rows of straight and decorative stitching.

Now that you've stitched your way through the projects in Part II, I hope you have learned to sew better. Are you motivated to use the many stitches, presser feet, and accessories available on your Viking? I also hope that you've had fun stitching along with me, that you have a bunch of completed projects to give away or to keep, and that you're inspired to learn more about The World of Sewing.

In Part III, you'll learn even more about specific presser feet and stitches. Then I share some useful mail-order resources and good books.

Besides collecting fabric and other sewing paraphernalia, I also collect sewing and needlecraft books. In listing them in the bibliography, I feel as if I'm introducing you to dear friends. I encourage you to get to know them better as you further refine your skills. They're not only a helpful reference, but a continuous source of inspiration.

Good-bye for now, and happy sewing.

STITCH AND PRESSER FOOT ENCYCLOPEDIA

- *Chapter Eight: Encyclopedia of Stitches*
- *Chapter Nine: Encyclopedia of Presser Feet*

Part III

STITCH AND PRESSER FOOT ENCYCLOPEDIA

ENCYCLOPEDIA OF STITCHES

● *Cassette A: Utility Stitches*

● *Cassettes B and C: Letters and Numbers*

● *Cassette D: Decorative Stitches*

● *Fix*

Most encyclopedias are organized alphabetically. This one is not. Instead, it is organized into groups of stitches, as the list above shows. This is the way the stitches on the Viking 1100 cassettes are organized. Of all the Viking models, the 1100 has the most stitches available, so you are assured the stitches on your Viking will be described, even if you have an older model. For each stitch in this encyclopedia, I give the name and the 1100 cassette letter and stitch number. For example, the feather stitch is A35; the train engine stitch is D11. Refer to Fig. 8.1 and compare the stitches on your Viking with the ones pictured on the Viking 1100 cassettes.

AUTOMATIC AND TRIMOTION™ STITCHES

Stitches are classified in two ways—automatic and Trimotion™. "Automatic" means the stitches feed through the machine in one direction, and the needle may also move from side to side "automatically." The zigzag (A12), woven blind hem (A30), and three-step zigzag stitch (A19) are examples.

"Trimotion" stitches, sometimes referred to as "stretch stitches," are made when the needle zigzags as the feed dogs move the fabric forward and backward. Because of the way they are made, Trimotion stitches stretch and return to shape when sewn on a knit fabric. Examples of Trimotion stitches are the feather stitch (A35) and smocking stitch (A26). Stitches are also divided further into utility and decorative classifications.

Fig. 8.1.
Viking 1100 stitch
cassettes A, B, C, and D.

Cassette A
Utility stitches and buttonholes.

Cassette B
Block letters and numbers.

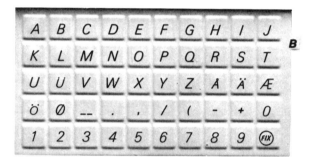

Cassette C
Script letters and numbers.

Cassette D
Decorative stitches and Pictograms.
See 1100 Sewing Book.

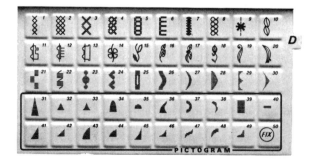

UTILITY AND DECORATIVE STITCHES

Utility stitches are those used most often for basic sewing and mending—straight stitch (A1,2,3,4), zigzag (A11,12,13), woven blind hem (A30), elastic blind hem (A29), three-step zigzag (A19), stitch-and-overcast (A23), overedge (A22), flatlock (A25), and a number of others.

Decorative stitches are used to embellish a piece of fabric, ribbon, or trim. Examples are the domino (D21), ribbon (D22), ball (D23), and heart (D24). On the Viking 900 series and 1100 there are also decorative stitches used for edge finishes, Satin Elements (stitches D31 – 49) used to create Pictograms, and decorative stitches on the B and C lettering cassettes designed for use with letters and numbers.

This encyclopedia describes both utility and decorative stitches and their uses. Let's start by taking a closer look at the most common utility stitch—the straight stitch.

CASSETTE A: UTILITY STITCHES
STRAIGHT STITCH (A1,2,3,4)

- Variable Needle Positions
- Automatic Backstitch
- Basting
- Easestitching
- Edgestitching
- Staystitching
- Stitch-in-the-Ditch
- Straight Seams
- Topstitching
- Twin Needle Hem
- Twin Needle Tucks (Pintucks)
- Understitching

The straight stitch is used primarily to sew straight seams on woven fabrics. The stitch length is changed depending on the weight of the fabric. Generally, for a finer fabric, a shorter stitch length is used. For heavier fabrics, a longer stitch length is used. When you turn on the 900 series or 1100 Vikings, a straight stitch is automatically selected at 2.5—the most common stitch length for a majority of fabrics.

Make a stitch sample for your notebook with each stitch length sewn on the same piece of fabric, so you can see how they differ. Label each length. Try stitching on different weights of fabric (Fig. 8.2).

Sew-How: *To keep your stitches straight and to count the number of stitches per inch, stitch various lengths on 1" (2.5cm) gingham. If you experience puckering, iron a piece of plastic-coated freezer wrap to the wrong side of a single layer of gingham.*

Fig. 8.2.
Try various stitch lengths
on a piece of fabric,
label each, and put in
your notebook.

Fig. 8.2.

Sew-How: *If your fabric puckers, shorten the stitch length. If the fabric waves out of shape, lengthen the stitch.*

VARIABLE NEEDLE POSITIONS (A1,2,3)

Topstitching is often easier when you move the needle position rather than moving the fabric one way or the other. Older model Vikings have infinite needle positions between right and left needle position. The 900 series Vikings have 13 needle positions; the 1100 has 25 needle positions.

To move the needle to the left on a 900 series, set the machine on a straight stitch and touch the stitch width button. With each touch, the needle moves little-by-little to the left. For right needle position, push the mirror image button, touch the stitch width button, and the needle moves little-by-little to the right.

To change needle position on the 1100, select A1 for left needle position, A2 for center needle position, A3 for right needle position. Then touch the stitch width button to move the needle between left, center, and right the distance desired. Each push of the button moves the needle slightly to the right or to the left.

Sew-How: *To change needle positions using the reinforced straight stitch (A8,9,10), select the function and move the stitch width as described above for the Viking 1100.*

Fig. 8.3.
Baste using contrasting
bobbin thread and a
loosened upper tension.
Pull bobbin thread to
remove stitches.

AUTOMATIC BACKSTITCH (A4)

The 1100 has another straight stitch function called automatic backstitch (A4). When selected the stitch takes an automatic backstitch at the beginning of the seam. At the end of the seam, push the STOP button so the threads tie off automatically. This way the automatic backstitch function repeats itself at the beginning of your next seam. If you forget to push the STOP button, you must push A4 each time you start a seam to backstitch automatically.

The following applications of the straight stitch are commonly used in pattern instructions.

BASTING

Basting is a line of temporary stitching used to join pattern pieces to check fit and appearance of the seam before final stitching. For easy removal, set your Viking as follows:

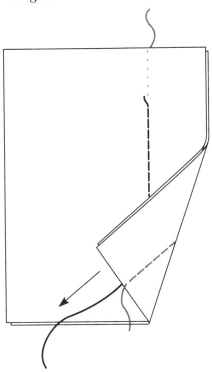

Fig. 8.3.

Machine Readiness Checklist	
Stitch:	straight (A2)
Length:	longest
Width:	0
Foot:	standard A metal zigzag
Needle:	70/10 or 80/12 universal
Thread:	all-purpose top and bobbin; contrasting color to fabric in the bobbin
Tension:	top, loosened slightly; bobbin, normal

Pull bobbin thread to remove stitches (it's easy to find because you used a different color bobbin thread). After basting, remember to reset your top tension to normal and change your bobbin thread to match the top (Fig. 8.3).

EASESTITCHING

Many projects require flat pieces of fabric to fit curved areas. Therefore, the flat fabric must be manipulated to fit by easestitching.

When easestitching, a longer fabric edge is joined to a shorter one with no folds or gathers visible from the right side of the project.

Fig. 8.4.
Pin fabric together and
pull bobbin thread to
adjust ease.

Fig. 8.5.
Hold your index finger
behind the foot so fabric
bunches up to
easestitch "plus."

Easestitching is used for setting in sleeves. It's used in a two-piece sleeve at the elbow, for easing a skirt or pant waistline into a waistband and in other areas as described in the pattern.

Machine Readiness Checklist

Stitch:	straight (A3)
Length:	2.5 (fine fabrics) to 3.5 (heavy fabrics)
Width:	0
Foot:	standard A metal zigzag
Needle:	80/12 universal
Thread:	all-purpose
Feed dogs:	up
Needle position:	far right
Tension:	normal; for more ease, tighten upper tension

1. On a single layer of the fabric to be eased, stitch between notches, guiding the raw edge at the 5/8" (1.5cm) seam line marked on your needle plate. Because you are sewing in right needle position and guiding the raw edge by the 5/8" (1.5cm) seam line, easestitches are inside the seam allowance and won't show once the seam is stitched.

2. Pin fabric pieces together matching notches. Pull bobbin thread to adjust ease as needed (Fig. 8.4).

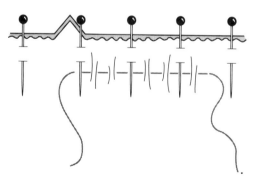

Fig. 8.4.

Sew-How: *For more ease, try the easestitch "plus" method. Set your machine as described above, but slightly tighten the upper tension. As you sew, hold your index finger behind the foot so the fabric bunches up (Fig. 8.5). Hold fabric until you can't hold it firmly any longer, release, and repeat. The fabric eases automatically without tucks or gathers. This is great for easing a set in sleeve or the edge of a circular or curved hemline.*

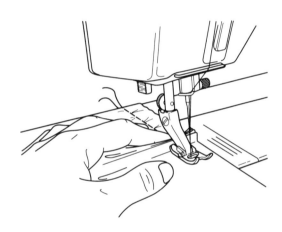

EDGESTITCHING

Edgestitching is a line of stitching 1/8" (3mm) or less from the finished edge and is generally stitched with thread matching the fabric. Edgestitch a collar, cuff, top of a waistband, hem edge, belt edges, the edge of a pleat, or tuck.

Fig. 8.6.
Edgestitch a collar, cuff,
top of waistband, belt
edges, the edge of a
pleat, or to make a tuck.
Place edge of fold
against the toe of the foot
and stitch.

Fig. 8.7.
To prevent fabric from
stretching out of shape,
staystitch curved and
bias cut edges 1/2"
(1.3cm) from raw edge.

Machine Readiness Checklist

Stitch:	straight (A2)
Length:	normal for the fabric
Width:	0
Foot:	blind hem D or metal zigzag A
Needle:	appropriate for fabric
Thread:	all-purpose
Needle position:	variable

1. Press edge to be edgestitched. Place edge of fold so it guides against the inside right toe of the blind hem D or metal zigzag A (Fig. 8.6).

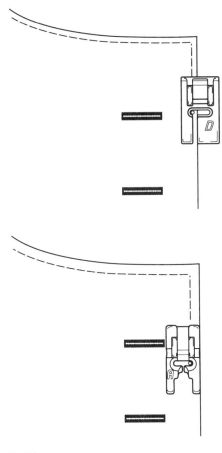

Fig. 8.6.

Sew-How: *For edgestitching a single thickness, use the buttonhole C foot. For edgestitching a front tab, collar, or pocket made of at least two fabric thicknesses, use the blind hem D foot. The raised edge on the underside of the D foot compensates for the added fabric thickness.*

2. Set your needle position so the needle is the desired distance from the edge and edgestitch. The foot enables you to edgestitch uniformly from the fabric edge (see Fig. 9.11).

STAYSTITCHING

Staystitching is a line of stitching just inside the seam allowance which keeps curved and bias cut edges from stretching out of shape as the fabric is handled during construction. Areas commonly staystitched are necklines, shoulders, and waistlines.

To staystitch, use a 2 length straight stitch (A2), and stitch 1/2" (1.3cm) from the raw edge on a single layer of fabric (Fig. 8.7). To prevent the fabric from distorting, staystitch in the direction of the arrows as shown.

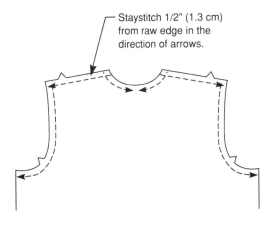

Staystitch 1/2" (1.3 cm) from raw edge in the direction of arrows.

Fig. 8.7.

Fig. 8.8.
Stitch-in-the-ditch to tack
down facings or finish
waistbands.

Fig. 8.9.
Topstitching on a pocket.

Sew-How: *When you pin a straight piece to a curved pattern piece (as you would when putting a collar on a neckline) staystitch around the curve 1/2" (1.3cm) from the raw edge. Then clip the curved seam line to the staystitching. The pattern piece fits better and the fabric will not ravel past the staystitching.*

STITCH-IN-THE-DITCH

Tack facings or finish waistbands by stitching-in-the- ditch (see Figs. 9.11, 9.12, 9.13). To do this:

1. Use the blind hem D or buttonhole C foot and a 3 length straight stitch (A2).

2. With the right side up, place the crack of the seam under the foot, centering it under the needle (Fig. 8.8).

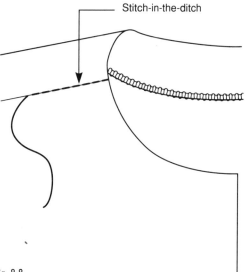

Stitch-in-the-ditch

Fig. 8.8.

3. Pull threads to the wrong side and tie them off.

STRAIGHT SEAMS

The straight stitch is used to sew a seam that will be pressed open on a woven fabric.

Machine Readiness Checklist	
Stitch:	straight (A2)
Length:	2.5 – 3.5
Width:	0
Foot:	standard A metal zigzag
Thread:	all-purpose
Needle:	70/10 or 80/12 universal
Tension:	normal
Fabric:	varies

With right sides together, sew a seam, stitching 5/8" (2.5cm) from the raw edge. To set the stitches, press over them so seam is flat and together. Then press seam open.

Sew-How: *If your seam line puckers, the thread may be too heavy for the fabric. Try using machine-embroidery thread with a 70/10 needle.*

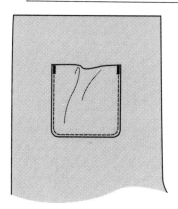

Fig. 8.9.

TOPSTITCHING

Topstitching is a line of stitches sewn on the top side of a project parallel to the finished edge or to a seam line. Topstitching differs from edgestitching because it's not sewn as close to the

Fig. 8.10.
Twin needle hem on a knit fabric looks as if it has been knitted into the fabric.

finished edge as edgestitching, and a longer stitch length is usually used. Topstitching can also be done with a variety of decorative top threads such as silk twist, polyester topstitching thread, or by using two threads through the same needle. Generally topstitching is used to embellish and is not necessary for the construction of a project (Fig. 8.9).

Machine Readiness Checklist

Stitch:	straight (A2)
Length:	3 – 4
Width:	0
Foot:	standard A or transparent B (appliqué)
Thread:	two threads through the same needle; or silk twist or topstitching
Needle:	80/12 universal, 90/14 topstitching for heavy threads
Tension:	normal for two threads through same needle; tighten top slightly for heavier threads

Sew-How: *Be consistent. Use the same stitch length to topstitch all parts of a project. If you have a mechanical machine, stop at a corner so the needle has hit its dead lowest point, and is on its way out of the fabric. This way, the stitch cycle is complete so you don't run the risk of skipping a stitch. Most electronic and computerized machines that can stop sewing with the needle in the fabric do this automatically.*

Interface three weights of fabric. Fold each in half on the lengthwise grain, and topstitch each using different stitch lengths. Make a note of the best stitch length for topstitching each fabric. Put these samples in your notebook.

TWIN NEEDLE HEM

Twin needles are used on top- and front-loading bobbin machines only. If your bobbin goes in the side of your machine, the needles sit in the machine incorrectly and will not work. This fast, professional way to hem a knit looks as if the hem has been knitted into the fabric (Fig. 8.10). For stretchy knits such as sweater knits, stretch terry, and velour, lengthen stitch to 4 – 4.5.

Fig. 8.10.

Machine Readiness Checklist

Stitch:	straight (A2)
Length:	2.5 – 3.5
Width:	0
Foot:	utility B or transparent (appliqué)
Thread:	all-purpose to match fabric
Needle:	twin, size 2.0/80(12)
Tension:	normal; for more pronounced tuck, tighten upper tension
Fabric:	woven or knit

Fig. 8.11.
Twin needle pintucks.

Fig. 8.12.
Understitching prevents
facing from rolling
toward the outside.

Sew-How: *To prevent threads from tangling through the upper tension, place one spool so thread pulls from the front of the spool; place the other spool so the thread pulls from the back of the spool.*

1. Fold hem up desired amount and press.

2. With the right side up, place fabric under foot the width of the hem, so foot is resting on a double layer of fabric. Stitch.

3. Trim excess fabric away from the underside.

Sew-How: *To prevent cutting a hole where it doesn't belong when trimming away the fabric close to the stitch, use a pair of scissors with one rounded blade or with a pelican-shaped blade. Position the scissors so the rounded or pelican-shaped blade is between the hem allowance and the wrong side of the project.*

TWIN NEEDLE TUCKS (PINTUCKS)

Set your machine as described above using the raised seam F foot. For a more pronounced tuck, tighten the upper tension, and cord the tuck using the raised seam guide and pearl cotton (see Figs. 9.13, 9.14).

With the right side up, sew on a single layer of fabric. The bobbin thread shares itself between the two top threads creating a zigzag stitch on the underside and a tuck on the right side of the fabric. For stretchy knits, lengthen stitch to 4 – 4.5.

Applications: Stitch with thread matching the fabric to create texture down the front of a knit sweatshirt, top or dress. Pintuck the front of an heirloom blouse or christening gown. Run multiple rows around the hem of a skirt for more body (Fig. 8.11). (See Fig. 9.13.)

Fig. 8.11.

UNDERSTITCHING

Understitching prevents the inside layer of fabric from rolling to the outside and is generally done on a facing edge.

After stitching and trimming the seam, press seam allowance toward the facing. With the right side up, stitch 1/8" (3mm) from the seam line using a straight stitch appropriate for the fabric (Fig. 8.12).

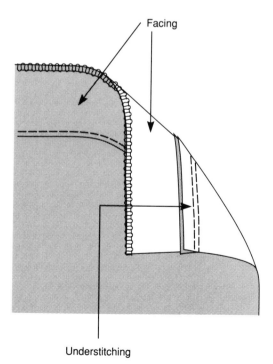

Facing

Understitching

Fig. 8.12.

Fig. 8.13.
Reinforced straight stitch
as a topstitch on jeans.

Understitching a facing first makes it easier to topstitch later. However, you may not always want to topstitch, so try the following SEW-HOW method.

Sew-How: *Instead of using a straight stitch to understitch a facing, use a three-step zigzag (A19 or 20) on a 1.5 length and a 4 – 5 width (see Fig. 8.40). This stitch flattens the bulk and makes the seam allowance lie flat so it may not be necessary to topstitch.*

TRICOT STITCH (A5,6,7)

The tricot stitch is recommended for seaming knits where the seam allowance will be pressed open, and for seaming very fine knits where the seam will be trimmed to 1/4" (6mm). A5 will stitch in left needle position, A6 in center needle position, A7 in right needle position.

Machine Readiness Checklist	
Stitch:	tricot (A5,6,7)
Length:	2.5
Width:	2
Foot:	standard A for fine knits; utility B for medium to heavy knits
Needle:	appropriate for fabric
Thread:	all-purpose
Tension:	normal

Place right sides together and stitch on the 5/8" (1.5cm) or 1/4" (6mm) seam line. Press seam flat and together, then press 5/8" (1.5cm) seam open or press 1/4" (6mm) seam to one side, toward the front of the garment.

Sew-How: *The tricot stitch is a great problem-solver stitch; if you have a difficult, slippery fabric, this stitch will generally produce a satisfactory seam.*

REINFORCED STRAIGHT STITCH (A8,9,10)

Sometimes referred to as the elastic straight stitch, this stitch was thought of as the original stretch stitch because it is strong enough to stretch with a knit seam, and recovers well after stretching. However, it is almost impossible to rip out if you make a mistake. The reinforced straight stitch takes two stitches forward and one back and is used to reinforce areas of stress such as underarm and crotch seams.

Lengthen it, and you get a beautiful topstitch like those seen on jeans and leather goods (Fig. 8.13).

Fig. 8.13.

Still another application is for linen collar, cuff, napkin, and tablecloth hems.

Fig. 8.14.
Reinforced straight stitch
used with the wing
needle as a hem finish
on linen collar.

Machine Readiness Checklist

Stitch:	reinforced straight (A8,9,10)
Length:	4 – 6
Width:	0
Foot:	standard A metal zigzag or Teflon H
Needle:	wing
Thread:	darning #70 or #120 weight (see Sources of Supply)
Fabric:	tightly woven cotton or linen

1.   Finish hem edge with the three-step zigzag or serpentine stitch (A19, 20; length, 1; width, 4) using all-purpose thread and a 70/10 universal needle. Fold hem up desired amount and press.

2.   Using a wing needle, rethread top and bobbin with darning thread. Topstitch hem so the foot is resting on a double layer of fabric (Fig. 8.14).

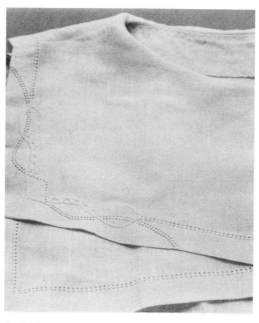

Fig. 8.14.

Sew-How: *The reinforced straight stitch is made by taking two stitches forward and one stitch back. It's important your machine is adjusted properly so the needle stitches back into the same hole creating the look in Fig. 8.14. If your stitching line is rough and the holes created by the wing needle are uneven, check your Operating Manual to see how the stitch length can be fine-tuned or elongated.*

ZIGZAG STITCH (A11,12,13)

- Left, Center, and Right Needle Positions
- Button Sewing
- Button and Belt Loops
- Couching with the Zigzag Stitch
- Gathering over a Cord
- 5/8" (1.5cm) Knit Seam
- Overcast a Raw Edge
- Speed Basting
- Thread Tacks

Add stitch width to a straight stitch and you have a zigzag stitch. It's used to make buttonholes, sew buttons, embroider, make belt loops, gather over a cord, stitch a knit seam, overcast a raw edge, satin stitch, tack down a facing, plus much more.

Fig. 8.15.
Zigzag stitch on varying
widths and lengths.

Fig. 8.16.
A tapered satin stitch in
left, center, and right
needle position.

To acquaint yourself with the stitch, sew row after row of zigzag stitches experimenting with the stitch width and length (Fig. 8.15). Record settings and keep your experiments in your notebook. Once you have a basic familiarity with the zigzag, you will master the following techniques.

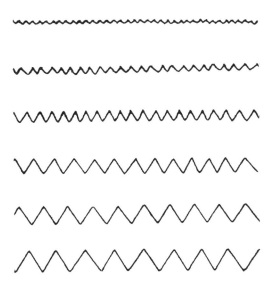

Fig. 8.15.

LEFT, CENTER, AND RIGHT NEEDLE POSITIONS

On the Viking 1100, select from zigzag stitches in three needle positions—left, center, and right. When the needle is in the left position (A11), the column of zigzag stitches guides under the left side of the foot. If you choose to taper a satin stitch (length 0.5; width 0,6,0), the stitch tapers from the left, out to the right, then back to the left again. Make a sample for your notebook.

When the needle is in the center position (A12), the column of zigzag stitches guides down the center of the foot. The tapered satin stitch tapers out equally to both sides, then back to the center again. Make a sample for your notebook.

When the needle is in the right position (A13), the column of zigzag stitches guides under the right side of the foot. If you taper a satin stitch in right needle position, the stitch tapers from the right to the left, then back to the right again. Make a sample for your notebook.

Application: Use the zigzag in left, center and right needle positions to gather over a cord or to topstitch. With the needle position variations you can put the column of zigzag stitches precisely where you want. Use the tapered satin stitch from left, center, or right needle position to taper a monogram or to stitch a stem or leaf (Fig. 8.16).

Fig. 8.16.

BUTTON SEWING

Use the zigzag stitch to sew a button on by machine (see Fig. 9.18). Unlike commercial machines that use a one-thread chain stitch to attach buttons, the conventional sewing machine has a top and bobbin thread so buttons are stitched securely. Sewing buttons by machine is also faster than sewing them on by hand.

*Fig. 8.17.
Button taped to fabric
with tapestry needle
between the holes.*

*Fig. 8.18.
Wrap a thread shank
between the button and
fabric.*

Machine Readiness Checklist	
Stitch:	zigzag (A11)
Length:	0
Width:	2 – 4 (test on your button)
Foot:	remove the foot and use the foot shank to anchor the button down
Feed dogs:	down
Needle position:	far left
Accessories:	transparent tape or glue stick, Fray-Check, tapestry hand needle

1. Mark button placement. Place button by taping it on or by dabbing the back with the glue stick.

Sew-How: *A thread shank between the button and the fabric allows room for the buttoned fabric. To make a thread shank, place a tapestry needle between the holes before taping over button (Fig. 8.17).*

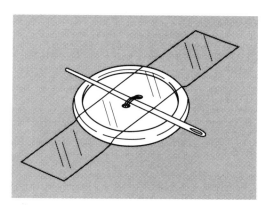

Fig. 8.17.

2. Turn the flywheel by hand so the machine needle stops in the left hole of the button and lower the presser bar lever.

3. Turn the flywheel by hand to check the needle clearance; adjust your zigzag width if necessary. Then stitch four to five zigzag stitches.

4. Move width to 0 and take a few stitches in place to anchor threads. Remove fabric and pull off enough thread to wrap a shank between the button and fabric (Fig. 8.18).

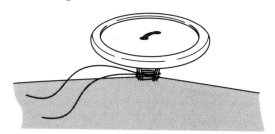

Fig. 8.18.

5. After wrapping shank, pull threads to the back, tie and clip them off at fabric. Dab Fray-Check on threads to secure them.

BUTTON AND BELT LOOPS

Rather than hand crocheting belt or button loops, zigzag over pearl cotton or multiple strands of thread.

Fig. 8.19.
Zigzag over pearl cotton
to make belt and button
loops.

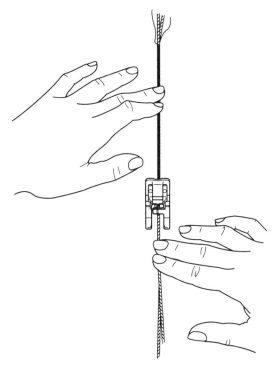

Fig. 8.19.

Machine Readiness Checklist

Stitch:	zigzag (A11 or 12)
Length:	0.5 – 0.8
Width:	widest
Foot:	transparent B (appliqué) or buttonhole C
Feed dogs:	up
Needle position:	center (A12) for B (appliqué) foot; left (A11) for buttonhole C foot
Thread:	all-purpose
Accessories:	pearl cotton to match thread, large-eyed tapestry needle

1. Place a double strand of pearl cotton or multiple strand of thread under the foot so 2 – 3" (5 – 7.5cm) are behind the foot.

Sew-How: *When using the C foot, guide pearl cotton under the left groove in the foot.*

---

2. Hold top and bobbin thread tails behind the foot, and zigzag over pearl cotton or thread so the stitches cover cord (Fig. 8.19).

3. Thread stitched cord through tapestry needle to insert in seam where desired. Knot both ends so loop will not pull out.

COUCHING WITH THE ZIGZAG STITCH

Couching is a way to attach cord, floss, yarn, or ribbon to the surface of a fabric for an edge finish or decorative treatment.

Machine Readiness Checklist

Stitch:	zigzag (A11 or 12)
Length:	1 – 2
Width:	wide enough to clear cord
Foot:	transparent B (appliqué), narrow braiding, or buttonhole C
Feed dogs:	up
Needle position:	left if using buttonhole C; center if using narrow braiding
Thread:	all-purpose to match cord or nylon monofilament

Place cord, floss, yarn, or ribbon on the right side of a single layer of fabric. Zigzag over cord to attach to the fabric (Fig. 8.20).

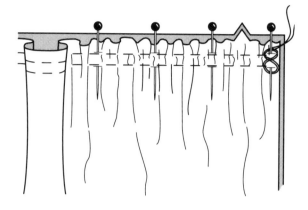

Fig. 8.21.

Fig. 8.20.

GATHERING OVER A CORD

To gather fabric, pattern instructions usually say to stitch two rows of straight basting stitches, which you then pull (Fig. 8.21). Often these threads break while you are pulling up the gathers. To prevent this, zigzag over a cord.

Machine Readiness Checklist	
Stitch:	zigzag (A11 or 12)
Length:	2 – 3
Width:	2 – 3 or wide enough to clear cord
Foot:	buttonhole C or narrow braiding
Feed dogs:	up

Needle	
position:	left for buttonhole C foot; center for narrow braiding foot
Accessories:	#8 or #5 pearl cotton or nylon fishing line

1. Place cord under groove of the foot on the wrong side of a single layer of fabric so 2 – 3" (5 – 7.5cm) extends behind it.

2. Guiding 1/2" (1.3cm) from the raw edge and on the wrong side of the fabric, zigzag over cord being careful not to catch cord in the stitching (Fig. 8.22).

3. Pull gathers up and adjust from both ends. Once fabric has been gathered to desired length, knot or anchor cord so gathers don't pull out. Although it is not necessary, you may remove the cord after stitching.

Fig. 8.22.
Zigzag over cord and
pull gathers up.

Fig. 8.23.
Use tiny zigzag to sew a
5/8" (1.5cm) seam
on a knit.

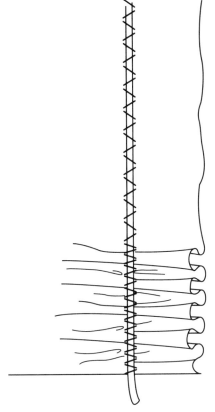

Fig. 8.22.

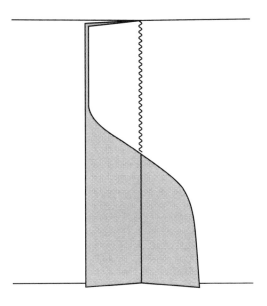

Fig. 8.23.

5/8" (1.5CM) KNIT SEAM

If a straight stitch is used to construct a knit, the thread often breaks. To prevent this, stitch the seam with a tiny zigzag stitch.

Machine Readiness Checklist	
Stitch	zigzag (A12)
Length:	1 – 2
Width:	1
Foot:	transparent B (appliqué)
Needle:	70/10 or 80/12 universal
Thread:	all-purpose
Tension:	normal

1. Place right sides together and stitch seam at the 5/8" (1.5cm) seam line (Fig. 8.23).

2. Press seam flat and together to blend the stitches. Then press seam open.

Sew-How: *If gathering a long ruffle, cut the cord or pearl cotton the length of the finished ruffle plus 4" (10cm). Mark the finished length of ruffle on the cord by pinning 2" (5cm) from the end of the cord. Then mark the cord into fourths between the pins. Your cord is anchored by pins at the beginning and end of the ruffle. Zigzag over cord as described above. While stitching, guide cord with your right hand while pushing gathers down the cord with your left, matching the marks on the fabric with the marks on the cord. This way, the ruffle is gathered to the exact length needed without wasting a lot of cord.*

Sew-How: *This stitch is difficult to rip so baste the seam together first (see Speed Basting below) to check the fit.*

Fig. 8.24.
Finish raw edge with a
zigzag and overcast J
foot.

OVERCAST A RAW EDGE

Although it isn't always necessary to finish the seams, overcasting a raw edge prevents raveling and the project looks more professional. The zigzag stitch can be used to overcast a raw edge; however, many fabrics curl or tunnel under the stitch. To minimize this curling, try the following method.

Sew-How: *The three-step zigzag (A19 or 20), double overlock (A24), or flatlock (A25) are preferred stitches for overcasting. If you have one of those stitches available, skip ahead to page 183 and read how to use them for overcasting.*

Machine Readiness Checklist

Stitch:	zigzag (A12)
Length:	1.5 – 2
Width:	widest
Foot:	overcast J
Needle:	appropriate for fabric
Thread:	all-purpose

Fig. 8.24.

1. Place single layer of fabric under the foot so the raw edge is even with the guide in the foot.

2. Overcast edge, guiding the fabric so the needle swings off the edge on the right (Fig. 8.24).

SPEED BASTING

This is a fast, easy method of basting knits together and the stitches pull out quickly after fitting.

Machine Readiness Checklist

Stitch:	zigzag (A12)
Length:	longest
Width:	widest
Foot:	transparent B (appliqué)
Feed dogs:	up
Needle position:	center
Thread:	top, all-purpose; bobbin, contrasting color to top thread
Fabric:	knits
Tension:	top, loose; bobbin, normal

1. Stitch seam at seam line indicated on pattern.

2. Check fit and permanently stitch the seam. Remove basting stitches by pulling bobbin thread (Fig. 8.25).

Sew-How: *Use water-soluble Thread-Fuse™ basting thread on the bobbin as a temporary seam. The stitches dissolve in water.*

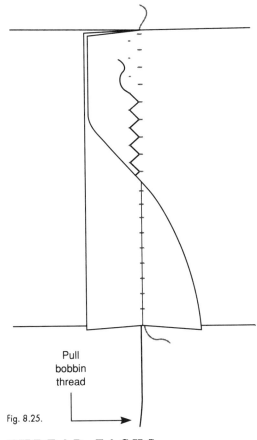

Fig. 8.25.
Remove speed basting
by pulling bobbin thread.

Fig. 8.26.
Attaching a ribbon or
yarn with thread tack.

Pull
bobbin
thread

Fig. 8.25.

THREAD TACKS

Tack a facing, bow, or small appliqué like this:

Machine Readiness Checklist	
Stitch:	zigzag (A11)
Length:	0
Width:	3 – 5
Foot:	transparent B (appliqué) or standard A metal zigzag
Feed dogs:	down
Needle position:	left
Thread:	all-purpose or cotton embroidery
Accessories:	Fray-Check

1. Place item to be tacked under the foot. Take four to five zigzag stitches. Move the width to 0 (Fig. 8.26).

2. Stitch a few locking stitches, remove the fabric, and pull threads to the back. Clip threads close to the fabric and dab them with Fray-Check.

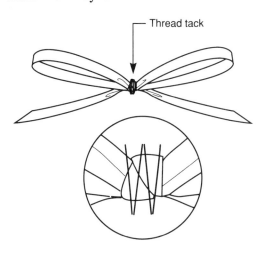

— Thread tack

SATIN STITCH (A14,15,16)

The satin stitch looks like a narrow satin ribbon stitched around appliqués and is used to monogram and embroider. Stitch different widths of satin stitches for your notebook.

Machine Readiness Checklist	
Stitch:	zigzag (A14,15,16)
Length:	0.3 – 0.8
Width:	2, 4, 6
Foot:	utility B or transparent B (appliqué)
Feed dogs:	up
Needle position:	center
Thread:	cotton embroidery or rayon embroidery
Fabric:	tightly woven cotton or cotton blend
Tension:	top, loosened slightly; bobbin, normal
Accessories:	iron-on freezer wrap or tear-away stabilizer

Fig. 8.27.
Varying widths of satin
stitching.

1. Iron freezer paper or pin stabilizer to the back of your fabric and set your machine for a 2 width satin stitch (A14). Stitch and examine, then adjust the stitch length so the stitches are next to, but not on top of, each other.

2. Repeat for 4 (A15) and 6 (A16) stitch widths (Fig. 8.27).

Fig. 8.27.

Sew-How: *The Viking 1100 has three preprogrammed satin stitch widths—2mm, 4mm, 6mm. If you want to override the program, adjust the width and length to your liking. The advantage of preprogramming is the guesswork is eliminated. Sew a sample of each stitch and put them in your notebook.*

Applications: Use the preprogrammed satin stitches for appliquéing, block monograms, flower stems, satin stitched edges, and cut work.

Satin Stitch Lettuce or Rolled Edge

The lettuce edge looks like the edge of a lettuce leaf when stitched on a knit. It's used on lingerie, ribbing edges and on children's clothing. When used on a woven, it looks like a rolled hem found on the edge of placemats, napkins, and scarves. When worked on the bias and stretched, it becomes a lettuce edge, too.

Machine Readiness Checklist	
Stitch:	zigzag (A15)
Length:	0.3 – 0.8
Width:	widest
Foot:	transparent B (appliqué) or buttonhole C
Feed dogs:	up
Thread:	all-purpose
Fabric:	single knits (e.g., interlock, jersey, tricot, ribbings)
Tension:	top, loosened slightly; bobbin, normal
Accessories:	round-nosed scissors

Method One

This technique works beautifully on nylon tricot or any single knit. When stretched across the grain, single knits curl to the right side.

1. To make the fabric roll, stretch the raw edge across the grain. Place rolled edge under the foot, holding the fabric in front of and behind the foot (Fig. 8.28).

Sew-How: *When using the buttonhole foot, guide the roll under the left groove for easy guiding.*

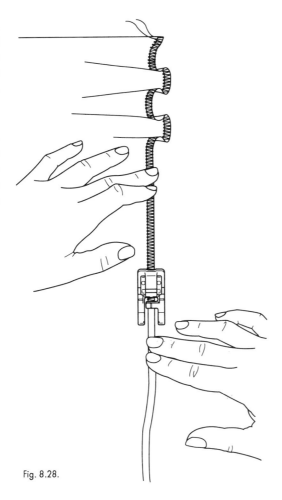

Fig. 8.28.
Zigzag over curled
edge, holding fabric in
front of and behind the
foot.

Fig. 8.29.
Tapered satin stitch
using the Automatic
(Satin Stitch) Taper stitch
on the Viking 1100.

Fig. 8.28.

3. Carefully trim the excess fabric to the stitching line.

4. After trimming, stretch the fabric across the grain.

AUTOMATIC (SATIN STITCH) TAPERS (A17)

If you don't have a practiced hand in tapering a satin stitch, the Viking 1100 has an automatic taper function. When you select this function, the satin stitch automatically tapers from center needle position to a 6 or narrower width. When you want it to taper back to 0, push the instant reverse button, and the stitch tapers evenly back to the center. Stitch a sample for your notebook (Fig. 8.29). Applications: Use A17 to taper stems, leaves, stitching on an appliqué, or a monogram.

Fig. 8.29.

RICKRACK STITCH (A18)

This stitch is more a decorative than a utility stitch; however, it is on the Viking 1100 A cassette so it is discussed here. Use the rickrack stitch where you would attach narrow rickrack or as a decorative seam.

2. Guide fabric so the needle stitches over the roll on the left and off the raw edge at the right.

Method Two

This is recommended for woven fabrics and single knits that run or are very stretchy, (e.g., ribbing, interlock, wool jersey, and Lycra® spandex).

1. Fold and press at least a 1/2" (1.3cm) hem.

2. Place fold halfway under the foot, right side up, so the needle catches the fabric on the left and swings off the fold at the right. Do not stretch the fabric while sewing. The stitches automatically push the fabric out of shape creating a ripple.

Rickrack "Ladder" Stitch as a Decorative Seam

Machine Readiness Checklist

Stitch:	rickrack (A18)
Length:	4.5 – elongated
Width:	4
Foot:	special marking (see Fig. 9.39)
Needle:	80/12 universal
Thread:	all-purpose or cotton embroidery
Tension:	top, loosened; bobbin, normal
Fabric:	suit-weight linen

1. Overcast raw edges with the three-step zigzag (A19, or 20). (See Fig. 8.35.)

2. Place fabric right sides together and sew at the 5/8" (1.5cm) seam line.

3. From the right side, pull seam open so the ladder stitches are seen (Fig. 8.30). For an open ladder seam, press seam open. For a closed ladder seam, press seam to one side.

Fig. 8.30.

THREE-STEP ZIGZAG (A19) AND SERPENTINE STITCH (A20)

- Attaching Elastic
- Mending
- Overcasting a Raw Edge
- Patching
- Tacking
- With Twin Needles
- Understitching

....

Next to the straight and zigzag stitches, I feel the three-step zigzag and the serpentine stitches are the most useful. They are closely allied and used in approximately the same way—so what is the difference?

The three-step zigzag takes three short stitches to the left, and three short stitches to the right—there is a sharp point where the stitch changes direction. The serpentine takes four stitches to the right, four to the left, but curves around the corner (Fig. 8.31). Because there are more stitches in the serpentine than the three-step zigzag, and the corner of the stitch is curved, it stretches more and is gentler to the fabric. Therefore the serpentine is recommended for knits and the three-step zigzag for wovens.

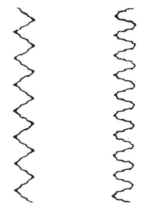

Fig. 8.31.

Applications: Use either stitch for attaching elastic, mending, overcasting a raw edge, patching, tacking down facings or trims, twin needle cable stitching, understitching, and much more.

Attaching Elastic

Pattern instructions usually say to stretch the elastic while attaching it to the fabric. When the needle stitches through the elastic, it causes the rubber to break down and the elastic to stretch out of shape. You can avoid this pitfall with the following method because the fabric rather than the elastic is stretched. For this reason, it works only on knits.

Machine Readiness Checklist

Stitch:	three-step zigzag (A19) or serpentine (A20)
Length:	1 – 1.5
Width:	4 – widest
Foot:	transparent B (appliqué)
Thread:	all-purpose
Fabric:	sweatshirt fleece, velour, stretch terry and other knit fabrics
Needle:	70/10 or 80/12 universal
Accessories:	vanishing marker, pencil with an eraser on the end

Note: *To do this technique properly, you must have about 1/2" (1.3cm) fabric on either side of the elastic. Therefore, when cutting fabric out, add 1/2" (1.3cm) to the top opening where elastic is to be stitched. This method also works the same no matter where the elastic is applied. However, for this example, the instructions are written as if you were applying elastic to the waistline.*

1. Cut elastic 3 – 5" (7 – 12.5cm) shorter than waistline measurement. Mark it into eighths with the vanishing marker. Mark garment waistline into eights.

Sew-How: *Double-check the length of waistline elastic before cutting to be sure it fits over your hips.*

---

2. Pin elastic to wrong side of fabric, matching eighth-marks and placing it 1/2" (1.3cm) from cut edge. Do not join elastic ends.

3. Place work under the foot and sew a couple of stitches to anchor elastic. Using index finger of both hands simultaneously, start sewing while pulling the fabric out sideways, exactly where the needle enters the fabric. Take four or five stitches, reposition your fingers, and repeat until the fabric is eased in place and elastic ends overlap (Fig. 8.32).

Sew-How: *For a firmer grip at the right, pull on the fabric using the eraser end of a pencil.*

---

4. Fold fabric over elastic so the three-step zigzag shows on the inside.

Machine Readiness Checklist

Stitch:	zigzag (A12)
Length:	1.2
Width:	1
Foot:	transparent B (appliqué) or utility B

Fig. 8.32.
Pin elastic to wrong
side, 1/2" (1.3cm) from
cut edge. Pull fabric out
sideways where the
needle enters the fabric,
and sew four to five
stitches. Repeat until
fabric is eased into
elastic.

Fig. 8.33.
"Wiggle" fabric into
place with left index
finger.

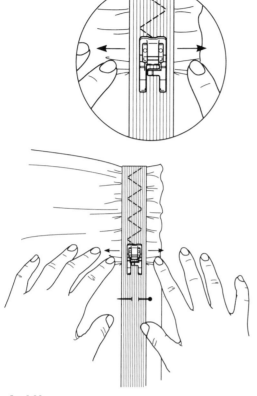

Fig. 8.32.

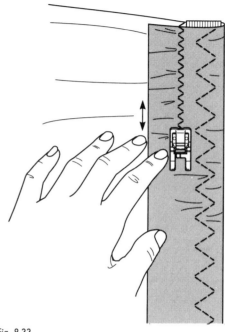

Fig. 8.33.

Mending

Mend a run or tear with the three-step
zigzag or the serpentine stitch.

Machine Readiness Checklist

5. Place waistline under foot, wrong side
up so the needle will be stitching just
under the elastic. Place index finger to
the left side of the foot. Sew to the left of
the elastic while wiggling the fabric back
and forth with the index finger of your left
hand (Fig. 8.33). The wiggling prevents
elastic from stretching out and eliminates
unnecessary puckers, tucks, or gathers
from being stitched in the right side of the
work.

6. Trim excess fabric away up to the
stitch.

Machine Readiness Checklist

Stitch:	three-step zigzag (A19) or serpentine (A20)
Length:	0.4 – 0.8
Width:	widest
Foot:	transparent B (appliqué) on medium to heavy fabric; standard A foot on lightweight fabrics
Thread:	all-purpose or 100% polyester one shade darker than fabric
Accessories:	a strip of fusible interfacing

Fig. 8.34.
Center run or tear under
the foot and mend with
the three-step zigzag
stitch.

Sew-How: *I mend old denim jeans using a gray color thread on the bobbin and a blue to match the fabric on the top. Then I tighten the upper tension slightly. The mend is almost invisible because the gray thread pulls slightly to the surface of the fabric giving a faded look to the denim.*

1. Fuse a strip of interfacing to the underside of tear. Center the run or tear under the foot and sew (Fig. 8.34). The stitches form over and across the tear, keeping the fabric flat and helping pull raveled threads in place.

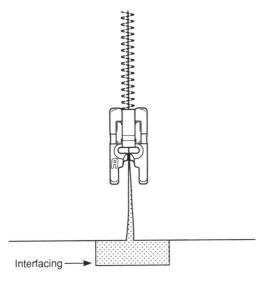

Interfacing →

Fig. 8.34.

2. If necessary, turn the fabric around and stitch another row of three-step zigzags or serpentine stitches next to the first until tear is repaired.

Overcasting a Raw Edge

Overcasting a raw edge with the zigzag stitch often causes tunneling. Because the three-step zigzag and serpentine stitches take three or four short stitches over and back, they keep raw edges flat. Overcast almost any type of fabric with either stitch.

Machine Readiness Checklist	
Stitch:	three-step zigzag (A19) or serpentne (A20)
Length:	0.8 – 1.5 (use shorter length on fine fabrics; use longer length on heavy fabrics)
Width:	widest
Foot:	standard A metal zigzag on fine fabrics; transparent B (appliqué) on medium to heavy fabrics

Test for best stitch length on fabric scrap. Place raw edge under the foot so the right swing of the stitch is just off the edge.

Sew-How: *After cutting, overcast raw edges before putting the project together. To overcast quickly, butt one pattern piece up next to the other without lifting the foot. When you're done, pattern pieces will look like a kite tail (Fig. 8.35). Then cut threads between the pieces before construction.*

Patching

The old-fashioned way to patch was to turn the raw edges in on the patch and stitch it over the hole by hand. This method is so slow, I found my mending pile getting unmanageable. Save time and put a patch on to stay with this following method.

Fig. 8.35.
To save time, butt one pattern piece up to the next when overcasting.

Fig. 8.36.
Stitch patch so three-step zigzag stitches cross each other at the corners.

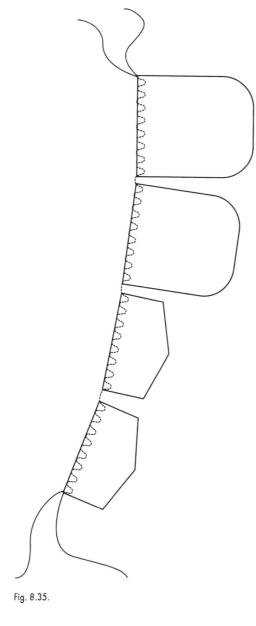

Fig. 8.35.

Machine Readiness Checklist

Stitch:	three-step zigzag (A19) or serpentine (A20)
Length:	0.5 – 1
Width:	widest
Foot:	standard A metal zigzag, Teflon H, or roller
Feed dogs:	up
Needle:	90/14 jeans for medium to heavy fabrics; 80/12 universal for lightweight fabrics
Thread:	all-purpose or cotton darning (see Sources of Supply)
Accessories:	glue stick

1. Cut patch large enough to cover the hole so the frayed fabric is covered. Don't turn under edges. Because the mending stitches are so close, the edges won't fray. This method cuts down on bulk.

2. Pin or glue-stick patch over hole. Starting at one corner, guide fabric so the right swing of the needle clears the raw edge of the patch. Sew to the corner, stopping with the needle on the far right side of the stitch (Fig. 8.36).

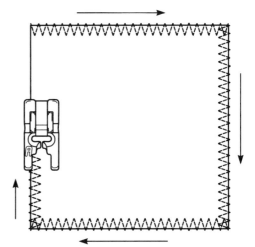

Fig. 8.36.

Fig. 8.37.
Stitch across and back a
few times to tack down a
facing, ribbon, or yarn
tie in a quilt.

3. Pivot patch and stitch second side. The stitches should cross each other in the corner for extra reinforcement.

4. Repeat for other two sides. Pull threads to the back and tie them off. Trim damaged fabric from the wrong side of the patch.

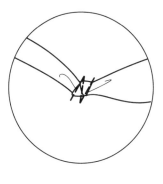

Sew-How: *If you have a free-arm machine, you can patch a knee or elbow without ripping out the seam as long as your stitch length has the continuous reverse feature (see your Operating Manual). To do this, sew the first two sides of the patch as described above, then use the continuous reverse to sew the second two sides of the patch.*

Tacking

Tack down a facing, ribbon, or yarn tie when tying a quilt, or attach a small appliqué.

Fig. 8.37.

Sew-How: *On the 900 series and the 1100 Vikings, push the finishing or STOP button so stitches lock off automatically.*

Machine Readiness Checklist	
Stitch:	three-step zigzag (A19) or serpentine (A20)
Length:	0
Width:	3 – widest
Foot:	transparent (B) appliqué
Feed dogs:	down
Needle position:	left

1. Place facing, yarn, ribbon, or appliqué on background or fashion fabric and under the foot.
2. Stitch across and back in the same place five or six stitches (Fig. 8.37). Move width to 0 and stitch a few stitches in one place.

3. Pull threads to the back and cut or tie them off.

Three-Step Zigzag and Serpentine with Twin Needles

Use thread matching the fabric to create a cable in a solid-colored fabric. I've used five to seven rows of cable stitching down the front of a stretch terry cloth sweatshirt and centered down each sleeve.

....

Fig. 8.38.
Use twin needles with the
three-step zigzag to
create a cable on a soft
knit.

Fig. 8.39.
Match twin needle,
three-step zigzag cable
stitches back to back.

Machine Readiness Checklist

Stitch:	three-step zigzag (A19) or serpentine (A20)
Length:	1 – 2
Width:	3 (wide enough for needles to clear the hole in the foot and needle plate)
Foot:	transparent B (appliqué)
Feed dogs:	up
Needle position:	center
Needle:	twin, size 2.0/80(12) or 2.5/80(12)
Thread:	all-purpose
Fabric suggestions:	stretch terry, velour, wool jersey, some medium-weight T-shirt knits
Accessories:	vanishing marker or dressmaker's chalk

Sew-How: *On the 900 series and 1100 Vikings, push the twin needle function button to narrow the width for twin needle sewing.*

1. Using the vanishing marker or dressmaker's chalk, mark where the center cable is to be stitched.

2. Sew the first row of cable stitches over the line marked in Step 1. Turn the fabric around and stitch the second row next to the first about a presser foot-width away (Fig. 8.38). (If you were to sew every line the same way, the fabric would distort.)

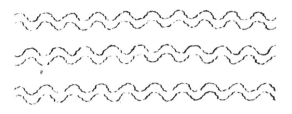

Fig. 8.38.

3. Continue to sew row after row of cable stitching, working from the center row of cable stitches out, until you have the desired effect.

Sew-How: *Once you have mastered this technique, match the stitches, back to back, and use this design as the center row of cabling (Fig. 8.39).*

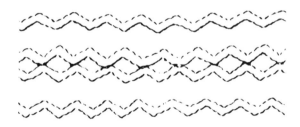

Fig. 8.39.

Understitching

Understitching prevents the inside layer of fabric from rolling to the outside and is generally done on a facing edge. You can understitch with the straight stitch, but the three-stitch zigzag or serpentine flattens the bulk of a faced edge better, so it's not always necessary to topstitch.

Fig. 8.40.
Understitch facings with
the three-step zigzag to
prevent them from rolling
out of place.

Stitch:	three-step zigzag (A19) or serpentine (A20)
Length:	1 – 1.5
Width:	widest
Foot:	standard A metal zigzag for lightweight fabrics; transparent B (appliqué) for medium and heavy fabrics

1. After stitching and trimming the seam, press seam allowance toward the facing.

2. With the right side up, place the foot so the right edge of the needle hole is at the seam line, and understitch (Fig. 8.40).

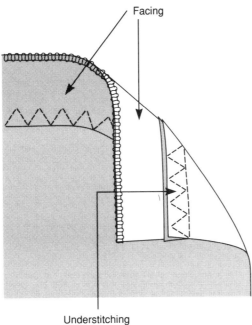

Facing

Understitching

Fig. 8.40.

UTILITY STITCH/OVERCAST AND STRETCH STITCHES

- Overcast Stitch (A21)
- Overedge Stitch (A22)
- Stitch and Overcast (A23)

187

- Double Overlock (A24)
- Flatlock (A25)
- Smocking Stitch (A26)
- Bridging Stitch (A27)
- Elastic Casing Stitch (A28)
- Knit Blind Hem Stitch (A29)
- Woven Blind Hem Stitch (A30)
- Automatic Button Sewing (A31)
- Machine Quilting Stitches (A32, 33)
- Arch Stitch (A34)
- Feather Stitch (A35)
- Heirloom Appliqué Stitch (A36)
- Programmed Bartack (A37)
- Automatic Mending and Darning (A38, 39, 40)

The following six stitches—the overcast (A21), overedge (A22), stitch-and-overcast (A23), double overlock (A24), flatlock (A25), and smocking stitch (A26)—are all used similarly, but are designed for specific fabrics.

OVERCAST STITCH (A21)

The overcast stitch is recommended for use to seam and overcast lightweight knits and light- and medium-weight wovens.

1/4" (6mm) Seams

Use this method on most knits and medium-weight wovens. As always, test on a swatch first.

Stitch:	overcast (A21)
Length:	2 – 2.5
Width:	5
Foot:	overcast J or transparent B (appliqué)
Needle:	75/11 stretch for knits; 80/12 universal for wovens
Thread:	all-purpose

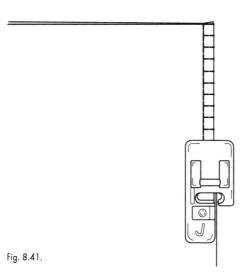

Fig. 8.41.
Stitch 1/4" (6mm) seam allowance so the stitch on the right swings off raw edges with the overcast stitch.

Fig. 8.42.
Guide seam allowance by the 1/2" (1.3cm) line in the needle plate and trim the fabric up to the stitch.

Fig. 8.41.

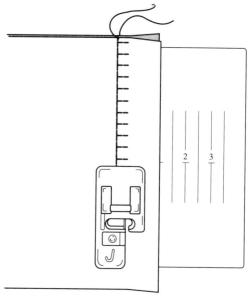

Fig. 8.42.

1. For a project cut with 1/4" (6mm) seam allowances, place right sides together so raw edges are to the right inside edge of the needle hole in the presser foot. The needle stitches into the seam allowance on the left and swings off the raw edge on the right (Fig. 8.41).

Sew-How: *For a project with 5/8" (1.5cm) seam allowances, place fabric under foot, guiding the raw edge by the 1/2" (1.3cm) line in the needle plate (Fig. 8.42). If you guide by the 5/8" (1.5cm) line in the needle plate, the stitch cheats you out of 1/8" (3mm) at each seam allowance. That doesn't sound like much, but multiply 1/8" (3mm) by eight cut edges and you have taken 1" (2.5cm) out of the total circumference. Your garment may be too snug for comfort.*

---

2. Trim excess fabric up to the stitch.

OVEREDGE STITCH (A22)

The overedge, sometimes called the overlock stitch, is designed for use on heavy, super-stretchy fabrics. Use it for 1/4" (6mm) seams on sweater knits, stretch terry cloth, ribbing, Lycra spandex swim wear, and biking fabrics.

Often these fabrics require stabilizing so seams will not droop or stretch out of shape. To do this, incorporate elastic thread, yarn, or pearl cotton in the seam.

Machine Readiness Checklist	
Stitch:	overedge (A22)
Length:	3
Width:	4 – 6
Foot:	transparent B (appliqué) or utility B
Needle:	80/12 universal
Thread:	all-purpose
Fabric:	stretch terry, velour, sweater knits
Accessories:	elastic thread, yarn, or pearl cotton

1. For a project cut with 1/4" (6mm) seam allowances, place right sides

Fig. 8.43.
To stabilize a knit seam, place a strand of elastic thread, yarn, or pearl cotton under foot and stitch with the overedge stitch.

together so raw edges are to the right inside edge of the needle hole in the presser foot. Put needle in fabric and raise the foot. (For a project with 5/8" [1.5cm] seams, see SEW-HOW under Overcast Stitch [A21], above.)

2. Cut a length of elastic thread, yarn, or pearl cotton the length of the seam, and place it under the foot. Put the foot down and stitch (Fig. 8.43). The needle stitches into the seam allowance on the left and off the raw edge at the right.

Fig. 8.43.

STITCH AND OVERCAST (A23)

The stitch and overcast is recommended for seaming medium-weight knits. It resembles a four-thread serger overlock, so it can also be used to topstitch T-shirt knits, wool jersey, and lightweight sweater knits and velour.

Machine Readiness Checklist	
Stitch:	stitch and overcast (A23)
Length:	3
Width:	5
Foot:	utility B or transparent B (appliqué)
Thread:	all-purpose

Follow instructions above (Overcast Stitch A21) for a 1/4" (6mm) or 5/8" (1.5cm) seams.

DOUBLE OVERLOCK STITCH (A24)

The double overlock stitch is recommended for overcasting a raw edge on a heavy woven such as denim, corduroy, or heavy duck. It can also be

used to seam and overcast a 1/4" (6mm) seam on these fabrics.

Machine Readiness Checklist	
Stitch:	double overlock (A24)
Length:	3
Width:	5 – 6
Foot:	utility B, transparent B (appliqué), or overcast
Thread:	all-purpose
Needle:	appropriate for fabric

1. To overcast a raw edge, place the right side of the fabric up, guiding the raw edge by the right inside edge of the needle hole in the foot.

2. Follow instructions (Overcast Stitch A21) for 1/4" (6mm) or 5/8" (1.5cm) seams.

FLATLOCK STITCH (A25)

- Edge Finish
- Lingerie Elastic Application

The flatlock resembles a 3-thread serger overlock. It is used on knits and wovens to overcast raw edges and to stitch and finish a 1/4" (6mm) seam in one operation. It is also used to topstitch T-shirts, sweatshirts, swim wear, and other active sportswear, and to apply lingerie elastic.

Edge Finish

This edge finish is recommended for loosely woven fabrics.

Machine Readiness Checklist	
Stitch:	flatlock (A25)
Length:	3
Width:	4 – 5
Foot:	overcast J or transparent B (appliqué)
Thread:	all-purpose

Fig. 8.44.
Finish edge of loosely
woven fabric with the
flatlock stitch.

Place raw edge under foot so the needle catches into the fabric on the left and swings just off the raw edge and over the guide in the foot on the right (Fig. 8.44).

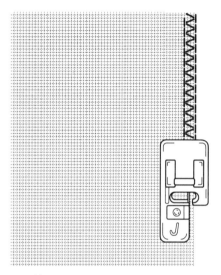

Fig. 8.44.

Lingerie Elastic Application with the Flatlock (A25)

Machine Readiness Checklist

Stitch:	flatlock (A25)
Length:	3
Width:	4 – 5
Foot:	transparent B (appliqué)
Needle:	70/10 or 80/12 universal
Thread:	all-purpose or nylon lingerie
Fabric:	nylon tricot or cotton single knit
Accessories:	1/2" (1.3cm) lingerie elastic, vanishing marker

Note: *To do this technique properly, leave about 1/2" (1.3cm) of fabric on either side of the elastic. It works only on*

knits or loosely woven fabrics cut on the bias. Cut lingerie with 1/2" (1.3cm) extra fabric at the top of waistline and at panty legs where elastic is to be sewn.

1. Measure elastic to fit comfortably around the waist or legs (usually 2 – 5" [5 – 12.5cm] smaller than garment opening). Mark elastic and opening into eighths using the vanishing marker.

2. Pin elastic to opening on the right side, 1/2" (1.3cm) down from the raw edge. Overlap and pin elastic ends at the side seams.

Sew-How: *Lingerie elastic wears longer when sewn on the outside of the garment because the fabric underneath protects it from perspiration and body oils.*

---

3. Place work under presser foot so the left side of the stitch falls on the fabric and the right side swings onto the elastic. Take a couple of stitches to anchor elastic.

4. Using index fingers of both hands simultaneously, start sewing while pulling the fabric out sideways, exactly where the needle enters the fabric. Take four or five stitches, reposition your fingers, and repeat until the fabric is eased into place and elastic ends overlap (Fig. 8.45).

5. Trim away excess fabric to the stitch. Stitch a ribbon over elastic ends to cover the overlap.

SMOCKING STITCH (A26)

This stitch can be used to stitch and finish a 1/4" (6mm) seam in one step on a lightweight knit as described above (Overcast stitch A21), as a decorative topstitch using two threads through the same needle, and to stitch overlapped seams in lacy fabrics (Fig. 8.46).

Fig. 8.45.
Place work so left side of stitch falls on the fabric and right side swings onto elastic. Pull fabric sideways where needle enters fabric and take four or five stitches. Repeat until fabric is eased into elastic. Trim excess fabric from behind elastic. Sew ribbon over elastic join.

Fig. 8.46.
Smocking stitch.

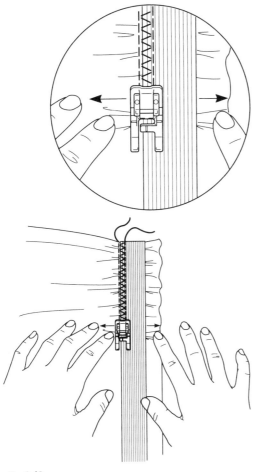

Fig. 8.45.

Fig. 8.46.

Machine Readiness Checklist

Stitch:	smocking (A26)
Length:	2.5 – 3
Width:	4 – 5
Foot:	standard A for fine fabrics, transparent B (appliqué) for heavier fabrics
Needle:	70/10 universal
Thread:	all-purpose or 100% cotton to match fabric
Fabric:	lace or lacy fabric
Accessories:	glue stick

1. On a flat surface, overlap a 5/8" (1.5cm) seam allowance by laying the wrong side of one fabric pattern piece against the right side of another.

Sew-How: *Use the glue stick to hold the seam together before stitching.*

2. Topstitch with the smocking stitch. Because the stitch is open-looking, the lacy fabric shows through the stitch.

3. Carefully trim seam allowances to the stitch on both sides of the overlapped seam.

Fig. 8.47.
The Bridging stitch.

BRIDGING STITCH (A27)

- Edge-to-Edge Piecing
- Fagoting

The bridging stitch resembles a hand stitch that was commonly used on crazy quilts years ago. It is used to piece together straight cut edges of leather, vinyl, Ultraleather™, or Ultrasuede™. It is also used for piecing straight edge lace or ribbon or to join two pieces of fabric or for fagoting (Fig. 8.47).

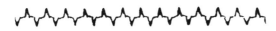

Fig. 8.47.

Bridging Stitch for Edge-to-Edge Piecing

This is a great way to join leather scraps together to make a belt, tote, or handbag. Also join straight edge ribbon and lace.

Machine Readiness Checklist	
Stitch:	bridging (A27)
Length:	1 – 1.5
Width:	6
Foot:	lace joining and edgestitching, transparent B (appliqué). See note

Needle:	appropriate for fabric
Thread:	appropriate for fabric
Fabric suggestions:	leather, suede, straight edge lace or trim, straight seam allowances folded back and pressed
Accessories:	Fray Check

Note: *The lace joining and edgestitching foot was not available at the time of publication, so ask your Viking dealer whether it is available.*

1. With right side up, butt the straight edge of leather, suede, lace, trim, or fabric against the guide in the foot, so one piece is against the right edge of the guide and one piece is against the left edge of the guide. Stitch the length of the join.

2. Pull threads to the wrong side and tie them off. Drop seam sealant on the knot.

3. For extra reinforcement, press a strip of fusible interfacing over the wrong side of the join.

Bridging Stitch for Fagoting

Fagoting is a method of attaching fabric to fabric, or fabric to trim, with a row of stitching. For even spacing, use the raised seam guide.

Machine Readiness Checklist

Stitch:	bridging (A27)
Length:	1 – 1.5
Width:	5 – 6
Foot:	standard A metal zigzag for fine fabrics; transparent B (appliqué) or utility B for medium to heavy fabrics
Needle:	appropriate for fabric
Thread:	all-purpose or 100% cotton
Feed dogs:	up, covered with raised seam guide
Tension:	normal

1. Fold seam allowances of two pieces of fabric to the wrong side and press.

2. With the right side up, snug the fold of each fabric piece against the guide in the plate. The space created between the two pieces of fabric by the raised seam plate keeps the spacing even.

3. Begin stitching. The needle catches a stitch in the fold on the left, then catches a stitch in the fold at the right. Continue stitching until fagoting is complete. Pull threads to the back and tie them off.

Use fagoting in heirloom sewing on a front yoke, down a sleeve, or at a hem.

ELASTIC CASING STITCH (A28)

- Encasing Elastic
- Sew on a Button
- Delicate 1/8" (3mm) Seam
- Shell Tuck

Use the elastic casing stitch (A28) as a way of encasing narrow 1/8" (3mm) wide elastic, sewing on a button, creating a delicate seam, and shell tucking fine woven and knit fabrics.

Encasing Elastic

Machine Readiness Checklist

Stitch:	elastic casing (A28)
Length:	1 – 1.5 as desired
Width:	5 – 6
Foot:	transparent B (appliqué), utility B, or open toe appliqué. See note
Needle:	appropriate for fabric
Thread:	all-purpose or nylon lingerie to match fabric
Tension:	normal
Fabric:	lightweight knit (tricot) or woven (handkerchief linen)
Accessories:	1/8" (3mm) elastic

Note: *The open toe appliqué foot was not available at the time of publication, so ask your Viking dealer whether it is available.*

Sew-How: *This is an easy way to attach elastic at the cuff of a little girl's dress sleeve. To do this, leave the sleeve open, attach the elastic 1" (1.5cm) above the finished edge of the sleeve, then seam the sleeve, catching elastic ends in the seam. The cuff shirrs in with a ruffle below the elastic.*

---

1. With the sole off the foot shank, thread elastic up and over the bar between the toes of the foot, and through the needle hole, so the elastic is under the heel of the foot.

2. Snap foot in place. On the wrong side of the fabric, encase elastic with the stitch, without stitching through the elastic.

Sew-How: *If you pull the elastic slightly while sewing, the fabric will shirr.*

3. Slide stitches down elastic for desired fullness. Stitch seam, catching elastic ends in the seam.

Sew on a Button with the Elastic Casing Stitch

Use this stitch instead of the zigzag to sew on a button. It takes three stitches on the left and three stitches on the right, thus automatically locking off the stitches in each hole of the button. (See Fig. 9.18.)

Delicate 1/8" (3mm) Seam

For a delicate 1/8" (3mm) seam in nylon tricot or handkerchief linen, try this:

Machine Readiness Checklist

Stitch:	elastic casing (A28)
Length:	0.5
Width:	5 – 6
Foot:	standard A metal zigzag or Teflon H
Needle:	70/10 universal
Thread:	100% cotton or nylon lingerie
Tension:	normal
Fabric:	nylon tricot, handkerchief linen

With right sides together, place seam allowance halfway under the presser foot. Stitch the seam so half of the stitch forms on the fabric, and the other half falls off the raw edges at the right.

Sew-How: *This is a very fine seam, so be sure the raw edges are cut straight and even. If they aren't, you may end up with a hole in your seam after sewing.*

Shell Tuck with the Elastic Casing Stitch

Shell tuck the hem edge of a slip, nightgown, or cuff.

Machine Readiness Checklist

Stitch:	elastic casing (A28)
Length:	1.5
Width:	5 – 6
Foot:	standard A metal zigzag or Teflon H
Needle:	70/10 universal
Thread:	all-purpose
Tension:	top, loosened slightly; bobbin, normal
Fabric:	nylon tricot, handkerchief linen, batiste, organdy

1. Fold and press hem up at least 1/2" (1.3cm).

2. With the right side up, place the fold halfway under the foot and stitch. Each time the needle zigs off the edge then zags back onto the fabric, a delicate shell is made.

3. Trim hem allowance to the stitch.

Fig. 8.48.
Varying widths and
lengths of the knit blind
hem stitch.

Fig. 8.49.
Place pins perpendicular
to and 1/4" (6mm) from
hem edge.

KNIT BLIND HEM STITCH (A29)

- Blind Hemming
- Decorative Edge Finish

Blind Hemming

The knit blind hem stitch is designed for hemming knit fabrics. Notice the narrow zigzag stitches between the wider ones (Fig. 8.48). This enables the stitch to stretch with the fabric, so you are less likely to catch your heel in a knit hemline and rip it out.

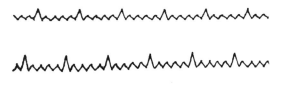

Fig. 8.48.

Machine Readiness Checklist

Stitch:	knit blind hem (A29)
Length:	0.7 – 1
Width:	2.5 – 3
Foot:	blind hem D
Needle:	70/10-11 universal
Thread:	all-purpose
Tension:	top, loosened; bobbin, normal
Fabric:	knit jersey, double knit, velour or stretch terry cloth

1. Measure hem, and cut raw hem edge so it is even. Pin hem up desired amount, placing pins perpendicular to and 1/4" (6mm) from hem edge (Fig. 8.49).

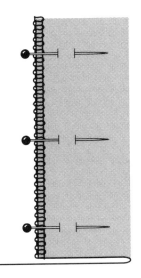

Fig. 8.49.

Sew-How: *Because the knit blind hem stitch is made of zigzag stitches, it is not necessary to overcast the raw hem edge. However, finish the hem edge of a woven using the three-step zigzag or flatlock stitch (see Figs. 8.35, 8.44).*

2. With gentle steam and a press cloth, press hem without pressing over pins.

3. Fold hem allowance to the outside, folding the hem back to where the pins enter the fabric. Place hem under foot so the body of the garment is to the left, and the 1/4" (6mm) extension is to the right of the needle.

Sew-How: *The fabric is guided the same for both elastic (A29) and woven blind hems (A30) (Fig. 8.50).*

Fig. 8.50.
Fold hem back to where
the pins enter the fabric.
Needle stitches on
extension, then takes a
small bite into the fold.

Fig. 8.51.
Corded knit blind hem
stitch as an edge finish.

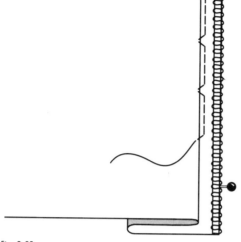

Fig. 8.50.

Fig. 8.51.

4. Begin stitching so the needle takes a few stitches on the extension, then a small bite into the fold, picking up a thread or two at the left. Remove pins before stitching over them. The less fabric the needle catches, the more invisible the hem, so use the narrowest width possible and loosen the upper tension. On lightweight fabrics, loosen the bobbin tension, too.

5. Press hem from the right side with steam and a press cloth.

Although it's not necessary, the finer the thread used when hemming, the more invisible the results. I like #50 weight cotton embroidery thread (see Sources of Supply).

Decorative Edge Finish

The knit blind hem stitch can also be used on a shorter stitch length and a wider width to create a stitch that looks like an eyelash or hand buttonhole stitch. Use it to topstitch an appliqué, create eyelashes on a puppet or toy (see Chapter 6), or cord the stitch for a two-toned decorative effect (Fig. 8.51).

Machine Readiness Checklist

Stitch:	knit blind hem (A29)
Length:	0.3 – 0.5
Width:	5
Foot:	transparent B (appliqué) or utility B
Feed dogs:	up
Needle:	70/10 or 80/12 universal
Thread:	all-purpose or machine embroidery (for a faster fill-in, use two threads through the same needle)
Tension:	top, loosened slightly; bobbin, normal
Accessories:	#5 or #8 pearl cotton

Fold and press a narrow 1/2" (1.3cm) hem. Place fold under the foot so the stitches on the right fall just off the edge of the fold.

Sew-How: *If you are using the knit blind hem stitch to appliqué, guide the straight edge of the stitch along the edge of the appliqué, so the stitches on the left cover the raw edge. For an edge finish, fold under at least a 1/2" (1.3cm) hem and press. Guide cord under the left side of the foot, and place the fabric under the foot so the stitches zigzag off the fold on the right.*

WOVEN BLIND HEM STITCH (A30)

- Blind Hemming
- Couched Saddle Stitch
- Shell Tuck and Corded Shell Tuck

Blind Hemming

The woven blind hem stitch (A30), sometimes referred to as the blind hem stitch, works like the elastic blind hem stitch (A29), but is designed for use on woven fabrics. The straight stitches between the zigzags make the woven blind hem stitch more stable and suitable for wovens. Set your machine, and blind hem your woven fabrics as described above for the knit blind hem (A29).

Sew-How: *Rather than using hem tape to finish the hem edge of a woven fabric, overcast the hem edge with the three-step zigzag (A19 or 20) or the flatlock stitch (A25). It saves time, minimizes bulk, and it's one less thing you need to find to match your fabric.*

Couched Saddle Stitch

This topstitching technique is used commonly on ready-to-wear coats and suits and is easy to duplicate.

Machine Readiness Checklist	
Stitch:	woven blind hem (A30)
Length:	1 – 1.5
Width:	1 – 2
Foot:	narrow braiding, hemmer, or transparent B (appliqué)
Feed dogs:	up
Needle:	80/12 universal
Needle position:	center
Thread:	nylon monofilament
Fabric:	wool coating, fleece, or suiting
Tension:	normal
Accessories:	#3, #5 pearl cotton, or six strand embroidery floss

Clip pearl cotton or floss into the braiding foot or hemmer or under the transparent B (appliqué) foot and topstitch. The straight stitches bury themselves in the fabric next to the floss, while the zigzag creates an indentation so each stitch looks 1/4" (6mm) long (Fig. 8.52).

Shell Tuck and Corded Shell Tuck

Shell tuck the edge of a half slip, skirt lining, neck edge, facing, or trim with the blind hem stitch.

Fig. 8.52.
Couched saddle stitch.

Fig. 8.53.
To shell tuck, place folded edge under foot with bulk to the right.

Fig. 8.52.

Machine Readiness Checklist

Stitch:	woven blind hem (A30)
Length:	1.5 – 2
Width:	4 – 6
Foot:	standard A metal zigzag for lightweight fabrics; transparent B (appliqué) for medium to heavy fabrics
Needle:	appropriate for the fabric
Thread:	all-purpose or cotton embroidery
Feed dogs:	up
Fabric:	nylon tricot, cotton knits, lining fabrics
Tension:	top, tightened slightly; bobbin, normal
Accessories:	#3 or #5 pearl cotton

900 Series and 1100 Notes:

Stitching a shell tuck with the bulk of the fabric to the right can be awkward. Instead, use the reverse blind hem stitch, or push the side-to-side mirror image button and guide the fabric so the bulk is to the left.

1. Turn up a hem and press. **Note:** If shell tucking a ribbing edge, do not press over folded edge because it may distort the ribbing.

2. Place folded edge under the foot so the bulk of the fabric is to the right. Place fold halfway under the foot and stitch (Fig. 8.53). **Note:** To prevent skipped stitches, the needle must swing completely off the folded edge.

To cord the shell tuck, lay a strand of pearl cotton at the fold and stitch. Again, the needle must swing off the fabric and over the cord.

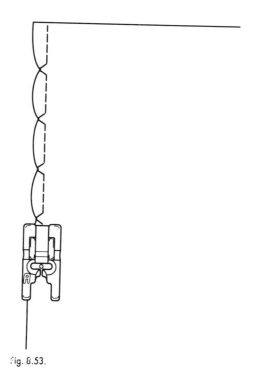

Fig. 8.53.

3. You can trim the excess fabric to the stitch; however, the edge may curl on a single knit. To avoid this, run a row or two of decorative stitching or a twin needle tuck a presser-foot width from the shell tuck; then trim excess fabric to the stitch.

AUTOMATIC BUTTON SEWING (A31)

Why is there an automatic button sewing function on the Viking 1100, when all you need is a simple zigzag stitch to sew a button on by machine? To save time. The function can be stored in one of the memories, so it stitches the same number of times between the holes, and automatically ties off the stitch for each button.

Machine Readiness Checklist	
Stitch:	automatic button sewing (A31)
Length:	0
Width:	4 or adjust for the button
Foot:	none—leave foot shank on the machine
Needle:	80/12 universal
Thread:	all-purpose
Pressure:	normal
Feed dogs:	down
Accessories:	button reed for heavy fabrics, glue stick or transparent tape

1. Glue stick or tape button in place.

2. Place fabric and button under the needle, and lower the foot shank down on the button. Turn the flywheel a couple of times by hand, and adjust the width so the needle clears the holes in the button as needed. Zigzag button on. Push the reverse button to lock stitches. Store the function in memory (see Operating Manual).

Sew-How: *To use the button reed, take two stitches to anchor button, raise the foot shank, then insert reed under the button and between the fabric. Lower foot shank and sew (see Fig. 9.18).*

MACHINE QUILTING STITCHES (A32, 33)

Rather than straight quilting, quilt a piece of fabric using the quilting scallop (A32) or quilting wave (A33).

Machine Readiness Checklist	
Stitch:	machine quilting (A32, 33)
Length:	3
Width:	6
Foot:	dual feeder
Needle:	90/14 stretch
Thread:	100% cotton sewing for cotton fabric; all-purpose for cotton/poly blends
Accessories:	water-erasable marker, edge guide

1. Pin or baste quilt sandwich together (top fabric, batting, backing fabric). Draw a line the width of the quilt across the grain. This is where you will start the machine quilting at the top of the quilt.

2. Attach the edge guide behind the presser bar and adjust it out the desired distance, so the rows of quilting will be evenly spaced.

3. Starting from the center of the line marked in Step 1, machine quilt the length of the fabric. Move the quilt to the right, and guide the edge guide over the first row of quilting. Repeat row after row of machine quilting until half of the project is stitched.

4. Turn your project around and machine quilt as before, starting from the center, working out to the other side.

ARCH STITCH (A34)

The arch stitch can be used as a machine quilting stitch as described above for A32 and A33. It can also be used as a decorative topstitch or as a shell tuck on the hem edge of a skirt lining or half slip.

Shell Tuck with the Arch Stitch (A34)

Machine Readiness Checklist	
Stitch:	arch (A34)
Length:	0.7
Width:	6
Foot:	standard A metal zigzag or buttonhole C
Needle:	70/10 universal
Thread:	all-purpose
Fabric:	nylon tricot, lining fabrics, sheer or lightweight woven
Accessories:	#5 pearl cotton

1. Fold at least a 1/2" (1.3cm) hem and press.

2. Place the fabric under the foot, right side up, and guide it so the stitches on the right fall off the folded edge.

3. To cord the edge, use the buttonhole C foot and guide the pearl cotton under the right groove of the foot.

FEATHER STITCH (A35)

Like the bridging stitch (A27), the feather stitch is similar to the hand feather stitch used to piece crazy quilts. Use it as a decorative topstitch on children's clothes, gifts, and table linens. The feather stitch is also beautiful when stitched with pearl cotton. This is called reverse embroidery because the pearl cotton or embroidery floss is put in the bobbin, and the fabric is decorated by sewing upside-down.

Reverse Embroidery with the Feather Stitch

Machine Readiness Checklist	
Stitch:	feather (A35) also try A27, A32, A33, A34, or A26
Length:	2.5 – 4
Width:	6
Foot:	transparent B (appliqué)
Needle:	80/12 universal or what is appropriate for the fabric
Thread:	top, all-purpose to match pearl cotton; bobbin, pearl cotton
Tension:	tighten upper tension slightly; bypass bobbin tension
Fabric:	medium-weight knit or woven
Accessories:	water-erasable marker

1. Wind a bobbin with pearl cotton. Tie a loop around the bobbin spindle, and hold the pearl cotton in your lap. Put the bobbin on the bobbin winder and push the foot control to slowly wind the bobbin. Guide the pearl cotton evenly on the bobbin by hand.

Fig. 8.54.
Reverse embroidery with
the feather stitch.

900 Series and 1100 Notes:

For the 900 series Vikings, thread the bobbin case as for all-purpose thread, and slightly loosen the tension screw on the bobbin case by turning the screw counterclockwise. The pearl cotton should pull through the tension smoothly with a slight drag on it. For the Viking 1100, thread bobbin case by bypassing the tension and threading the pearl cotton up through the slot in the top of the bobbin case. Put bobbin case in the race as normal, then bring bobbin thread up by turning the flywheel one complete turn by hand.

2. Test sew on a scrap and adjust the top tension so the pearl cotton does not loop. Mark where you want to sew on the wrong side of the fabric, and guide by the line. Turn your work over. Aren't the results beautiful (Fig. 8.54)? This is an easy way to create a trim or braid.

Fig. 8.54.

HEIRLOOM APPLIQUÉ STITCH (A36)

- Hand Appliqué
- Fine Seam and Overcast
- Delicate Edge Finish

This simple stitch can be used in a variety of ways. First, it can be used to simulate a hand appliqué stitch. Set it on the mirror image function, and it becomes a fine seam and overcast, perfect for seaming batiste, organdy, organza, handkerchief linen, nylon tricot, and lining fabrics. Use it as a delicate edge finish on lightweight wovens and knits.

Hand Appliqué with the Heirloom Appliqué Stitch (A36)

Machine Readiness Checklist

Stitch:	heirloom appliqué (A36)
Length:	1.5 – 2
Width:	2
Foot:	standard A metal zigzag
Needle:	70/10 universal
Thread:	100% cotton machine embroidery to match base fabric
Tension:	top, loosen slightly; bobbin, normal
Fabric:	lightweight woven
Accessories:	glue stick

1. Cut out appliqué shape, adding 1/4" (6mm) seam allowances.

2. Turn appliqué seam allowance to the wrong side and press.

3. Glue-stick the appliqué to the base fabric.

Sew-How: *Apply the glue stick to the appliqué when the fabric is warm for a better stick.*

---

4. Guide your work so the straight part of the stitch falls just off the folded edge of the appliqué. Stitch around appliqué, matching stitches at the beginning and end. Pull threads to the back and tie them off.

Sew-How: *For a shadow appliqué, cut appliqué the exact size needed. Glue-stick appliqué to the base fabric. Lay a piece of sheer fabric over appliqué, and stitch around appliqué so the stitch is along the raw edge. The fabric will not ravel because the sheer fabric overlays the appliqué. The overlay also softens the appliqué color.*

Fine Seam and Overcast with the Heirloom Appliqué Stitch

Machine Readiness Checklist

Stitch:	heirloom appliqué (A36)
Length:	2
Width	2
Foot:	standard A metal zigzag
Needle:	70/10 universal
Thread:	100% cotton sewing
Tension:	top, loosened slightly; bobbin, normal
Fabric:	organza, organdy, batiste, tricot, handker-chief linen

1. Cut pattern pieces out with a 5/8" (1.5cm) seam allowance.

2. Push the side-to-side mirror image button, so the straight part of the stitch is on the left. Place right sides together, and stitch the seam at the 5/8" (1.5cm) seam line. Trim away seam allowance to the stitch.

A Delicate Edge Finish with the Heirloom Appliqué Stitch

Machine Readiness Checklist

Stitch:	heirloom appliqué (A36)
Length:	1.5 – 2
Width:	2
Foot:	buttonhole C
Needle:	70/10 universal
Thread:	100% cotton machine embroidery
Tension:	top, loosened slightly; bobbin, normal
Fabric:	shirt-weight cotton, handkerchief linen

1. Fold and press a narrow 1/2" (1.3cm) hem and press. (This technique can also be used at the edge of a collar, cuff, or tuck.)

2. Place the fold under the buttonhole C foot so the fold is against the inside of the right toe. The needle will take one stitch on the fabric and a couple of stitches over the fold to create a delicate thread chain.

3. Trim away hem allowance to the stitch if this technique was used at a hem edge.

Other Applications: Apply a piece of straight edge lace using the heirloom appliqué stitch, guiding the straight part of the stitch along the straight edge of the lace.

Hem a napkin, placemat, or collar using the wing needle, fine thread, and the heirloom appliqué stitch. Fold and press hem. Topstitch so the straight part of the stitch is parallel to the hem edge. Trim excess hem allowance to the stitch.

PROGRAMMED BARTACK (A37)

Use the programmed bartack to reinforce pocket corners, the bottom of fly front zippers, and plackets or to tack drapery pleats or attach belt loops.

Machine Readiness Checklist	
Stitch:	programmed bartack (A37)
Length:	2
Width:	1.5
Foot:	transparent (B) appliqué
Needle:	appropriate for the fabric
Thread:	all-purpose

Place pocket corner or area in need of reinforcement under the foot and sew. The stitch sews vertical straight stitches, then overcasts with a row of zigzag stitches.

AUTOMATIC MENDING AND DARNING (A38,39,40)

The automatic darning stitch (A38) stitches the length of the tear and changes direction when you push the reverse button. It then takes twelve passes up and down over the hole.

The automatic mending stitch (A39) takes a few tiny stitches side to side and is designed to repair a tear. For a ravelly tear, shorten the stitch to 1.5.

The automatic mend and darn stitch (A40) combines the two functions. First it mends with the tiny stitches from side to side. Then it darns the length of the tear with an up and down darning stitch and stops after twelve passes.

Sew-How: *For a "pucker-proof" mend or darn, stretch your work in a hoop before sewing.*

BUTTONHOLES (A41 – 49)

- Automatic Buttonholes (A42)
- Corded Buttonholes
- Specialty Buttonholes (A41-49)

Today's Vikings and their buttonhole feet make sewing buttonholes easier than ever. In this section, we will look at the basic automatic bartack buttonhole, a corded buttonhole, and the specialty buttonholes available on the 900 series and 1100 Vikings (see Fig. 8.1, cassette A).

Sew-How: *The buttonhole C foot has three marks on the left toe. Most patterns that recommend horizontal buttonholes start them 1/2" (1.3cm) from the finished edge. Line the center mark on the C foot with the finished edge of the fabric, and the buttonholes will start 1/2" (1.3cm) from the finished edge.*

Use the lines on the left toe to make a buttonhole to fit your button. Place button on top of the foot so the edge of the button lines up with the front of the needle hole in the foot. Stitch the buttonhole so the first column of stitches reaches the mark in the foot, just beyond where the other edge of the button falls (see Fig. 9.8).

Fig. 8.55.
Corded buttonhole.

Automatic Buttonholes (A42)

Most Vikings built in the last 15 years make an automatic bartack buttonhole—made in one, two, or four steps without having to turn the fabric. Each model has its own method. Check your Operating Manual.

Corded Buttonholes

Corded buttonholes look better and wear longer than ordinary buttonholes. Use them on coats, suits, and areas that receive a lot of stress and wear.

1. Set your Viking to make a bartack buttonhole (A41 or 42).

2. Select a pearl cotton, embroidery floss, or multiple strand of thread to match the fabric and thread. Place the cord, over the prong on the back of the buttonhole C foot and under the grooves, so the loop is at the stress point of the buttonhole.

3. Stitch the buttonhole making sure the zigzag stitches cover the cord but don't pierce it. Do not pull on cord while making the buttonhole because the cord moves with each stitch.

900 Series and 1100 Notes:

Before making the second bartack on the 900 series and Viking 1100, lift the foot and pull the pearl cotton loop up to the first bartack. Cross pearl cotton ends over one another at the other end of the buttonhole, and stitch the second bartack. Clip cord off at the fabric. The reinforced bartack stitches over the cord so it won't pull out when the buttonhole is used.

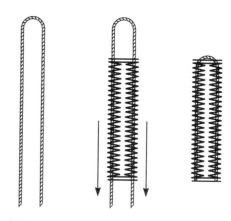

Fig. 8.55.

4. For other Viking models, pull the loop to the bartack. Then pull free ends of the cord to the back or between the facing and fashion fabric to tie them off (Fig. 8.55).

Sew-How: *To cut buttonholes open, use the back of your ripper to score the fabric between the two rows of stitching (Fig. 8.56). This opens the cutting space. Then use a buttonhole cutter and block to cut the buttonhole open. If you don't have a buttonhole cutter, use the ripper, sometimes called a buttonhole knife, to cut the buttonhole open. Put the point of the ripper in the middle of the buttonhole, then bring it up through the fabric in front of the bartack as if it were a pin (Fig. 8.57). Cut. Repeat for the other end of the buttonhole, cutting from the center out. This way you don't inadvertently cut through the bartack. Trim out any fraying threads; then put a little Fray-Check or seam sealant on the inside of the buttonhole.*

Fig. 8.56.
Use the back of your ripper to score the cutting space and separate the two sides of the buttonhole.

Fig. 8.57.
Use a ripper to cut the buttonhole open.

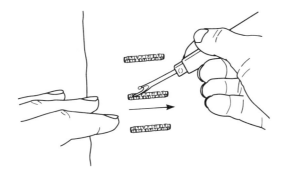

Fig. 8.56.

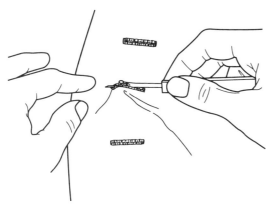

Fig. 8.57.

Specialty Buttonholes

The bartack buttonhole with added cutting space (A41) is designed for use on heavy tailored garments. The added cutting space enables you to cut it open without cutting the threads. Cord this buttonhole for strength.

The bartack buttonhole (A42) is designed for most light- and medium-weight fabrics. Cord this buttonhole for strength.

The European or lapel buttonhole (A43) is designed for men's lapels or a Chanel-type jacket. It can be corded for extra strength and for a raised appearance. To cord it, follow the instructions above for cording a buttonhole (Fig. 8.55), but do not cross the ends of the cord before making the tapered bartack at the

beginning of the buttonhole. Simply stitch the second bartack and clip cord off close to the fabric.

The round end buttonhole (A44) is designed for light blouse-weight fabrics and children's clothing. Although it can be corded, the cord must be clipped off close to the fabric at both bartacks.

The heavy reinforced buttonhole (A45) is the strongest utility buttonhole available on the Viking 1100. It is recommended for use on woven work clothes or on heavy, stabilized knits.

The medium reinforced stretch buttonhole (A46) is recommended for light- and medium-weight knits and wovens. The Trimotion stitch allows the buttonhole to stretch, and there is less chance that the buttonhole will "fish mouth" out of shape on a knit. Cord it as described above for corded buttonholes (see Fig. 8.55). Do not use the buttonhole sensor (see Fig 9.9) with this buttonhole.

The heirloom buttonhole (A47) is recommended for use on fine fabrics such as batiste, organza, and handkerchief linen. Use it on your heirloom or French hand-sewn projects.

Choose between the **square-end (A48)** and the **tapered-end (A49) keyhole buttonholes.** Both are recommended for use on tailored jackets, coats, and menswear.

The leather buttonhole (A2) comes up on the Program Display when you select "leather" and "buttonhole" on the Sewing Advisor. It is a straight-stitch box which is sewn and cut open and used on leather, Ultrasuede™, or Ultraleather™. Do not use the buttonhole sensor (see Fig. 9.9) with this buttonhole.

CASSETTES B AND C: LETTERS AND NUMBERS

The Viking 990 and 1100 have interchangeable cassettes with block and script letters and numbers. See your Operating Manual on programming these stitches shown in Fig. 8.1, cassettes B and C.

The Viking 1100 can also correct, insert, or remove letters from a program. See page 85 in your 1100 Operating Manual for specific details.

Rather than tell how to program letters and numbers, I will give you some ideas on where to use lettering.

1. Nancy Zieman, host of the popular TV program "Sewing with Nancy" embroiders the pattern number in the hem of the garment. That way, if someone asks what pattern number it is, she takes a quick peek and tells her.

2. Stitch the name and birth date of your baby on a ribbon, and stitch it in the hem of the christening gown. This ribbon can be the "something old" or "something blue" when the child grows up and marries, and can be stitched in the hem of the bride's wedding gown. I made one for my son and stitched it in the waistband of his christening suit, so when the time comes, I hope his bride will want it stitched into the hem of her gown.

3. Stitch name tags for children's birthday parties or name cards at an adult's tea or dinner party.

4. Make your own designer labels, or label clothing that will be sent to the cleaner's, laundry, or summer camp.

5. Incorporate lettering into a decorative border sewn at a hem, pocket, placket, waistband, or the length of suspenders.

Sew-How: *The Viking 1100 can store up to 63 stitches per program, and the stitches from one cassette can be combined with letters and numbers from another cassette on the same program. This means you can spell out a name, then run a couple of decorative stitches on the same program. On both the 990 and 1100, the decorative stitches found on the lettering cassettes are designed specifically for use with the lettering.*

CASSETTE D: DECORATIVE STITCHES

- Cross Stitches (D1, 2 3)
- Mock Smocking Stitch (D4)
- Hemstitches (D5, 6, 7, 9; A8, 9, 10)
- Hemstitches (D5, 6, 7, 9; A8, 9, 10)
- Honeycomb (D8)
- Open Decorative Stitches (D10 – 20)
- Closed (Satin) Decorative Stitches (D21 – 25)
- Satin Edge Stitches (D26 – 30)
- Pictograms (D31 – 49)

There are two types of decorative stitches—closed and open. Closed means the stitches are close together and are variations on the satin stitch. Examples are the domino (D21), heart (D24), ball (D23), and the satin edge stitches (D26 – D30) (Fig. 8.58). On the Viking 1100, many of the closed satin stitches can be elongated up to five times their length without loosing the stitch density.

Fig. 8.58.
Closed (satin) decorative
stitches; domino (D21),
heart (D24), and ball
(D23).

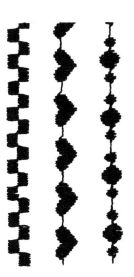

Fig. 8.58.

The beauty of open decorative stitches is seeing the stitch and the fabric under it. Examples are stitches D10 – D20.

In this section we will take a closer look at the decorative stitches on cassette D and their applications. Again, the Viking 1100 has the greatest number of stitches in the line; you should find some of them on your model. Compare and make stitch samples for your notebook. Also look in Part II, The World of Sewing, for even more applications for your decorative stitches.

CROSS STITCHES (D1,2,3)

These cross stitches emulate hand cross stitches and can be programmed to create a beautiful border.

Use stitch D3 as a topstitch over gathers to create a hand-smocked effect. See the Viking 1100 **Pictograms and Sew Much More**, page 39, for additional stitch applications.

MOCK SMOCKING STITCH (D4)

Use this stitch with the wing needle and stitch row after row on a lightweight woven, guiding rows a presser foot width

away to create the look of smocking. This stitch is featured on the Swedish blouse on page 40 in the Viking 1100 **Pictograms and Sew Much More** book.

Machine Readiness Checklist	
Stitch:	mock smocking (D4)
Length:	2
Width:	6
Foot:	transparent B (appliqué)
Needle:	wing
Thread:	rayon embroidery to match fabric
Tension:	top, normal or tighten slightly for more puckering; bobbin, normal
Fabric:	lightweight woven cotton broadcloth or batiste
Accessories:	water-erasable or vanishing marker

Sew-How: *If you are smocking an area such as a cuff, collar, or yoke, smock the fabric first, then cut out the pattern piece.*

1. Draw a line the length of the fabric following the straight of grain using the water-erasable or vanishing marker.

2. Sew the first row of smocking, centering the presser foot over the line. Sew successive rows next to each other, a presser foot width apart.

3. Cut out pattern piece after smocking the fabric.

HEMSTITCHES (D5,6,7,9; A8,9,10)

Hemstitches should not be confused with blind hem stitches because they look like a row of holes found at hems of heirloom linen napkins, table linens, linen finger tip and hand towels. Hemstitching can also be used as a lace insertion on French hand-sewn projects.

The holes are the predominant feature of these stitches because a wing needle and fine thread are used. The wing needle, which has wings on either side, pokes a large hole in the fabric. The stitch takes a few passes in and out of the same hole, which binds the hole open so holes will not close after the fabric is cleaned or laundered. The fine thread is used so it will not fill up the holes with each stitch.

Although the Viking 1100 has the stitches mentioned above preprogrammed on a 3 – 6 stitch width, I prefer a 2 – 3 stitch width. Make stitch samples for your notebook and write your preferred width setting for each stitch.

Stitch D5 is known as the Turkish hemstitch, D6 as the Point de Paris, D7 as the Entredeaux or Venetian hemstitch and emulates purchased Entredeaux used for lace insertion. D9 is the daisy and looks lovely when stitched between rows of tucks or rows of lace insertion.

Sew-How: *The reinforced straight stitch (A8,9,10) can be used for lace insertion or as a hem finish. Use the wing needle, darning thread, and set the length at 4 – 5.*

Machine Readiness Checklist

Stitch:	one of the hemstitches (D4,5,6,7,9; A8,9,10)
Length:	2.5 – 4.5
Recommended width:	2 – 3
Foot:	standard A metal zigzag or Teflon H
Needle:	wing
Thread:	100% cotton size #70 or #120 darning or hemstitching thread, top and bobbin
Tension:	top, loosened slightly; bobbin, normal
Fabric:	lightweight woven cotton or linen

1. To stitch a row of hemstitching between two rows of tucks, stitch tucks first so they are a presser foot width apart (see Fig. 8.11). Also see the Viking 1100 **Pictograms and Sew Much More** pages 43 – 49, for alternate tucking techniques.

2. On a single layer of fabric, stitch a row of hemstitching following the lengthwise grain.

Sew-How: *Hemstitching also looks well sewn on the bias (Fig. 8.59).*

---

3. To sew a hem, fold hem up desired depth and press. Topstitch from the right side using one of the hemstitches, so the foot rests, and stitch sews, on a double layer of fabric. Trim excess hem allowance to the stitch.

Fig. 8.59.
Hemstitches.

Fig. 8.60.
Honeycomb stitches.

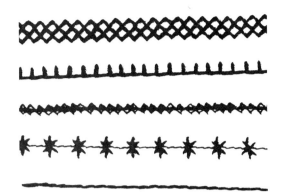

Fig. 8.59.

Sew-How: *The daisy (D9) can be sewn using a size 80/12 universal needle, and regular sewing or rayon embroidery thread as a decorative stitch.*

LACE INSERTION WITH THE VENETIAN, POINT DE PARIS, OR TURKISH HEMSTITCHES (D5,6,7)

1. Set your machine as described above. Using a straight edge lace, pin or baste lace on the right side of the fabric where desired. Stitch, guiding the straight edge of the lace. Repeat for the other side.

2. Carefully trim away fabric under lace up to the stitch.

Sew-How: *The Point de Paris (D6) can also be used to appliqué lace or to stitch a piece of straight edge lace to the hem edge of a ruffle. To do this, guide the straight part of the stitch along the straight edge of the lace. Trim excess hem allowance to the stitch.*

HONEYCOMB (D8)

The honeycomb stitch (Fig. 8.60) looks very much like the smocking stitch (A26, see Fig. 8.46) and is used in the same ways. It can also be used with the wing needle. However, because the needle stitches in each hole only once, a regular weight sewing thread or rayon embroidery thread can be used.

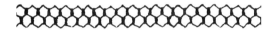

Fig. 8.60.

Sew-How: *The holes in this stitch are not bound open by the stitch, so they may close up a bit once the fabric is cleaned or laundered.*

OPEN DECORATIVE STITCHES (D10 - 20)

The beauty of open decorative stitches is in looking at the stitch and the fabric through it. The open decorative stitches (D10 - 20) can be used alone, in combination with each other, or used with the Pictograms. Make a stitch sampler for your notebook using one or all of these combinations. For more ideas, see pages 1 and 2 in the **Pictograms and Sew Much More** book for your Viking 1100.

CLOSED (SATIN) DECORATIVE STITCHES (D21 – 25)

Closed decorative stitches look like variations on the satin stitch. Use them to topstitch over ribbon or cord. Use them with the 7-hole cording foot to create unique trims and braids (see Fig. 9.27).

In Part II, the closed satin stitches are referred to as the domino (D21), ribbon (D22), ball (D23), heart (D24), and eyelet buttonhole stitch (D25).

Sew-How: *The center part of the eyelet buttonhole stitch can be trimmed out, and a narrow ribbon threaded through the stitch like an eyelet.*

SATIN EDGE STITCHES (D26 – 30)

Use the satin edge stitches to finish the edge of a collar, cuff, or ruffle.

Machine Readiness Checklist	
Stitch:	satin edge stitches (D26,27,28,30)
Length:	0.3 for D26, 27, 30; 3 for D28
Width:	6
Foot:	standard A metal zigzag or Teflon H
Needle:	90/14 stretch
Thread:	rayon embroidery
Tension:	top, loosened slightly; bobbin, normal
Fabric:	light- to medium-weight cotton or linen
Accessories:	tear-away stabilizer

1. Cut out collar or cuff, leaving on the seam allowance. Interface the upper collar or upper cuff piece following the pattern instructions.

2. Place collar or cuff pieces, WRONG sides together. If this is a cuff, turn the seam allowance under on the under-cuff, which will be attached to the sleeve, and press.

3. Begin satin edge stitching on the 5/8" (1.5cm) seam allowance. Push the STOP or finishing button when you get close to the corner so the stitch stops at the end of the cycle before turning the corner. Pivot and finish stitching.

4. Trim away excess seam allowance up to the stitch.

Sew-How: *You can also use this technique on a single layer of fabric by placing a piece of tear-away stabilizer under the fabric. Remove the tear-away, then trim excess seam allowance to the stitch.*

Straight Edge Scallop (D29)

This satin edge stitch (Fig. 8.61) looks best on an edge when used in the side-to-side mirror image setting and when sewn on a folded edge. Set your machine as described above, with the side-to-side mirror image. Lengthen the stitch slightly for soft knits.

Fold a hem edge or tuck. Stitch so the stitches on the right fall just off the fold. Notice how it creates a gentle scallop from a straight edge. Use this delicate finish on the hem edge of a nightgown, bridal tulle, or lightweight cottons and linens. Also use it as an appliqué stitch.

Fig. 8.61.
Straight edge scallop on
a folded edge.

Fig. 8.61.

PICTOGRAMS (D31 – 49)

To make a Pictogram, use one or combine a number of the Satin Elements (D31 – 49) available on the D cassette for the Viking 1100, and the number 2 cassette for the Viking 990. On the 1100 Viking, many of the Satin Elements can be elongated to five times their original length without losing the stitch density.

Use the Satin Elements to create Pictogram flowers, people, animals, or geometric motifs. For more Pictogram ideas, see the **Pictograms and Sew Much More** book for your Viking 1100. Also see the Pictogram Idea Books for the Viking 990 and **Know Your Viking** by Jackie Dodson with Jan Saunders (Chilton, 1988).

FIX (A,B,C,D50)

At the end of each Viking 1100 cassette, there is a FIX function button. It's used for programming decorative stitches and, unlike the STOP function, which stops sewing the end of a stitch or program, the FIX function takes a few locking stitches at the end of a stitch or program, then continues on, pausing between the stitches. This function is used primarily for creating two-color embroidery designs (see Viking's **Pictograms and Sew Much More** sewing book).

ENCYCLOPEDIA OF PRESSER FEET

Today's top-of-the line 900 and 1100 series Vikings come with between ten and thirteen standard presser feet and accessories. Why so many? To help you sew better. But which one is used for what purpose? This encyclopedia suggests ways to use each foot in both practical and decorative applications. But first, you need to understand the anatomy of the presser foot.

There are two parts to a presser foot—the shank and the foot or sole. The shank holds the foot in place and provides a hinge so the foot can tip on and off varying thicknesses of fabric. Presser feet for older Vikings are fixed to the foot. Presser feet on newer models snap on and off for easy changing.

The purpose of a presser foot is to hold the fabric firmly against the feed dogs, aid in proper stitch formation, and protect your fingers from the needle. Presser feet are also designed for different uses so let's take a closer look at one.

The underside of the foot has a toe and heel (Fig. 9.1). The underside is the most important part because it helps guide the fabric and stitches so they feed smoothly over the feed dogs. The toe or toes are on the front of the foot in front of the needle. The heel is on the back of the foot behind the needle. Let me show you how important the presser foot can be.

Fig. 9.1.
Underside toe and heel
of presser foot.

Fig. 9.2.
Underside of button
sewing foot.

Fig. 9.3.
Underside of the utility
B foot with wide
channel at the heel.

Fig. 9.1.

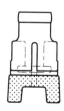

Fig. 9.2.

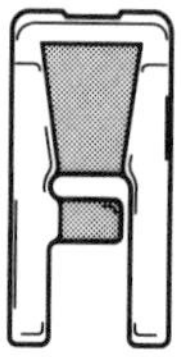

Fig. 9.3.

Fig. 9.4.
Standard A metal
zigzag foot with
ooth, flat underside.

When I taught machine embroidery, I showed the class a satin stitch—a wide zigzag stitch sewn very close together. When finished, satin stitching should look like a narrow strand of satin ribbon and have a smooth, rounded appearance, like the stitches you see on monogrammed towels.

Everyone tried it. But one of the students used her button sewing foot and wondered why the fabric wouldn't move. Look at the underside (Fig. 9.2). Notice the flat bottom, short toes and the rubber sleeve or grip put there so the button will not slip out. You can imagine why this woman was having some difficulty—the foot could not move over the satin stitches.

The proper foot to use is the utility B or transparent B (appliqué) foot (Fig. 9.3). The underside has a wide channel behind the needle which allows the stitches to form and the fabric to move smoothly under it without flattening the stitches into the fabric. Before we get ahead of ourselves, let's take a look at the six best and most common Viking feet—the standard A metal zigzag, utility B, transparent B (appliqué), buttonhole C, blind hem D, and zipper E.

STANDARD ACCESSORIES: THE SIX BEST FEET

- Standard A Metal Zigzag
- Utility B
- Transparent B (Appliqué)

- Zipper E
- Buttonhole C
- Blind Hem D

STANDARD A METAL ZIGZAG FOOT

This foot is made of metal, and the underside is smooth and flat—no grooves or ridges (Fig. 9.4). It is designed to stitch very fine fabric or very heavy fabric because it holds the fabric firmly against the feed dogs.

Has your machine ever "eaten" the fabric? This foot helps prevent the problem. It offers support around the needle to prevent it from pulling and pushing fabric up and down with every stitch. On fine fabrics it also helps prevent puckering. On heavy fabrics it helps prevent skipped stitches.

Application: Most inexperienced sewers leave this foot on all the time, but it makes sewing harder. When you teach yourself to sew better, you will use this foot for about 30 percent of garment construction.

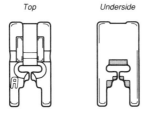

Top   Underside

Fig. 9.4.

Fig. 9.5.
In left or right needle position, the needle holes provide support around three sides of the needle to prevent puckering and skipped stitches.

Fig. 9.6.
Utility B foot with wide channel on the underside.

Fig. 9.7.
The transparent B (appliqué) foot, is made of a transparent material for good visibility and has a wide channel in the heel.

Fig. 9.8.
The standard buttonhole C foot has two narrow channels in the heel and one open channel in front of the needle hole on the underside.

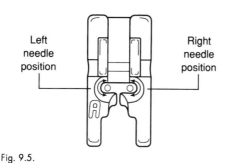

Left needle position

Right needle position

Fig. 9.5.

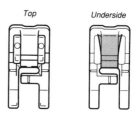

Top   Underside

Fig. 9.7.

Sew-How: *If you are using a new, appropriately sized needle for the fabric and experiencing puckering or skipped stitches, use the standard A metal zigzag foot and decenter the needle to the far left or far right. This way, the needle hole in the foot and needle plate provide support around three sides of the needle, rather than two sides, as is the case when the needle is in the center position (Fig. 9.5).*

UTILITY B FOOT

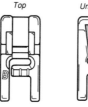

Top   Underside

Fig. 9.6.

Sometimes called an embroidery foot, the metal utility B foot has a wide channel carved out of the heel on the underside (Fig. 9.6). This channel allows decorative stitches (e.g., satin stitch A14, 15, 16, 17; domino D21; ball D23) to be sewn and the fabric to move smoothly without flattening the stitches into the fabric. The channel also flairs out at the heel to help turn smooth curves and corners. Use the lines on the top in front of the needle as reference points.

Application: Use this foot to embroider on lightweight fabrics because

it provides more pressure on the fabric than the transparent B (appliqué) foot described below. You may also want to apply a Teflon guide plate to the bottom of this foot for embroidering on leather, vinyl, suede or other sticky fabrics.

TRANSPARENT B (APPLIQUÉ) FOOT

Sometimes referred to as a transparent embroidery foot, the transparent B (appliqué) foot is made of a synthetic material that allows you to see what's going on under it—excellent for machine appliqué and embrioidery. This foot also has a wide channel carved out of the underside (Fig. 9.7) so decorative stitches are sewn and move smoothly under the foot without being flattened in the fabric.

Application: Use this foot for most of the embroidery stitches sewn with a presser foot. Also use it for seaming techniques in medium and heavy wovens and knits.

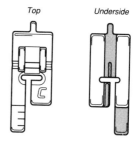

Top   Underside

Fig. 9.8.

BUTTONHOLE C FOOT

This foot has two narrow channels in the heel and one open channel in front of the needle hole on the underside (Fig. 9.8). After the first column of stitches is made,

Fig. 9.9.
The buttonhole sensor
has an underside like
the buttonhole C foot,
but there is a
measuring wheel that
insures one-step
buttonholes are made
the same length, time
after time, regardless
of the fabric weight,
weave, or number of
thicknesses.

the foot rides on the narrow column of stitching so the two sides of the buttonhole are parallel. Since buttonholes on the Viking feed backward first, you can always start your buttonholes at the same distance from the edge of the fabric by using one of the markings on the left toe.

This foot also has a bar on the heel for cording. Corded buttonholes (see Fig. 8.55) are more durable and generally look better than uncorded buttonholes.

Application: Unlike many other brands of buttonhole feet, the C foot works well on lightweight fabrics because the needle is supported around three sides. However, because there is not a mechanism to insure all the buttonholes come out the same size (except on the Viking 990 and 1100, on which you can program your buttonhole length) mark buttonhole length carefully before stitching.

Also use this foot to stitch-in-the-ditch (see Fig. 8.8). Guide the inside right toe by the "ditch" in the seam. The ridge on the underside of the right toe spreads the seam, allowing you to stitch perfectly in the ditch.

BUTTONHOLE SENSOR

The buttonhole sensor comes as standard equipment and presently can be used only with the Viking 1100 (Fig. 9.9). It attaches like a normal sole, and a small cable plugs into the machine above the presser bar next to the light cover. The underside looks like the buttonhole C foot, but there is a measuring wheel that insures one-step buttonholes are made the same length, time after time, regardless of the fabric weight, weave, or number of fabric layers.

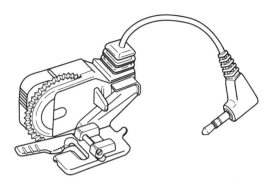

Fig. 9.9.

Application: Use the buttonhole sensor on all buttonhole styles except A2, the leather buttonhole, and A46, the medium reinforced buttonhole.

To use the sensor, plug it in and set the measuring wheel at the white mark. When it is set properly, the Programdisplay will show you. The buttonhole length is preset for a 1.5cm (5/8") buttonhole. To lengthen, push the ELG+ button and the buttonhole increases in length by 2mm. Four buttonhole lengths are preset:

16mm = approximately 5/8"

18mm = approximately 3/4"

20mm = approximately 3/4"

22mm = approximately 1-1/8"

Buttonhole lengths will vary depending on fabric weight.

BLIND HEM D FOOT

The underside of the D foot is higher on the left than on the right. This way when the fabric is folded for blind hemming, there is enough room under it for the double layer of fabric (Fig. 9.10). The blind hem stitch on the Viking 1100 and the 900 series machines are preprogrammed for use with the D foot so the needle won't pick up too much fabric when blind hemming. If used properly, it ensures almost invisible results on most fabrics (see Figs. 8.48, 8.49, 8.50).

Fig. 9.10.
The underside of the blind hem D foot is higher on the left than right. When fabric is folded for blind hemming, the double layer of fabric guides smoothly under it.

Fig. 9.11.
Use the blind hem D foot for edgestitching, topstitching, or making traditional pintucks. Snug right toe or guide against edge of fold and stitch.

Fig. 9.12.
A, The zipper E foot snaps on and off to move from side to side. B, Use the zipper foot to cover and attach piping in a seam on clothing, pillows, or slipcovers.

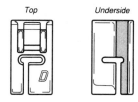

Top   Underside

Fig. 9.10.

Application: Besides blind hemming, use this foot for edgestitching, topstitching, or making traditional pintucks. Snug the inside of the right toe against the edge of the fabric. Move the needle position as far left as desired and stitch (Fig. 9.11).

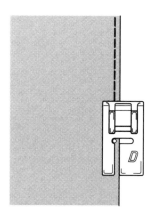

Fig. 9.11.

ZIPPER E FOOT

If you have avoided a pattern because it called for a zipper, the E foot will help. It snaps on so the toe is on the left or on the right. This way you can stitch either side of the zipper without riding over the zipper the coil.

Application: Use the E foot to sew in zippers and to cover and attach cord or piping in a pillow or slipcover (Fig. 9.12).

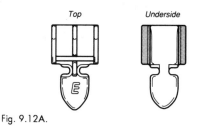

Top   Underside

Fig. 9.12A.

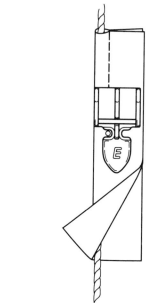

Fig. 9.12B.

OTHER STANDARD ACCESSORIES

- Raised F Seam Foot
- Raised Seam Guide
- Overcast J Foot
- Teflon H and Glide Plates
- Edge Guide
- Button Reed

RAISED SEAM F FOOT

The raised seam F foot (Fig. 9.13) is used with twin needles to create pintucks found on dressy blouses or shirts, christening gowns, and French hand-sewn garments. The underside has three grooves which track over previous rows of pintucking, so the rows are parallel and evenly spaced. Here's how to use it:

Fig. 9.13.
The raised seam F foot and guide is used with twin needles to stitch multiple rows of pintucks parallel to one another. The underside has three grooves. After the first tuck is stitched, the remaining rows ride in the first groove so they are parallel to the first.

Fig. 9.14.
Stitch multiple rows of tucks, starting from the center row out.

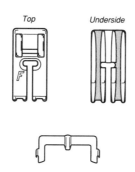

Top   Underside

Fig. 9.13.

Machine Readiness Checklist

Stitch:	straight (A2)
Length:	2 – 2.5
Width:	0
Foot:	raised seam F
Feed dogs:	up
Needle position:	center
Thread:	100% cotton or all-purpose
Fabric:	light- to medium-weight cotton, cotton blend, wool jersey, cotton T-shirt knit
Tension:	for more pronounced tuck, tighten upper tension
Accessories:	vanishing marker or dressmaker's chalk

1. Mark tuck placement on the right side of a single layer of fabric with vanishing marker or dressmaker's chalk, marking center row only.

2. Stitch the first tuck on the line marked in Step 1.

3. Stitch second row next to first, guiding the fabric so the first tuck rides in one of the channels in the foot.

Stitch as many rows of tucking as desired, working from the center row out (Fig. 9.14).

Fig. 9.14.

Sew-How: *If you plan a lot of tucks on a pattern that doesn't call for them, stitch the tucks first, then center the pattern on top of the tucks and cut out the project. This ensures the garment will not be too tight.*

Applications: Pintuck blouses, shirts, or children's clothing. Use this as a way to create texture on a solid fabric, matching the thread to the fabric. This foot also works well for rolling and whipping in French hand-sewn edges (see explanation below) because the space between the toes is wide enough to enable a fine piece of fabric to roll before whipping the edges. Here's how:

Fig. 9.15.
The overcast J foot, sometimes called an overedge foot, has a wire on the top and has a narrow channel behind the wire on the underside. The stitch forms over the wire and keeps the fabric flat to prevent tunneling.

Machine Readiness Checklist	
Stitch:	zigzag (A12)
Length:	1
Width:	4
Foot:	raised seam F
Needle:	70/10 universal
Thread:	100% cotton darning
Tension:	top, tight; bobbin, normal
Fabric:	cotton bastiste or handkerchief linen

Rolled and whipped edges are always used in conjunction with French hand sewing. The fabric must have a finished edge so it will not pull away when attached to a piece of lace or entredeux.

1. Cut a 2" (5cm) scrap of the same fabric you will roll and whip.

2. Guide the raw edge of the scrap so it is halfway under the presser foot. Stitch, holding the threads from the top and bobbin until the fabric begins to roll. When you approach the end of the scrap, butt the good fabric up to it so it rolls exactly at the beginning of the edge.

3. Cut off scrap to attach fabric to lace or entredeux.

RAISED SEAM GUIDE

For a more pronounced pintuck, use the raised seam guide with the raised seam F foot and twin needles. It snaps over the feed dogs and, when threaded with pearl cotton, guides the cord so it ends up under the twin needles pintuck.

OVERCAST J FOOT

Have you overcast a raw edge with a zigzag stitch and ended up with the fabric tunneled under it? Then use the overcast J foot. When the zigzag stitch is used on a 4 to 6 width, the stitch forms over the bar on the right, keeping thread tension even during stitch formation to prevent tunneling (Fig. 9.15).

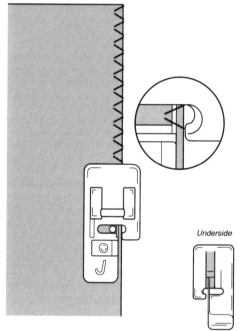

Underside

Fig. 9.15.

Applications: Use this foot with the zigzag (A12), overcast (A21), flatlock (A25), rickrack (A18), or any stitch that causes tunneling on a 4 width or wider. Use it not only for overcasting seams, but also for 1/4" (6mm) seams with the stitches mentioned above.

Fig. 9.16.
The Teflon H foot has a
flat, smooth underside
and is coated with
Teflon so it will not
stitck on leathers,
vinyls, and other sticky
fabrics.

Fig. 9.17.
A, Edge guide slips
behind the foot shank
and adjusts out 3"
(7.5cm) to the right of
the needle. B, The
quilting guide adjusts
out to the right or left
of the needle to keep
many rows of quilting
straight and even.

TEFLON H FOOT AND GLIDE PLATES

The H foot has a flat, smooth underside and is coated with Teflon so it will not stick on leathers, synthetic leathers and suedes, and sticky vinyls (Fig. 9.16). It offers support around the needle so the fabric is not pushed and pulled with every stitch, thus preventing skipped stitches.

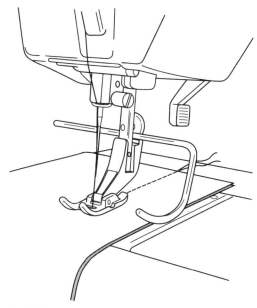

Fig. 9.17A.

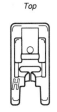 

Top   Underside

Fig. 9.16.

The Teflon glide plates are shaped to fit the zipper E foot, buttonhole C foot, and standard A metal zigzag foot, so these feet stitch smoothly on the leather-type fabrics. You can also trim glide plates to fit other soles, if necessary. To attach a glide plate, peel the paper from adhesive backing, then stick it to the bottom of the sole.

Applications: Construct leather and leather-like projects using the Teflon H. foot. Also use it for sewing slippery linings, acetates, and silks to prevent the underlayer of fabric from feeding faster than the top layer.

EDGE GUIDE

Do you have trouble sewing straight? The edge guide will help. It slips behind the foot shank and adjusts out 3" (7.5cm) to the right of the needle (Fig. 9.17A,B). Use it also as a quilting guide so multiple rows of stitching are straight and evenly spaced. Quilt your own fabric using the straight stitch (A1, 2, 3), zigzag (A11, 12, 13), three-step zigzag (A19), or other decorative stitches.

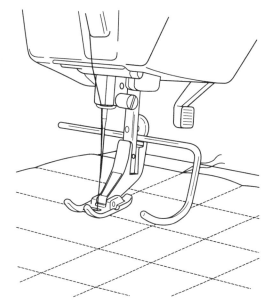

Fig. 9.17B.

Sew-How: *If you are quilting many rows, the underlayer of fabric may pucker or come out shorter than the rest of the piece. Prevent this by using the dual feed foot (see Fig. 9.29).*

Fig. 9.18.
With reed and button
in place, stab needle
into the left hole, lower
presser bar, and stitch.

Applications: Use as a seam guide or anytime you are stitching wider from the edge of the fabric than what is marked on the needle plate. The edge guide also is helpful for stitching deep hems or cuffs and for topstitching and quilting.

BUTTON REED

Did You Know? The three buttons on jacket sleeves were stitched there to discourage soldiers from wiping their mouths and noses on their sleeves.

Button Reed for Sewing on Buttons

This accessory is sometimes called a clearance plate. It has two ends, one thicker than the other, which provide space for a shank so the button stands away from the fabric. A button shank prevents the buttonhole from gapping and pulling too hard on the button and fabric. Use the thicker end for heavy fabrics. Use the thinner end for medium weight fabrics.

Machine Readiness Checklist	
Stitch:	zigzag (A11)
Length:	0
Width:	3 – 6 (may vary with button)
Foot:	none (leave foot shank on)
Feed dogs:	down
Needle position:	far left
Accessories:	glue stick

1. Mark button placement. Dab the glue stick on the back of the button and place it on button reed.

2. Place reed and button on fabric under the foot or foot shank. Stab the needle into the left hole and lower the presser bar lever (Fig. 9.18). If sewing on a four-hole button, start with the holes closest to you.

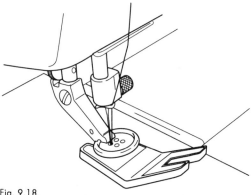

Fig. 9.18.

3. Move the flywheel by hand to check needle clearance, adjust the stitch width if necessary, then stitch four to five zigzag stitches. If sewing a four-hole button, lift presser bar and move the fabric to stitch the back two holes.

4. Move stitch width to 0 and stitch two to three stitches to lock them off. Remove fabric by pulling off enough thread to wrap a shank between the button and fabric.

5. Poke top and bobbin threads between button and fabric, then thread them through a hand needle. Wrap a shank (see Fig. 8.18). Pull free ends through to the back of the fabric and tie them off.

Sew-How: *To eliminate the need to tie off threads, bring threads to the back and snip them close to the back of the fabric and dab them with a spot of Fray Check.*

Fig. 9.19. A, Use button reed as a wedge under toes as you approach and come off a thickness. To start sewing on a thick edge, place needle in fabric, raise the presser foot, wedge button reed under heel, then lower presser foot. B, When coming off a thickness, leave the needle in your work, raise the presser foot and wedge reed under toes. Lower presser foot and stitch through the heavy seam.

Did you know? Regardless of button size, 90 percent of the holes in buttons are the same distance apart. Why? Button manufacturers use the same equipment to make the holes in most buttons, whatever the diameter.

Button Reed as a Wedge

Sewing up and over heavy seams on a jean hem or attaching a belt loop is tough because the foot stalls on the way up and coasts on the way down the thickness. This happens because the foot is not level with the feed dogs.

Use the button reed as a wedge under the heel of the foot as you approach a thickness (Fig. 9.19A) and under the toes as you come off the thickness (Fig. 9.19B).

1. As the toes tip up, stop with the needle in the fabric and lift the foot. Slip the wedge under the heel and lower presser foot.

2. Stitch across the thickness until the toes begin to tip down. Stop with the needle in the fabric and lift the foot again.

3. Slip wedge under the toes and take a few stitches until the back of the foot is off the thickness. Remove wedge.

This technique prevents stitch distortion and keeps the needle from breaking on the foot as it pivots on and off the thickness.

When starting a seam or topstitching on a heavy fabric, place needle at the edge of the fabric and the reed under the heel of the foot. This way the foot doesn't have to climb uphill to start sewing.

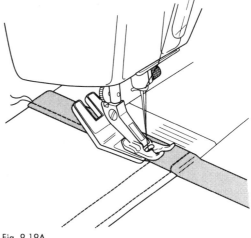

Fig. 9.19A.

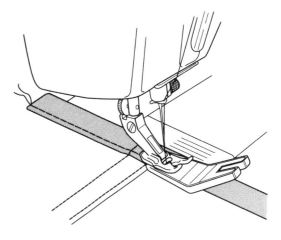

Fig. 9.19B.

Sew-How: *Even though it may look as if the foot is down, remember to lower the presser foot on the wedge to engage the upper tension. Otherwise the stitches will not form properly.*

Fig. 9.20.
Bias binders are used
for applying flat or
prefolded bias tape,
binding, or trim. With
binder off machine,
thread V- shaped cut
through funnel.

EXTRA ACCESSORIES

- Bias Binder
- Braiding Feet
- Circular Sewing Attachment
- Cording Foot
- Darning Foot
- Dual Feeder
- Eyelet Plates

- Gathering Foot
- Hemmer
- Hemstitch Fork
- Lace Joining and Edgestitching Foot
- Open-Toe Appliqué Foot
- Piping Foot

- Roller Foot
- Ruffler
- Rug Foot
- Special Marking Foot
- Straight Stitch Foot
- Weaver's Reed

BIAS BINDER

A bias binder is used for applying flat or prefolded bias tape, binding, or trim. Available for most machines, the bias binder has a funnel and guide to fold the binding over the base fabric before it reaches the needle.

Some bias binders are used only with a straight stitch; others can be used with a zigzag or decorative stitch; still others are adjustable to accommodate varying widths of tape or binding.

Machine Readiness Checklist	
Stitch:	straight (A2), zigzag (A12), or decorative
Length:	varies
Width:	varies
Foot:	bias binder
Thread:	all-purpose
Fabric:	prequilted or medium to heavy woven
Tension:	normal
Needle position:	varies
Accessories:	1/2" (1.3cm) flat or prefolded bias tape

1. Unfold 3" (7.5cm) of one end of a length of bias tape and press flat.

2. On the pressed end, fold tape in half the long way and make a V-shaped cut so the point of the cut is at the fold (Fig. 9.20).

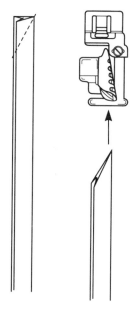

Fig. 9.20.

Fig. 9.21.
Slip base fabric into
slot in center of funnel.

Fig. 9.22.
Narrow braiding foot
has a narrow channel
on the underside
behind the needle and
a clip or guide on top
to guide yarn, pearl
cotton, or narrow
cord.

Fig. 9.23A.
Couch interesting yarn
in a plaid, stripe or
scrolled design using
the narrow braiding
foot.

3. With the binder off the machine, thread tape through the funnel so the point of the cut is to the right. **Note:** If you are having trouble threading the funnel, use a hand needle and doubled thread to stitch through the point of the V and pull the point through the funnel.

4. Put binder on the machine and pull the feed end of tape so it extends about 2" (5cm) behind the foot.

5. Slip the base fabric into the slot in the center of the funnel.

6. Adjust your needle position so the needle stitches inside the folded edge of the tape (Fig. 9.21).

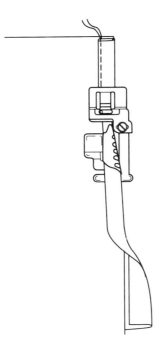

Fig. 9.21.

Application: Bind the edges of double-faced quilted fabric for placemats or an unlined jacket. Stitch on bias tape or Seams Great™ for a Hong Kong seam finish or hem.

BRAIDING FEET

Narrow Braiding Foot

Sometimes referred to as a narrow cording foot, this foot is not usually standard, but I feel it's a necessity. The top of the foot has a guide to hold narrow cord, such as pearl cotton, yarn, or cordonnet. The underside has a narrow channel behind the needle which flairs out at the heel, enabling you to stitch around curves and corners smoothly (Fig. 9.22).

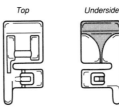

Top   Underside

Fig. 9.22.

Applications: Use this foot to cord an edge that will be satin stitched later. To gather, use this foot to zigzag over a cord so you don't catch the cord in the stitch. Create your own fabric by using a solid base fabric and couch interesting yarn in a plaid, stripe, or scrolled design (Fig. 9.23A).

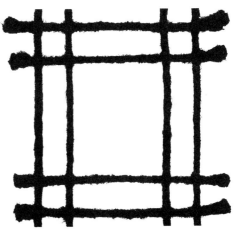

Fig. 9.23A.

Fig. 9.23B.
Child's artwork enlarged and appliquéd as a wall hanging. The outline is done with the narrow braiding foot threaded with black yarn and couched with a straight stitch using nylon monofilament thread top and bobbin.

Fig. 9.24.
The underside of the standard braiding foot has a channel wider than that on the narrow braiding foot to feed braid straight.

Fig. 9.25.
Embellish jackets or children's clothing and costumes with braid, heavy yarn, cord, trim, or soutache braid.

Outline an appliqué with yarn or cord by straight stitching through it (Fig. 9.23B). Because the clip or guide holds the cord in place, you can stitch in any direction and be assured of stitching through the cord to anchor it properly. For truly invisible results, use nylon monofilament thread top and bobbin. This way all you see is the cord or yarn and not the stitches used to attach it to the fabric.

Fig. 9.25.

The standard braiding foot works on the same principle as the narrow braiding foot, but the channel on the underside is wider and feeds the braid straight.

Sew-How: *If you are doing a lot of braid application, you may find it helpful to use the braiding guide with the braiding foot. It attaches behind the foot shank, like the edge guide, and has a curlicue for the braid to feed through.*

Application: Embellish jackets, children's clothing, and costumes with braid, or couch over heavy yarn, cord, or trim.

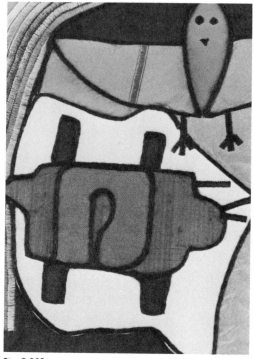

Fig. 9.23B.

Standard Braiding Foot

The standard braiding foot is often just called a braiding foot. The opening in front of the needle is large enough to accommodate middy or soutache braid (Figs. 9.24, 9.25).

CIRCULAR SEWING ATTACHMENT

Sometimes referred to as a circular sewing or circular embroidery device, the circular sewing attachment is used to stitch perfect circles for patches, and embroidered covered buttons, to aid in circular embroidery and appliqué, and to make scallops (Fig. 9.26).

It attaches behind the presser bar, like a quilting or edge guide, and is used with a thumbtack and tape.

1. Attach guide behind the presser bar to the circle radius desired. With the foot up, tip guide toward you.

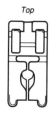 

Top   Underside

Fig. 9.24.

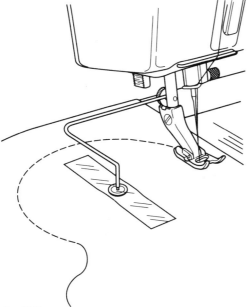

Fig. 9.26.
Tape thumbtack
upside-down on the
bed of your machine
the radius distance
away from the needle.

Fig. 9.26.

2. Stick a piece of tape on the thumbtack so the sticky side is against the flat side of the tack, and the point is up. Push the point of the tack into the hole in the circular sewing attachment, then tip it down so flat side of the tack is against the bed of your machine. Lower the presser foot and stick the tack on the bed of your machine. Lift presser foot again.

3. Iron plastic coated freezer wrap to the wrong side of the fabric or stretch fabric in a hoop. If you are using a heavy, closely woven fabric, this step may not be necessary.

4. At the center of the circle, pierce the fabric with the point of the tack. Lower presser foot.

5. Stitch around the circle matching stitches at the beginning and end. Use a straight stitch, zigzag, or other decorative stitch.

Applications: Outline a perfect circle to use as an appliqué, stitch concentric circles of decorative stitching for a round belt buckle, or make scallops.

CORDING FOOT

The cording foot is sometimes referred to as a five-hole or seven-hole foot, depending on how many holes are in front of the needle (Fig. 9.27). The underside looks like the utility B foot, with a wide groove behind the needle.

Before attaching to the foot shank, thread sole with pearl cotton, embroidery floss, metallic thread, baby yarn or any fine cord through two or more holes, and stitch over them using an open embroidery stitch (daisy D9, arch A34) or a closed satin stitch pattern (domino D21, ribbon D22, ball D23). The holes keep the cords in line and untangled, regardless of the direction you sew.

Applications: Create your own trims; decorate hemlines, pockets, or placemats; or use short lengths to texture a solid fabric.

Fig. 9.27.
The cording foot has
five or seven holes in
front of the needle and
a wide groove on the
underside behind the
needle. Create trims
and decorative
hemlines using the
cording foot and one
or more of the
decorative stitches
available on your
Viking.

Fig. 9.28.
The darning foot is
transparent for good
visibility.

Fig. 9.29.
The dual feeder, or
dual feed foot, has a
top set of feed dogs to
prevent fabric from
shifting or slipping and
the underlayer from
coming up short. Use
the dual feeder for
matching plaids and
stripes or for quilting
or sewing long
drapery seams and
hems.

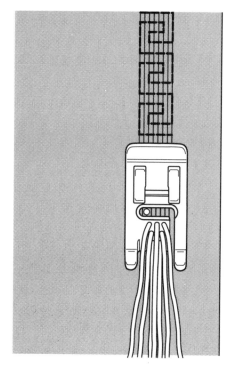

Fig. 9.27.

DARNING FOOT

As the name implies, the darning foot is
used for free-machine darning. It is made
of a transparent material for good
visibility (Fig. 9.28). The purpose of the
foot is to insure proper stitch formation,
minimize skipped stitches and puckering,
and protect your fingers while moving the
fabric freely under the needle.

Fig. 9.28.

To use it, drop the feed dogs and release
the pressure to the "darn" setting. When
you put the foot down and the needle is
up, the darning foot rests about 1/8"

(3mm) above the fabric. When the needle
is in the fabric, the bar of the foot rests
on the needle clamp screw and the foot
rests on the fabric surface during stitch
formation. This prevents the fabric from
pulling up and down with each stitch.

Sew-How: *Because of this spring-
action, the foot is noisy.*

Applications: Use the darning foot
to gain confidence when learning free-
machine embroidery or for darning heavy
or fine fabrics.

DUAL FEEDER

Sometimes referred to as a walking or
dual feed foot, the dual feeder has a top
set of feed dogs to prevent the top layer of
fabric from shifting and slipping and the
underlayer from coming up short (Fig.
9.29). The dual feeder works best with
the straight stitch, but can also be used
with other stitches. Some stitches are
better than others. Experiment for the
best choices.

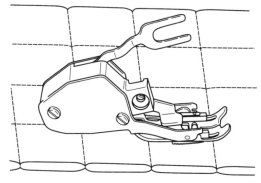

Fig. 9.29.

1100 NOTES: The Viking 1100 has two machine quilting stitches on the A cassette—A32, the quilting scallop, and A33, the quilting wave. Both work well with the dual feeder for quilting.

Applications: Use the dual feeder for matching stripes and plaids and for sewing napped and slippery fabrics. Use it for quilting so all fabric layers feed evenly. Finally, use the dual feeder when sewing long seams and hems, or attaching pleater tape to draperies or curtains.

EYELET PLATES

Eyelet plates come in 4mm and 6mm sizes, and are used with an awl to make thread eyelets (Fig. 9.30).

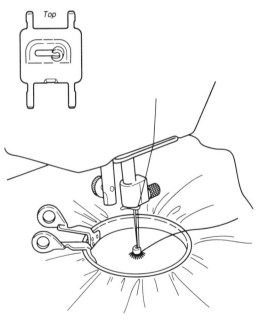

Fig. 9.30.

1. Remove presser foot and foot shank. Drop feed dogs.

2. Place the eyelet plate over feed dogs.

3. Tighten fabric in a hoop, and poke a hole with the awl where the eyelet is to be sewn.

Sew-How: *Rather than cutting a hole for an eyelet, use an awl. It separates threads in the fabric without cutting them so that the eyelet will not ravel. To make perfectly formed eyelets, the hole in the fabric should be small and fit snuggly around the tube in the plate.*

---

4. Push the hole over the tube in the plate and lower the presser foot. Set your machine for a zigzag stitch, length 0, width 2 – 4. Take one stitch and pull the bobbin thread to the surface of the fabric. Take a couple more stitches in one place to lock threads, then cut them off at the fabric. Begin sewing and turn the fabric slowly to overcast the hole.

Applications: Thread ribbon, lace, cord, or trim through eyelets. Use them to create designs like a bunch of grapes or flower centers. Create your own eyelet fabric. Once you have perfected making eyelets with the zigzag stitch, use Satin Element stitches such as a triangle (D32), or half-circle (D35) to create decorative eyelets.

Fig. 9.31.
The underside of the gathering foot is raised behind the needle and has a slot in front of the needle. To gather and attach a ruffle at the same time onto a flat piece, place ruffle under foot right side up. Slip flat piece into slot, right side down, and straight stitch.

Fig. 9.32.
The hemmer has a scroll-shaped feeder on top and a straight groove the width of the finished hem on the underside.

GATHERING FOOT

This foot gathers light- to medium-weight fabric automatically while sewing. The underside is raised behind the needle, and the slot in front of the needle enables the user to gather and attach the ruffle simultaneously (Fig. 9.31).

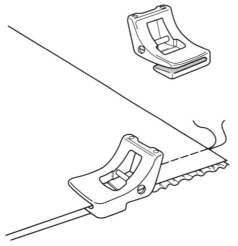

Fig. 9.31.

To use it, set your machine for a straight stitch. The amount the fabric gathers is determined by the weight of the fabric, stitch length, and upper thread tension. Use a fine fabric, a long stitch, and a tighter tension for a lot of gathers. Use a medium-weight fabric, a short stitch, and normal tension for finer gathers.

To gather and sew a ruffle onto a flat piece of fabric, place the fabric to be gathered under the foot, right side up, then put the foot down. Slip the flat piece into the slot, right side down, and stitch. Everything is stitched in one step.

Sew-How: *Sometimes the stitching may not be straight and even, so you may prefer to gather the ruffle separately, then attach it to the flat fabric piece.*

To determine how much gathering you need, stitch a test piece. Start with a strip of fabric 10" (25.5cm) long. This way, if the fabric gathers to 5" (12.5cm), you know to use a 2:1 ratio. Thus you would use a 50" (127cm) length of ruffle to attach to a 25" (63.5cm) waistband. **Note:** A gathering foot should not be confused with a ruffler. Both accessories gather, but a ruffler can also pleat (see Fig. 9.37).

Applications: Gather ruffles for children's clothing, curtains, dust ruffles, tablecloths, or blouses.

HEMMER

Sometimes referred to as a rolled hemmer, a hemmer is used to stitch the narrow, rolled hems commonly found on shirttails. The top has a scroll-shaped feeder; the underside, a straight groove (Fig. 9.32).

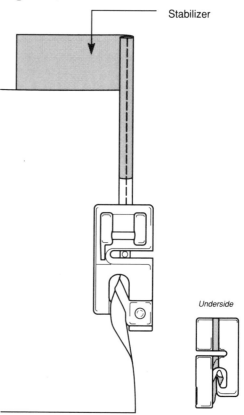

Stabilizer

Underside

Fig. 9.32.

Viking hemmers are available in 2, 3, and 5mm sizes—which is the width of the grooves on the underside of each foot. The width of a groove determines the finished hem width. **Note:** The wider the finished hem, the easier a hemmer is to use.

Sew-How: *To start stitching the rolled hem on the edge of the fabric, overlap a 3" (7.5cm) square of tear-away stabilizer and stitch it to the raw edge of the fabric at the starting end of the hem. Start rolling the stabilizer into the scroll of the hemmer. Then remove the tear-away after stitching.*

1. Roll and press a few inches of the hem to get started.

2. Feed the stabilizer into the scroll and begin sewing. With your right hand, hold the fabric up and slightly to the left of center, curling the edge of the fabric before it enters the scroll.

3. Stitch slowly and carefully to finish hem. Remove stabilizer. **Note:** This takes some practice, so try it on a scrap first.

Applications: Roll shirt and ruffle hems. On tricot, use the hemmer to roll and shell tuck an edge at the same time (see Fig. 8.53). Use the scroll to guide cord, yarn, pearl cotton, or narrow trim for a corded edge finish.

HEMSTITCH FORK

This accessory looks like a large bobby pin and is used for fagoting with the straight stitch (Fig. 9.33).

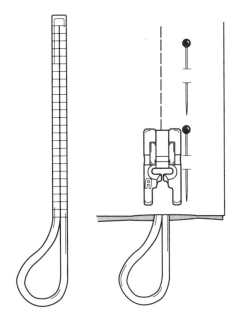

Fig. 9.33.

Machine Readiness Checklist	
Stitch:	straight
Length:	2 – 4
Width:	0
Foot:	standard A metal zigzag or rug
Needle:	80/12 universal
Thread:	100% cotton or all-purpose
Feed dogs:	up
Tension:	loosen halfway between normal and 0
Fabric:	tightly woven linen or linen-like

1. Pin your fabric, right sides together, placing pins parallel to, and 1/8" (3mm) from, the raw edge.

2. Slip the fork between the layers of fabric so the loop of the fork is toward you and the fork is snugged up to the pins.

Fig. 9.34.
Pieced collar made
with the hemstitch fork.
Decorative stitching on
either side of fagoting
keeps seams flat
during cleaning and
pressing.

3. Place the fork under the needle, put the needle down between the tines, and lower the foot. Stitch slowly to the loop in the fork. Stop with the needle down, lift the foot, and pull the fork toward you.

Sew-How: *If using the rug foot, the ridge in the foot fits between the tines in the fork (see Fig. 9.38).*

---

4. Lower foot again, stitch to the loop, pull the fork toward you. Continue until the line of stitching is complete.

5. Remove the fork and press the seam open. The folds will separate, and you will see a threaded ladder between them. If desired, topstitch seam allowances on either side of the ladders.

Applications: Use this method to join seams on baby clothes, French hand-sewn (by machine) blouses, collars, pocket tops, yokes, or anywhere you want an interesting seam. Piece fabrics together for a collar, tablecloth, or front tab (Fig. 9.34).

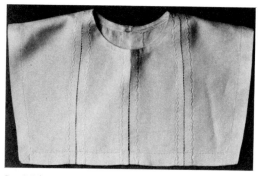

Fig. 9.34.

LACE JOINING AND EDGESTITCHING FOOT

The lace joining foot is designed for joining together straight edge lace or trim with the bridging (A27), three-step zigzag stitch (A19), or serpentine stitch (A20) (see Fig. 8.31). It can also be used for stitching close to and an even distance from the fabric edge—helpful for topstitching, edgestitching, and staystitching.

The underside has a blade in the center. To use it, simply butt the straight edge of one piece of lace against one side, the straight edge of another piece of lace against the other side, and stitch. The edges of the lace are next to each other, so they will not overlap, plus the join is strong and even.

To use this foot for edgestitching, butt the edge of the fabric against the blade in the foot, and decenter the needle as far to the left of the edge as desired. **Note:** This foot was not available at time of publication, so ask your Viking dealer to show it to you.

Applications: Join straight edge laces and trims. Piece leathers, suedes, vinyl, and synthetic suedes and leathers for handbags and belts. Edgestitch or topstitch evenly from the fabric edge.

OPEN-TOE APPLIQUÉ FOOT

The metal open-toe appliqué foot, sometimes called a decorative stitching foot, has a 6mm (1/4") channel in the heel on the underside, and two long toes in the front. It provides an excellent view of your work, important when stitching curves and corners of an appliqué, but offers no support in front of the needle.

Fig. 9.35.
The piping foot has a wide groove on the underside to hold and cover cord used for upholstery, pillows, or slipcovers. At publication, another piping foot with an even wider tunnel on the underside was on the drawing board. Ask your local dealer when it will become available.

Fig. 9.36.
The roller foot has rollers that roll against the fabric and act like a track on a bulldozer for sewing heavy fabrics.

Application: Use this foot on medium-weight fabrics for machine quilting and appliqué. If using finer weight fabric, use a tear-away stabilizer under the work, or fuse the appliqué to the base fabric with Wonder-Under to prevent puckering and skipped stitches. **Note:** This foot was not available at time of publication, so ask your Viking dealer to show it to you.

PIPING FOOT

The underside of the piping foot has a wide groove designed to cover cord used to edge upholstery and pillow seams (Fig. 9.35). It is also used to insert piping. Although you can use the zipper foot for either purpose, the piping foot makes it easier, and the stitching is more accurate.

 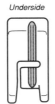

Top   Underside

Fig. 9.35.

To cover cord, cut the fabric on the bias the width of cord plus 1-1/4" (3.2cm) or unfold bias tape. Sandwich cord in the fabric or bias tape, then place it under the foot so the cord fits in the groove. Decenter the needle so the line of stitching snugs up against the cording and stitch.

To attach the finished cord or piping evenly, and without catching it in the seam, this foot is a must.

Applications: Pipe yokes and pockets, tote bags, handbags, backpacks, pillows, hemlines, or slipcovers, or use it when reupholstering—almost anywhere there is a seam. Also use the piping foot for an exposed zipper application (see Fig. 7.9).

ROLLER FOOT

The roller foot has textured rollers that roll against the fabric and act like the track on a bulldozer for sewing heavy fabrics (Fig. 9.36). The rollers move freely between the foot and feed dogs, so the foot rides easily over varying thicknesses.

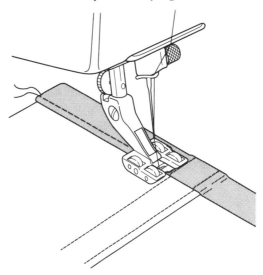

Fig. 9.36.

Applications: Use the roller foot for sewing uneven thicknesses of heavy fabrics—for example, hemming jeans or attaching belt carriers to a waistband. The roller foot also works well on denim, upholstery, and drapery fabrics and on sticky leathers and vinyls.

Fig. 9.37.
Ruffler.

Fig. 9.38.
The rug foot has a ridge on the underside that rides in the hemstitch fork and weaver's reed.

Fig. 9.39.
The special marking foot, sometimes called a tailor tacking or looping foot, has a raised bar in front which causes the thread to stand away from the fabric. The underside has a high, deep groove. To mark a pattern piece, stitch, pull fabric apart so thread loops are between two layers of fabric, then clip the thread.

RUFFLER

Rufflers haven't changed much from the days of the treadle machine (Fig. 9.37). They are adjustable and designed to ruffle or pleat the fabric to the desired fullness. Remember to stitch a sample first because once stitched, ruffles or pleats are not adjustable. **Note:** A ruffler should not be confused with a gathering foot (Fig. 9.31). Both accessories gather, but a ruffler can also pleat.

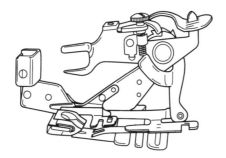

Fig. 9.37.

Applications: Stitch ruffles for square dance dresses, costumes, tablecloths, curtains and children's clothing.

RUG FOOT

The rug foot has a ridge on the underside that rides between the tines in the hemstitch fork or in the channel of the weaver's reed. The ridge prevents you from going off the track and breaking a needle (Fig. 9.38).

Applications: Use rug foot for piecing fabric strips with the hemstitch fork or for making fringe with the weaver's reed (see instructions above and below).

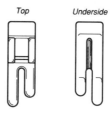

Top   Underside

Fig. 9.38.

SPECIAL MARKING FOOT

Sometimes called a fringe, tailor tacking, or looping foot, the special marking foot has a bar in the front that sticks up, off the fabric (Fig. 9.39). When used with the zigzag stitch, the bar causes the thread to stand away from the fabric. The underside has a high, deep groove, which allows the thread loops to stand up once stitched.

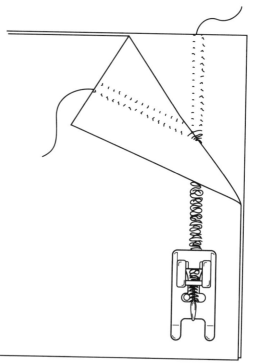

Fig. 9.39.

Applications: Use for pattern marking and making chenille fringe.

Special Marking Foot for Marking

Use it for tailor tacking.

Machine Readiness Checklist

Stitch:	zigzag (A12)
Length:	1 – 2
Width:	3 – 4
Foot:	special marking
Feed dogs:	up
Needle:	80/12 universal
Thread:	all-purpose or cotton embroidery
Fabric:	medium-weight woven or knit
Tension:	top, loosened slightly; bobbin, normal

1. Place fabric right sides together, with the tissue pattern on top, and stitch where fabric is to be marked. Carefully pull off tissue pattern piece.

2. Pull fabric apart so the thread loops are between the two layers of fabric, then clip threads. The threads accurately mark both pieces of fabric.

Special Marking Foot for Chenille

Make chenille fringe for flowers, eyelashes, or grass or to texture an existing piece of fabric. Use it also for appliqués or a freely embroidered design.

Set your machine as described above, but shorten the stitch length to 0.4 – 0.5. If you are covering a large area on one layer of fabric, fill it in faster by using two threads through the same needle and lengthen the stitch to about 0.8. You may have to iron freezer wrap to the wrong side of the fabric to prevent puckering.

To make a circle or square, start in the middle and work out.

STRAIGHT STITCH FOOT

The straight stitch foot is often used on very fine or very heavy fabrics. The reason? It's flat on the underside, so it offers even pressure and support around the needle (Fig. 9.40).

Top 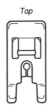 Underside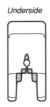

Fig. 9.40.

Sew-How: *It is not necessary to use a straight stitch foot when straight stitching, provided you are using the appropriate needle for the fabric and the proper stitch length. (See Table 1.1.)*

To achieve similar results, use the flat-bottomed standard A foot, and decenter your needle to the left or right. Also, use a fine needle and short stitch length for fine fabrics; use a heavier needle and longer stitch length for heavier fabrics.

Applications: Use this foot if you have tried everything else and are still experiencing skipped stitches, puckering, or uneven stitches. Also use it to topstitch difficult fabrics.

Fig. 9.41.
Use the 30mm or
45mm weaver's reed
and straight stitch
carefully down open
channel. Slide yarn
off reed. Leave yarn
looped or cut loops for
shaggier look.

Sew-How: *If your fabric puckers, shorten the stitch length. If your fabric waves out of shape, lengthen the stitch. This rule works with the straight stitch, zigzag, or any other stitch available on your sewing machine.*

WEAVER'S REED

The weaver's reed is available in two sizes—30mm for narrow fringe and 45 mm for wider fringe (Fig. 9.41). To use it:

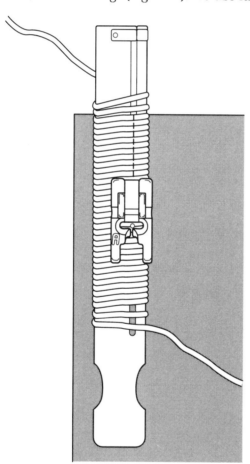

Fig. 9.41.

Machine Readiness Checklist	
Stitch:	straight (A2)
Length:	3 – 4
Width:	0
Foot:	standard A metal zigzag or rug
Needle:	80/12 or 90/14 universal
Thread:	all-purpose
Fabric:	wide bias tape, medium-weight woven, or pillow ticking, adding-machine tape (optional)
Accessories:	water-erasable marker

Weaver's Reed for Making Fringe

1. Draw a line down the center of the wide bias tape with the water-erasable marker.

2. Close the clip at the end of the toes and wrap the reed with yarn. Do not cut the yarn. Place wrapped reed on the bias tape, so the channel is to the right and centered over the line marked in Step 1. Carefully stitch down the open channel. Stop with the needle in your work.

3. Open the clip on the reed. Lift the foot. Slide yarn off the reed, pulling the reed toward you and stopping with the toes of the reed 1-1/2" (3.8cm) behind the needle. Wrap the reed again. Lower the presser foot. Stitch down the channel, slide yarn off, wrap and stitch to the end of the tape.

4. Leave yarn looped, or cut loops for a shaggier look.

Sew-How: *If making yards and yards of fringe, use Robbie Fanning's method. Robbie measures the length of fringe she wants from a roll of adding-machine tape. Then she stitches her fringe to the tape. This keeps the fringe from twisting, and it's easy to apply. Simply pull off the paper and stitch the fringe to the object.*

Weaver's Reed for Rug Making

Sew-How: *Jackie Dodson, author of* **Know Your Viking** *and* **Twenty Easy Machine-Made Rugs** *(Chilton, 1990), recommends using pillow ticking as a rug base because it is a closely woven, medium-weight fabric, and the stripes help you guide for straight rows of stitching.*

1. Cut pillow ticking the size of finished rug and overcast the raw edges using the three-step zigzag stitch (length 1, width 4 – 5). Set your machine as described above, and wrap the reed with yarn, bias cut fabric strips, ribbon, baby yarn, or pearl cotton.

2. You will be stitching rows of weaver's reed fringe following the lengthwise grain. Starting in the upper left corner, place the channel of the wrapped weaver's reed over one of the stripes in the pillow ticking, backstitch, then stitch fringe the length of the rug. Cut yarn at the end of the row, backstitching securely at the end of the fringe.

3. Wrap reed again, and place the channel 1/2 – 3/4" (1.3 – 2cm) to the right of the first row of fringe. The closer together the rows, the thicker the rug. Work successive rows from left to right, so the bulk of the rug is to the left.

4. Leave loops alone or cut for more texture.

Applications: Make weaver's reed fringe for doll or clown hair, or stuffed animal fur. Stitch fringe to a strip of wide bias tape or adding machine tape to set in a hood or pocket top or to sandwich between a jacket front and front facing. For finer fringe, wrap fork with 1/4" (6mm) ribbon, heavy yarn, or fabric strips cut on the bias. Heavier fringe can be used to make rugs and textured fringe for home decorating projects.

SOURCES OF SUPPLY

The following source list tells where you can find or write away for information on sewing machines, threads, and other sewing supplies you may not have at your local sewing store. For an extensive list and specific sewing needs, see *Sew, Serge, Press -- Speed Tailoring in the Ultimate Sewing Center,* by Jan Saunders (Chilton, 1989) and *Innovative Serging,* by Gail Brown and Tammy Young (Chilton, 1989).

VIKING INFORMATION

Husqvarna A.B.
s561 81
Huskvarna, Sweden

Viking Sewing Machines
A division of V.W.S., Inc.
11760 Berea Road
Cleveland, OH 44111

Viking publishes a wide range of educational materials too numerous to list here. Check with your local dealer. Of particular interest are:

• 1100 Owner's Handbook and Fabric Kit
• 990 Viking Owner's Handbook and Fabric Kit
• 600 Series Owner's Handbook and Fabric Kit
• 340D/340/300 Owner's Handbook and Fabric Kit
• Pictogram Idea Book (comes with the 990 Viking)
• Your Second Pictogram Idea Book
• Your Third Pictogram Book

KEY RING KITS

Showcase Keychain
Prime Arts Ltd., Inc.
Cincinnati, OH 45236

THREADS

Ask your local retailer or send a preaddressed, stamped envelope to the companies below to find out where to buy their threads.

Extra-fine

• *Assorted threads*
Robison-Anton Textile Co.
175 Bergen Blvd.
Fairview, NJ 07022

• *DMC 100% cotton, Sizes 30 and 50*
The DMC Corp.
107 Trumbull Street
Elizabeth, NJ 07206

• *Dual-Duty Plus Extra-fine, cotton-wrapped polyester*
J. & P. Coats/Coats & Clark
Consumer Service Department
P.O. Box 1010
Toccoa, GA 30577

• *Iris 100% rayon*
Art Sales
4801 W. Jefferson
Los Angeles, CA 90016

• *Iris 100% silk -- see Zwicky*

• *Madeira 100% rayon*
Madeira Threads
56 Primrose Drive
O'Shea Industrial Park
Laconia, NH 03246

• *Mettler Metrosene fine machine embroidery cotton, size 60/2*
Swiss-Metrosene, Inc.
7780 Quincy St.
Willowbrook, IL 60521

• *Natesh 100% rayon, lightweight*
Aardvark Adventures
P.O. Box 2449
Livermore, CA 94550

• *Paradise 100% rayon*
D & E Distributing
199 N. El Camino Real #F-242
Encinitas, CA 92024

• *Sulky 100% rayon, sizes 30 and 40*
Speed Stitch, Inc.
P.O. Box 3472
Port Charlotte, FL 33949
or
V.W.S., Inc.
11760 Berea Road
Cleveland, OH 44111

• *Zwicky 100% cotton, size 30/2; white and black darning thread*
V.W.S., Inc.
11760 Berea Rd.
Cleveland, OH 44111

• *Zwicky 100% silk*
V. W. S., Inc.
11760 Berea Rd.
Cleveland, OH 44111

Ordinary
• *Dual-Duty Plus, cotton-wrapped polyester --* see Dual-Duty Plus Extra-Fine

Also Natesh, heavyweight, Zwicky in cotton and polyester, Mettler Metrosene in 30/2, 40/3, 50/3, and 30/3, and Metrosene Plus

See addresses above.

Metallic
YLI Corp.
45 West 300 North
Provo, UT 84601

Troy Thread & Textile Company
2300 W. Diversey Ave.
Chicago, IL 60647

MACHINE-EMBROIDERY AND SEWING MACHINE SUPPLIES
(marking and cutting tools, hoops, threads, patterns, books, etc.)

Aardvark Adventures
P.O. Box 2449
Livermore, CA 94550
 also publishes "Aardvark Territorial Enterprise"

Clotilde, Inc.
1909 S.W. First Ave.
Ft. Lauderdale, FL 33315
 (Clo-Chalk, Needle Lube)

Craft Gallery Ltd.
P.O. Box 8319
Salem, MA 01971

D & E Distributing
199 N. El Camino Real #F-242
Encinitas, CA 92024

June Tailor, Inc.
2861 Highway 175
Richfield, WI 53076
 tailor board, hams, mits, press cloths, etc.

Nancy's Notions
P.O. Box 683
Beaver Dam, WI 53916

National Thread & Supply Corp.
695 Red Oak Road
Stockbridge, GA 30281

Patty Lou Creations
Rt. 2, Box 90-A
Elgin, OR 97827

Sew-Art International
P.O. Box 550
Bountiful, UT 84010

Sew/Fit Company
P.O. Box 565
LaGrange, IL 60525

Sewing Emporium
1087 Third Ave.
Chula Vista, CA 92010

Speed Stitch, Inc.
P.O. Box 3472
Port Charlotte, FL 33952

The Fabric Carr
P.O. Box 32120
San Jose, CA 95152

The Perfect Notion
566 Hoyt Street
Darien, CT 06820

Treadleart
25834 Narbonne Ave.
Lomita, CA 90717

MISCELLANEOUS

Applications
871 Fourth Ave.
Sacramento, CA 95818
 release paper for appliqué

Berman Leathercraft
145 South St.
Boston, MA 02111
 leather

Boycan's Craft and Art Supplies
P.O. Box 897
Sharon, PA 16146
 plastic needlepoint canvas

Clearbrook Woolen Shop
P.O. Box 8
Clearbrook, VA 22624
 Utrasuede scraps

Folkwear Patterns
The Taunton Press
63 South Main Street
Box 5506
Newtown, CT 06470 - 5506
 timeless fashion patterns

Kid Sew Patterns
1176 Northport Drive
Columbus, OH 43235
 children's patterns and teaching materials

Kids Can Sew
P.O. Box 1710
St. George, UT 84771 - 1710
 children's patterns and teaching materials

To Sew
P.O. Box 974
Malibu, CA 90265
 beginning sewing kits for children of all ages

MAGAZINES

Aardvark Adventures
P.O. Box 2449
Livermore, CA 94550
 newspaper jammed with information about all kinds of embroidery, design, and things to order

Fiberarts
50 College Street
Asheville, NC 28801
 gallery of the best fiber artists, including those who work in machine stitchery

Sew It Seams
P.O. Box 2698
Kirkland, WA 98083 - 2698

Sew News
P.O. Box 1790
Peoria, IL 61656
 monthly tabloid, mostly of fashion garment sewing

Threads
Box 355
Newton, CT 06470
 glossy magazine on all fiber crafts

Treadleart
25834 Narbonne Ave.
Lomita, CA 90717
 bimonthly publication about machine embroidery

BIBLIOGRAPHY
BOOKS

Ambuter, Carolyn, *The Open Canvas*, Workman Publishing, New York, 1982.

Betzina, Sandra, *Power Sewing*, and *More Power Sewing*, Sandra Betzina, San Francisco, CA, 1985, 1990.

Bishop, Edna Bryte, and Marjorie Stotler Arch, *The Bishop Method*, W & W Publishing Company, Memphis, TN, 1966.

Brown, Gail, and Pati Palmer, *The Complete Handbook for Overlock Sewing*, Palmer/Pletsch Inc., Portland, OR, 1985.

Coffin, David Page, *The Custom Shirt Book*, David Page Coffin, P.O. Box 1580, La Jolla, CA 92038, 1985.

Dodson, Jackie, *Know Your Viking*, Chilton Book Company, Radnor, PA, 1987.

_____, *Know Your Sewing Machine*, Chilton Book Company, Radnor, PA, 1988.

Fanning, Robbie and Tony, *The Complete Book of Machine Quilting*, Chilton Book Company, Radnor, PA, 1980.

Griffin, Barb, *Pizzazz For Pennies*, and *Petite Pizzazz* Chilton Book Company, Radnor, PA, 1986, 1990.

_____, *St. Nick's Knacks*, Country Thread Designs, 1988.

Habeeb, Virginia, *Ladies' Home Journal Art of Homemaking*, Simon & Schuster, New York, 1973.

Hazen, Gale Grigg, *Owner's Guide to Sewing Machines, Sergers, and Knitting Machines*, Chilton Book Company, Radnor, PA, 1989.

Jabenis, Elaine, *The Fashion Director*, John Wiley & Sons, New York, 1972.

Maddigan, Judy, *Learn Bearmaking*, Open Chain Publishing, Menlo Park, CA, 1989.

Palmer, Pati, Gail Brown, and Sue Green, *Creative Serging Illustrated*, Chilton Book Company, Radnor, PA, 1987.

Reader's Digest, *Complete Guide to Sewing*, The Reader's Digest Association, Inc., Pleasantville, New York, 1976.

Saunders, Janice S., *Illustrated Speed Sewing*, Speed Sewing Ltd., Centerline, MI, 1985.

_____, *Sew, Serge, Press: Speed Tailoring in the Ultimate Sewing Center*, Chilton Book Company, Radnor, PA 1989.

Shaeffer, Claire B., *The Complete Book of Sewing Shortcuts*, Sterling Publishing, New York, 1981.

_____, *Claire Shaeffer's Sewing S.O.S.*, Open Chain Publishing, Menlo Park, CA, 1988.

_____, *Claire Shaeffer's Fabric Sewing Guide*, by Claire Shaeffer, Chilton Book Company, 1989.

Simplicity, *New Simplicity Sewing Book*, Simplicity Pattern Company, New York, 1979.

Simplicity, *Simply the Best Sewing Book*, Simplicity Pattern Company, New York, 1988.

Singer Instructions for Art Embroidery and Lace Work, foreword by Robbie Fanning, Open Chain Publishing, Menlo Park, CA, 1989.

Singer, *Singer Sewing Update 1988*, Cy DeCosse Inc., Minnetonka, MN, 1988.

Vogue, *The New Vogue Sewing Book*, Butterick Publishing, New York, 1980.

Zieman, Nancy, with Robbie Fanning, *The Busy Woman's Fitting Book*, Open Chain Publishing, 1989.

_____, *The Busy Woman's Sewing Book*, Open Chain Publishing, 1989.

VIDEO TAPES

Betzina, Sandra, "Power Sewing Video," available in BETA or VHS. Power Sewing, P.O. Box 2702, San Francisco, CA 94126.

Clotilde, Clotilde's T.V. Teaching Segments Series #1 - #6, BETA or VHS. Clotilde Inc., 1909 S.W. First Ave., Ft. Lauderdale, FL 33315.

_____, Clotilde's Seminar Videos, "Sew Smart for the $500 Look," "Smart Tailoring," "Ultrasuede and Other Leather-like Fabrics," BETA or VHS. Clotilde, Inc., 1909 S.W. First Ave., Ft. Lauderdale, FL 33315.

Salyers, Donna, "Sew a Wardrobe in a Weekend," "Re-Do A Room in a Weekend," "Super Time-Saving Sewing Tips," "Craft and Gift Ideas." The Congress Video Group, 10 East 53rd St., New York, N.Y. 10022.

Tailor, June, "Pressing Matters." June Tailor, P.O. Box 208, Richfield, WI 53076.

Zieman, Nancy. Nancy has devoted five pages in her current catalog to her video tapes available which are too extensive to list here. Nancy's Notions, P. O. Box 683, 333 Beichl Ave., Beaver Dam, WI 53919.

VIDEO TAPES FROM VIKING

- 1100 Viking Owners Handbook - VHS
- 990 Viking Owners Handbook - VHS
- 340D/340/300 Viking Owners Handbook VHS
- Pictograms and Sew Much More - VHS
- 560ED Viking Owners Handbook -VHS

Video tapes with Viking sewing machines and Huskylocks. Order direct from supplier listed below:

Kaye Wood (Log Cabin and Reversible Quilts)
4949 Raw Road
West Branch, MI 48661
517/345-3028

Mary's Productions (Designer Sweatshirts)
Box 87, Dept. V
Aurora, MN 55705

Theta's School of Sewing (Charted Needle Design on Viking 990)
2209 NW 46th
Oklahoma City, OK 73112

Islander School of Fashion Arts (Industrial Shortcuts of Home Sewing)
P.O. Box 5216
Grants Pass, OR 97526

INDEX

Index

Index

Index